Studies in Diversity Linguistics

Chief Editor: Martin Haspelmath
Consulting Editors: Fernando Zúñiga, Peter Arkadiev, Ruth Singer, Pilar Valenzuela

In this series:

ISSN: 2363-5568

Grammaticalization in the North

Noun phrase morphosyntax in Scandinavian vernaculars

Östen Dahl

language
science
press

Östen Dahl. 2015. *Grammaticalization in the North*: *Noun phrase morphosyntax in Scandinavian vernaculars* (Studies in Diversity Linguistics 6). Berlin: Language Science Press.

This title can be downloaded at:
http://langsci-press.org/catalog/book/73
© 2015, Östen Dahl
Published under the Creative Commons Attribution 4.0 Licence (CC BY 4.0):
http://creativecommons.org/licenses/by/4.0/
ISBN: 978-3-944675-57-2
ISSN: 2363-5568

Cover and concept of design: Ulrike Harbort
Typesetting: Felix Kopecky, Sebastian Nordhoff
Fonts: Linux Libertine, Arimo
Typesetting software: XƎLᴬTEX

Language Science Press
Habelschwerdter Allee 45
14195 Berlin, Germany
langsci-press.org

Storage and cataloguing done by FU Berlin

Freie Universität Berlin

To the memory of
Ulrika Kvist Darnell

Contents

Contents

Contents

Preface

This book has a rather long history – the research it is based on started more than fifteen years ago, and it has existed as a downloadable PDF on Stockholm University's web site for a number of years. I was afraid that the cost of a regular publication would in effect make it less accessible to readers. The downside has been that it has been less visible. I am therefore grateful for the opportunity to have it included in the series Studies in Diversity Linguistics. The text is essentially the same as that of the 2010 version, with some minor revisions and updates. Many people have helped me in various ways during my work on this book. It is likely that I will forget to mention some of them here, but I hope to be able to list at least the most important of them. One major data source has been what I refer to in the book as the "Cat Corpus" – a parallel corpus of texts in about 50 Swedish vernaculars. I want to thank Rickard Franzén, Anne Markowski, Susanne Vejdemo, and Ljuba Veselinova, who helped me in building it (as well as helping me in other ways), but also above all Rut "Puck" Olsson, the author of the Cat stories and the undefatigable collector of translations of them, who passed away in 2014. Another data source was a "translation questionnaire"; I want to thank Christina Alm-Arvius (deceased in 2013), Margit Andersson, Erika Bergholm, Ann-Marie Ivars, Henrik Johansson, Maria Linder, Eva Olander, Eva Sundberg, and Cecilia Yttergren for providing and collecting responses to the questionnaire from different parts of the Swedish dialect area. In addition, the participants in a course that I gave before the turn of the millennium used the questionnaire and also collected other valuable data; thanks are thus due to Gunnar Eriksson, Mikael Parkvall, Anne-Charlotte Rendahl, Nawzad Shokri, and Bernhard Wälchli. I also want to thank Gerda Werf and Bengt Åkerberg, who have taught me much of what I know about Elfdalian. A very special mention here should be reserved for Ulrika Kvist Darnell, who undertook to read and comment on the manuscript in careful detail, which improved the text significantly in both form and content. Tragically, Ulrika was not to see the final result of her work; in December 2009, she passed away, at the age of 43. I have decided to dedicate this book to her. Finally, thanks are due to Martin Haspelmath, Sebastian Nordhoff, and Felix Kopecky for turning a somewhat rough samizdat publication into a professionally looking monograph. Generous financial support is acknowledged from the Swedish Bank Tercentenary Fund and the Swedish Research Council.

Abbreviations in glosses

The abbreviations are compatible with (i.e. are a superset of) the list of standard abbreviations included in the Leipzig Glossing Rules (http://www.eva.mpg.de/lingua/files/morpheme.html).

1	first person	NEG	negation
2	second person	NOM	nominative
3	third person	OBL	oblique
ACC	accusative	PART	partitive (case)
ALL	allative (case)	PARTART	partitive article
AN	animate	PASS	passive
ANT	anterior	PL	plural
ART	article	POSS	possessive
CMPR	comparative	PP	perfect participle
CS	construct state	PDA	preproprial definite article
DAT	dative	PIA	postadjectival indefinite article
DEF	definite (article)	PRAG	pragmatic particle
DEM	demonstrative	PROG	progressive
DU	dual	PRS	present
F	feminine	PST	past
GEN	genitive	Q	question particle/marker
IMP	imperative	REFL	reflexive
INDF	indefinite (article)	REL	relative (pronoun)
INF	infinitive	SBJ	subject
		SBJV	subjunctive
INFM	infinitive marker	SG	singular
IPFV	imperfective	SUP	supine
M	masculine	SUPERL	superlative
N	neuter	WK	weak form of adjective

Common symbols in vernacular examples

â	a very fronted [a] or [æ]
Ö, ô, ө, 8	a central schwa-like vowel with somewhat varying quality
L, ḷ, ḻ, ɫ, 1	a voiced retroflex flap (according to Swedish terminology *tonande kakuminal lateral* or in everyday language *tjockt l* 'thick l')
N	a retroflex *n*
λ, hl	an unvoiced *l* (usually historically derived from *sl*)
´	marks an "acute" pitch accent (also referred to as "Accent 1")
`	marks a "grave" pitch accent (also referred to as "Accent 2")

Doubling of vowels (*aa*) is often used to denote a "circumflex" accent, but in Finland Swedish vernaculars instead means that the vowel is long.

1 Introduction

1.1 What this book is about

The two Swedish parishes of Älvdalen and Överkalix enjoy certain fame for harbouring the most "incomprehensible" of all traditional Swedish dialects; indeed, the distance from Standard Swedish is great enough for it to be more natural to think of them as separate languages. Although the geographical distance from Älvdalen to Överkalix is almost a thousand kilometres, and the two varieties have developed in quite different directions, there are still a number of striking similarities between them. Given their generally conservative character, it is not surprising to find many features that have been retained from older periods of North Germanic and which can also be found in other geographically peripheral Scandinavian varieties. More intriguing, however, are phenomena that are only marginally present, if at all, in attested earlier forms of Scandinavian languages and that must thus represent innovations. Most of these concern the grammar of noun phrases and nominal categories, e.g. many distinctive and unexpected uses of the definite forms of nouns, the use of incorporated adjectives, and the use of the still surviving dative case in possessive constructions. These phenomena are, or were, were, and sometimes still are found over large areas in Northern Sweden and the Swedish-speaking areas in Finland and Estonia – a dialect area that I shall refer to as the "Peripheral Swedish area".

In the dialectological tradition, the phenomena referred to here are often mentioned but usually only in passing. It is only fairly recently that researchers have begun to investigate them more systematically, mainly from a synchronic point of view. I find that adding a diachronic dimension is worthwhile from at least two perspectives. The first perspective is that of typology and the study of grammaticalization processes: the paths of development in question are relatively infrequent and have so far not been studied in detail anywhere else. The second perspective is that of Scandinavian history: we are dealing with innovations that have taken place outside of the assumed "mainstream" language history represented in written sources. A major challenge is thus to present plausible hypotheses about their origin and spread. In this book, I shall approach the Northern

Swedish phenomena from both these perspectives. Since our knowledge about the synchronic facts is still rather patchy, in spite of the pioneering work of researchers such as Lars-Olof Delsing, I must also devote considerable attention to the descriptive side of the problem.

After the introductory chapter, I give a brief overview of the geographic, historical, and linguistic background to "Peripheral Swedish" in Chapter 2. Chapter 3 then discusses the expansion of the definite forms. It is the longest chapter, which reflects the central role of the phenomena described—two major types of definite markers found in the North Germanic languages: (i) free definite articles appearing in initial position in the noun phrase, and (ii) bound suffixes on the head noun (sometimes extended to headless adjectives). In the Peripheral Swedish area, preposed articles tend to be weakly represented, whereas suffixes have greatly expanded their domain of use. §3.1 gives a background to the expansion of suffixes by a summary of earlier literature on the topic, a discussion of the grammaticalization processes behind definite articles in general, and what is known about the genesis of definite marking in North Germanic. §3.3–§3.10 discusses the different types of extended uses found in the Peripheral Swedish area and their distribution in time and space. The major types are:

- generic uses: *Guldið ir dyrt* 'Gold is expensive' (Älvdalen, Ovansiljan).

- "non-delimited uses": *Ä add vurti skårån upå snjom* 'there was a hard crust on the snow' (Sollerön, Ovansiljan)

- after quantifiers: *Han drack mycke öle* 'He drank a lot of beer' (Sorsele, Southern Västerbotten)

- in low referential singular count nouns: *Å dåm hav öitjon* 'And they have a dinghy' (Sideby, Southern Ostrobothnia)

- in instrumental prepositional phrases: *An jat suppo mi stjed'n* 'He ate soup with a spoon' (Orsa, Ovansiljan)

Importantly, each of these types has its own geographical distribution. I reject the treatment of the extended uses as "partitive articles" , wholly separate from other uses of definite forms, both because several of the types cannot really be regarded as having partitive meaning, and because there is in fact a continuum between the more typical uses of definites and the extended ones.

§3.11 reviews some earlier attempts to explain the extended uses of definite forms: the generative treatment in Holmberg & Sandström (2003) and the attempt to invoke influence from Fenno-Ugric in Rießler (2002). In §3.12, I try to reconstruct the paths by which the extended uses have arisen, hypothesizing that generic uses have been the major bridgehead for further developments.

Chapter 4 treats attributive constructions with a focus on definitive marking in noun phrases with adjectival attributes. Standard Swedish normally uses double articles in such constructions, i.e. both a preposed and a suffixed article in the same noun phrase, as in *den svarta hästen* 'the black horse'. However, the preferred construction in the Peripheral Swedish area involves incorporation of the adjective in the noun, which is then marked only by a suffixed article, as in *swart-estn* 'the black horse' (Älvdalen, Ovansiljan). But this is not the whole story: there is also a tendency for new preposed articles to develop out of demonstrative pronouns; furthermore, other alternatives show up in special contexts, some of which were discussed in detail in Dahl (2003). I agree with earlier authors that the rise of adjective incorporation was connected with the more general process of apocope, with the caveat that we need a better understanding of how the compound stress occurring with incorporated adjectives arose.

Adnominal possessive constructions, which display a remarkable diversity in Scandinavian languages, are treated in Chapter 5. The major constructions used with lexical possessors in the Peripheral Swedish area are as follows:

- "*s*-genitives" or "deformed genitives" using a generalized phrasal suffix or clitic such as -*s*; historically a genitive ending and analogous to the s-genitives of standard Scandinavian and also English

- constructions involving a possessor NP in the dative:
  - the "plain dative possessive", where the possessor NP usually follows the head noun: *skoN paitjåm* 'the boy's shoe' (Skelletmål, Northern Westrobothnian)
  - the "complex dative possessive", where a marker of possibly pronominal origin is suffixed to the possessor noun, which is in the dative and preposed to the head noun: *kullum-es saing* 'the girls' bed' (Älvdalen, Ovansiljan)

- "h-genitives" in which the postposed possessor NP is preceded by a possessive pronoun: *kLänninga hännasj Lina* 'Lina's dress' (Skelletmål, Northern Westrobothnian)

- prepositional constructions: *Fresn at a Momma* 'Granny's cat' (Lit, Jämtland)

- incorporation of the possessor into the head noun: *pappaskjorta* 'father's shirt' (Lövånger, South Westrobothnian)

In the final section of Chapter 5, pronominal possession is briefly discussed. Here, the major parameter of variation is the position of the possessive pronoun, with the Peripheral Swedish varieties in general preserving the original position after the noun.

In Chapter 6, I look for a plausible account of the historical origin of the innovations behind the grammatical phenomena in the Peripheral Swedish varieties discussed in the earlier chapters, arguing that many of them spread from central Sweden, where they were later reverted due to the influence from prestige varieties coming from southern Scandinavia. I point to other grammatical and lexical innovations with a similar geographical distribution, some of which have already been hypothesized to have a similar story behind them, and also show that there is a significant correlation between the distribution of conservative and innovative features in the Peripheral Swedish area. Finally, I give a sketch of the demographic, historical and linguistic situation in medieval central Sweden as a background to the later developments.

Chapter 7 summarizes some of the most important conclusions of wider significance that can be drawn from the earlier chapters.

As I mentioned, some varieties in the Peripheral Swedish area are different enough from the standard and from each other to merit being regarded as separate languages. The distinction between languages and dialects is a notoriously vexatious one. In this particular case (which is of course far from unique), the varieties under discussion vary considerably with respect to their distance from the standard language. On the one hand, it seems wrong to refer to *älvdalska* and *överkalixmål* as dialects, in particular as dialects of Swedish; on the other hand, it would be rather strange to think of every parish in Sweden as having its own language. To circumvent this terminological problem, I shall use "vernacular" because this word has a venerable tradition as a general term to designate a local, non-standard variety as opposed to a standard or prestige language, irrespective of the linguistic distance between these two (originally, of course, the vernaculars were non-standard in relation to the prestige language Latin).[1] For the sake of variation, I shall sometimes use "(local) variety" instead.[2]

---

[1] In Swedish, the perhaps slightly old-fashioned word *mål* has the advantage of being neutral to the language-dialect distinction and is thus often a suitable way of referring to vernaculars.

[2] In addition, I shall at times give the most distinctive vernacular Älvdalen a privileged position by referring to it in the Latinate form, "Elfdalian".

1.2 Remarks on methodology

The main focus of both traditional dialectology and historical linguistics was on sounds; this meant that attention to grammar was largely restricted to the expression side of morphology, that is, to the shapes of word forms, whereas the meanings of morphological categories and their role in a larger grammatical context were neglected to a large extent. The phenomena to be discussed in this book were no exception: as I mentioned in the preceding section, in most works, they were usually only mentioned in passing (if at all), without any attempt at detailed analyses.

This lack of attention to major parts of grammar reflects the general profile of linguistic research in the 19th and early 20th century, but we have to acknowledge that there is also another reason for the reluctance to analyze syntactic and functional phenomena: it is simply rather difficult to get adequate data. Before the advent of modern recording technology, the syntax of spoken language could not really be studied systematically. Researchers had to rely on what they heard or thought they heard. Furthermore, grammatical intuitions in a non-standard variety are difficult to use as empirical material because informants tend to be biased by their knowledge of the standard norm and are mostly unused to thinking in terms of grammaticality with respect to their native variety. These problems are still with us today and are aggravated by the fact that many speakers no longer have a full competence in the local variety due to the on-going shift to more acrolectal forms of the language.

In spite of technological innovations, recordings of natural speech and proper transcriptions of such recordings are usually hard to come by. Early on, large numbers of recordings were made with now obsolete techniques. These are presently inaccessible, awaiting digitalization in the archives. Even where properly transcribed versions of spoken material exist, the volume is often not large enough to guarantee a sufficient number of occurrences of the phenomenon that interests the researcher. This is especially true if someone wants to study one and the same phenomenon in a number of different varieties.

In this situation, it is natural to look for other kinds of written material than transcriptions of recorded speech. The total amount of texts written in traditional non-standard Swedish varieties is in fact quite impressive. Obviously, however, the coverage is very uneven and the reliability of the data is often questionable. The oldest materials, from the 17th century onwards, tend to be "wedding poems" and the like, which were often written in a local vernacular according to the fashion of the time. However, the bound form of these texts is likely to have promoted influences from the standard language. Later, during the heyday of the dialectological movement around the turn of the previous century, a large number of texts were written down and published by dialectologists. However, it is not always clear how these texts came about. Some of them seem to be composed by non-native speakers, and whether they bothered to check the correctness of the text with native speakers is hard to tell.

In addition, even when texts were obtained from informants, the methodology applied sometimes seems rather questionable from the modern point of view. The well-known Swedish dialectologist Herman Geijer wrote some comments on his transcription of the text [S11] that are quite revealing in this respect. The text, "En byskomakares historia", is about twenty pages long, and contains the life-story of Gunnar Jonsson, a village shoemaker from the parish of Kall in western Jämtland. It was taken down in 1908. In his comments, Geijer describes his method as follows: Jonsson spoke for a while,[3] and then paused to let Geijer write down what he had said. "When memory was insufficient" Geijer "incessantly" asked for advice. After the day's session, the whole text was read out to Jonsson, but "no essential changes or additions were made at this point". Jonsson started out trying to speak Standard Swedish, but after a few sentences switched to his dialect, "which is to some extent individual and rather inconsistent". Hence, Geijer felt he could not write it down literally: "His language has naturally been considerably normalized in my rendering, partly intentionally, partly unconsciously". Jonsson's language, according to Geijer's comments, was not only a mixture of standard language and dialect, but also a mixture of dialectal forms "at least from the two parishes where he has been living". As an example of the normalization he found necessary, he notes in his comments that the two pronunciations of the word *men* 'but' used by Jonsson, [mɛn] and [mæn], were rendered in the final text with the standard spelling, thus neglecting the variation. It would have been pointless, Geijer claims, to try to render variation of this kind in a longer text. On the other hand, Geijer says that he left a few cases of inconsistency in the text "on purpose", apparently expecting some negative reactions to this. "In spite of the broad transcription and the normalization applied here, and in spite of the inconsistency that I insist on as a matter of principle, in contradistinction to many other transcribers", he hoped that the text would be useful as a sample of a dialect which had not been well represented before. Geijer's formulation suggests that other researchers applied a much more radical form of "normalization" of transcribed texts and that it was indeed customary to "correct" forms that did not

---

[3] "G.J. hade under föregående uppteckningar vant sig vid att berätta ett lagom långt stycke i sänder."

seem to be in accordance with the researcher's assumptions of what the dialect should be like. It is obvious that this throws doubt on the general reliability of older dialect texts.

1.3 Sources

Like my area of investigation, my set of sources is rather open-ended and extremely varied. The main categories are as follows:

1.3.1 Dialectological literature

This is in itself a varied category, including overviews, papers on specific topics and descriptions of individual vernaculars. The literature on Swedish dialects is vast, but as noted already, the problems that are central to my investigation have generally not been given too much attention. Quite a few individual vernaculars have received monograph treatment, but the quality of these works varies considerably. In recent decades, many vernaculars have been described by their own speakers. Although these works tend to concentrate on vocabulary and sometimes display a rather low degree of linguistic sophistication, they do contain valuable information that is not found anywhere else. Many relevant example sentences can be found in dialect dictionaries.

1.3.2 Published and archived texts

This is a particularly open-ended category, in the sense that I have looked at more texts than could be conveniently listed, but in most cases my reading was rather cursory: I looked for interesting examples, but did not try to do a complete analysis. It should be added that in addition to the reliability problems discussed in the previous section, many of the texts are not easy to read, let alone to convert to an electronic format – in particular this goes for hand-written materials in the archives.

1.3.3 Questionnaires

At a fairly early stage of the investigation, I constructed a translation questionnaire of 73 sentences and expressions which has been filled out by informants from different parts of the area of investigation, although the coverage could certainly have been more complete. A number of questionnaires were collected by the participants in a graduate course that I gave in 1998 (most extensively for

Ostrobothnian, as reported in Eriksson & Rendahl 1999: II:147, and by the authors of a term paper at the University of Umeå, as reported in Bergholm, Linder & Yttergren (1999). A similar questionnaire was constructed by Ann-Marie Ivars and distributed to a number of speakers of Swedish varieties in Finland; she kindly put the results at my disposal (see also Ivars 2005).

1.3.4 The Cat Corpus

Rut "Puck" Olsson, who is herself a native of the province of Hälsingland, became interested in the local language of Älvdalen in Dalarna when she was a school teacher there, and managed to learn Elfdalian well enough to pass for a local person. In order to promote interest in the endangered vernacular, she wrote a short story for children, *Mumunes Masse* 'Granny's Cat', in Elfdalian, which was later followed by a continuation, *Mier um Masse* 'More about Masse'. Furthermore, she persuaded speakers of other vernaculars to translate the stories into their own native varieties. These efforts are still continuing, but at present the first story exists in close to fifty versions (not all of which have been published), and the second story in eight. Obviously, many of the translators have had little or no experience in writing in the vernacular, and influence from Standard Swedish is unavoidable, but this material is still unique in containing parallel texts in a large number of varieties, many of which have not been properly documented. I decided to create a parallel corpus of Swedish vernaculars and had the texts scanned and converted to a suitable format. The ultimate goal is to tag all the words in the corpus with translations and word-class and morphological information; this work is still under way. For this present work, I have mainly used the translations of the first story, which is about 6500 words long. Naturally, the coverage of the Cat Corpus is not complete (see Map 3). Fortunately for my purposes, Northern Sweden is well represented, in particular Dalarna and the Dalecarlian area; but equally unfortunately, there is so far no translation from Finland.

1.3.5 Informant work and participant observation

Muchvaluable information has also been received by informal questioning of speakers of different varieties and by observation of natural speech, in particular during my visits to Älvdalen.

1.4 Remark on notation

In general, examples quoted from other works are rendered in the original notation; any attempt at unification would create more problems than it would solve. Common symbols are explained on page xiii.

I have made an exception for Elfdalian examples from Levander (1909) written in *landsmålsalfabetet*, the Swedish dialect alphabet created in 1878 by J.A. Lundell which, in spite of being quite advanced for its time, is very hard to read for the non-initiated and also quite cumbersome typographically. Instead, I have tried to use the orthography recently proposed by the Elfdalian Language Council ("Råðdjärum") as much as possible. (I have also re-written a few other examples in *landsmålsalfabetet* in a similar fashion.)

2 Peripheral Swedish: Geographic, historical and linguistic background

2.1 Geography

Sweden is traditionally divided into three major regions: Götaland, Svealand, and Norrland (see Figure 2.1), and since these regions are mentioned in all weather forecasts, people are quite aware of the division. Götaland and Svealand are commonly presumed to correspond to the lands of the two ethnic groupings Götar and Svear which are believed to form the basis of the Swedish people. However, present-day Götaland also includes the originally Danish and Norwegian provinces that became Swedish territory in the 17th century. The third region, Norrland – literally "the north land" – has no connection with any specific ethnic grouping (although it houses Finnish and Saami minorities), but rather represents the peripheral areas to the north that were colonized by Swedish-speaking people rather late. Although its area (242,735 sq. kms) is more than half of that of Sweden, it has only about 13 per cent of the population (1.16 million in 2013) and a population density of about 5 persons per square kilometre (compared to about 30 for the rest of Sweden). Sweden's record as a traditional colonial power is somewhat meagre, but Norrland has undoubtedly served the role of a substitute for overseas colonies, much like Siberia for the Russian empire. Today, in spite of its impressive natural resources (such as forests, iron ore and water power), Norrland is plagued by high rates of unemployment and decreasing population figures.

The delineation of Norrland, as officially defined, is somewhat arbitrary, however. Historically, the southernmost province of Norrland, Gästrikland, was part of Svealand. But what is more important is that a large number of natural and cultural borderlines all bisect Sweden in roughly the same way, with the northern part including not only Norrland but also a large part of Svealand, notably the province of Dalarna, and parts of the provinces of Värmland and Västmanland. This cluster of borderlines is usually referred to by the Latin phrase *limes norrlandicus* 'the Norrlandic border' (see Figure 2.1), and coincides fairly well with the isotherm for a January average temperature of -7°C. From the point of view of vegetation, *limes norrlandicus* delimits the "northern coniferous area", which is part of the huge taiga belt covering most of northern Eurasia. Deciduous trees such as oak and ash stop at the *limes norrlandicus,* and so did towns and nobility in the Middle Ages. The *limes norrlandicus* also coincides with the southern limit of the North Scandinavian transhumance system (seasonal movement of cattle, Swedish *fäbodväsendet*), further indicating the impact of this natural borderline on cultural practices.[1] This border is still very much a socio-cultural reality today, as evidenced by the fact that municipalities with less than 40 per cent in favour of Sweden joining the European Union in the 1994 referendum were overwhelmingly situated north of the *limes norrlandicus.*

For simplicity, I shall refer to the area north of the *limes norrlandicus* as "Northern Sweden". This term, then, is not synonymous to "Norrland". *Limes norrlandicus* is not frequently mentioned in the Swedish dialectological literature, but some isoglosses do follow it quite closely. Compare e.g. *limes norrlandicus* as shown in Figure 2.1 with the southern limit of the "North Scandinavian medial affrication" as shown in Figure 6.1 (p. 204) and the southern limit of the area with predominantly postposed pronominal possessors in Figure 5.4 (p. 199). It is clear that the natural conditions of Northern Sweden have not only influenced the inhabitants' way of living but have also – indirectly – been important for linguistic developments.

The linguistic phenomena discussed in this book occur mainly in Northern Sweden, as defined in the preceding paragraph, as well as in the Trans-Baltic parts of the Scandinavian dialect continuum (Finland, Estonia), particularly the Finnish province of Österbotten (Ostrobothnia, Pohjanmaa), and extending in some cases also to the islands of Gotland and Öland in the southern Baltic. I shall refer to this area as the PERIPHERAL SWEDISH area. It has been pointed out to me that the term "peripheral" may be interpreted as having negative associations; this is most certainly not the intention here – in particular I do not want to imply that the vernaculars spoken in the Peripheral Swedish area have a peripheral role to play relative to standard or acrolectal varieties.[2]

---

[1] The Swedish term *fäbod* is translated in dictionaries as "summer pasture", but this is a bit misleading since it refers to the whole complex of buildings and surrounding grazing fields that were used during the summer period. For this reason, I use the term "shieling", which has an analogous use in parts of Britain, as a translation of *fäbod* and the corresponding vernacular terms (such as Elfdalian *buðer*).

[2] The EU-supported Northern Periphery programme happens to delimit its area of activity in a way that makes it coincide quite closely in Sweden with the Peripheral Swedish area as I have defined it. (See map at http://www.northernperiphery.eu)

Figure 2.1: Traditional geographical divisions in Sweden

2.2 Administrative, historical and dialectological divisions

The first-level administrative units in Sweden and Finland are called *län* (Swedish) or *lääni* (Finnish). These will be referred to as "counties". The second-level unit is called *kommun* in Swedish and *kunta* in Finnish, translated as "municipalities". However, in dialectology, the traditional partitioning into *landskap* (translated as "province"), *härad* (translated as "judicial district") and *socken* (translated as "parish") is more useful.

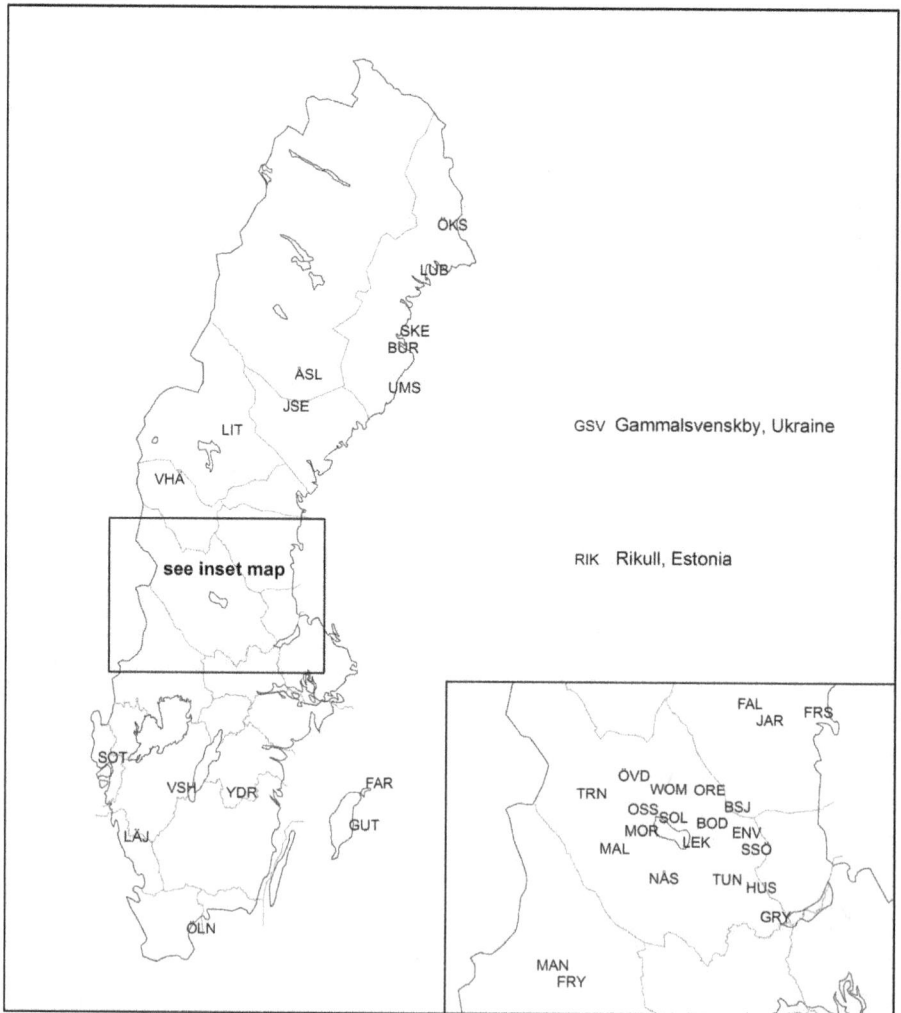

Figure 2.2: Vernaculars represented in the Cat Corpus.

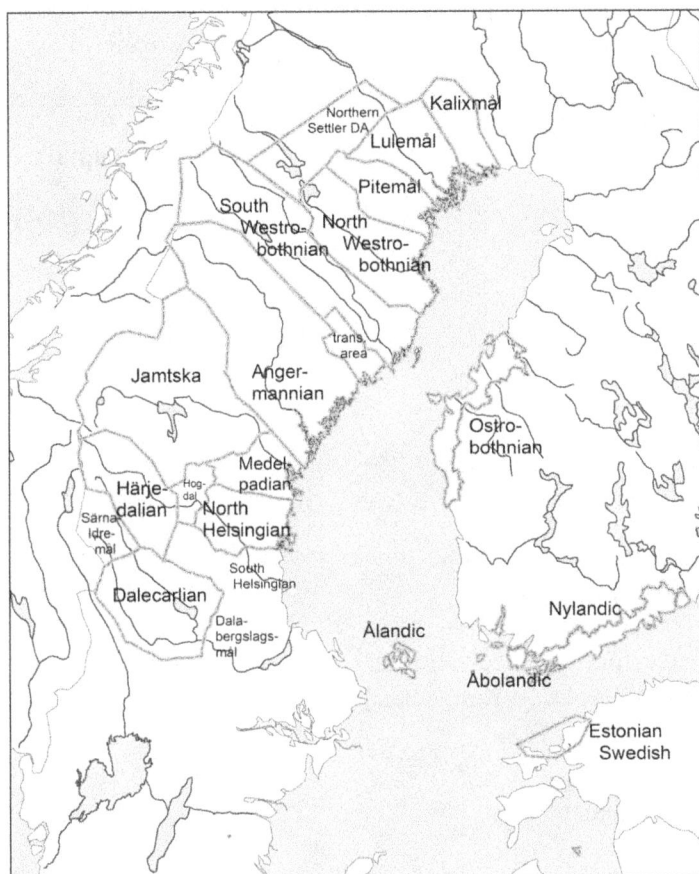

Figure 2.3: Dialect areas in the Peripheral Swedish Area.

I will use the Swedish toponyms for all these units throughout. When referring to dialects or dialect areas, however, I will sometimes use Latinized forms
such as "Dalecarlian" and "Westrobothnian", particularly in those cases where
the dialectological unit does not coincide with the geographical one.

Examples from individual parishes will in general be identified by the name
of the parish (in some cases also by a village name), followed by an abbreviation
for the dialect area or province in parentheses. Sometimes, however, sources
use traditional denominations of vernaculars, which may cover areas which are
larger or smaller than a parish (e.g. Lulemål, Önamål). For the vernacular spoken
in Älvdalen, Dalarna, I use the Latinized name "Elfdalian", which is currently
gaining ground as an English term, although it has received a competitor in the
alternative name "Övdalian".

Table 2.1: Vernacular groupings in and around the Peripheral Swedish area

---

Norrbothnian (*norrbottniska*)

- Kalixmål

- Lulemål

- Pitemål

Westrobothnian (*västerbottniska*)

- Northern Westrobothnian (*nordvästerbottniska*)

- Southern Westrobothnian (*sydvästerbottniska*)

- Angermannian-Westrobothnian transitional area (*övergångsmål*)

Northern Settler dialect area

Angermannian (*ångermanländska*)

Jamtska (*jämtska*)

Medelpadian (*medelpadska*)

Helsingian (*hälsingska*)

Dalecarlian (*(egentligt) dalmål*)

- Ovansiljan

- Västerdalarna

- Nedansiljan

Dalabergslagsmål

Ostrobothnian (*österbottniska*)

- Northern Ostrobothnian

- Central Ostrobothnian

- Southern Ostrobothnian

Southern Finland Swedish vernaculars

- Åbolandic

- Nylandic

- Ålandic

Estonian Swedish vernaculars (including Gammalsvenskby, Ukraine)

"Norwegian" vernaculars

- Härjedalian

- Särna-Idremål

2.3 Linguistic situation

2.3.1 Scandinavian in general

According to the traditional view, the Scandinavian languages (also referred to as "Nordic" and "North Germanic") are divided into two branches, West Scandinavian, comprising Icelandic, Faroese, and Norwegian, and East Scandinavian, comprising Danish and Swedish. The two branches are thought to have formed around 1000 AD. This classification is not very easy to apply to the present-day languages, however. Due to the prevalence of Danish in Norway during the half millennium of Danish rule there, and the efforts during the 19th century to re-create Norwegian as a written language, Norwegian today has two written standards, *bokmål* and *nynorsk,* with the former being fairly close to Danish and the latter being based mainly on rural vernaculars. Consequently, in some treatments *bokmål* is seen as an East Scandinavian language and *nynorsk* as a West Scandinavian language, which is counterintuitive since both varieties are not only very close to each other but also much more similar to Danish and Swedish than to Modern Icelandic. If one also takes the various spoken vernaculars in continental Scandinavia into account, it becomes clear that the standard languages Danish, Swedish, and Norwegian Bokmål and vernaculars spoken in the insular part of Denmark, urbanized areas in Norway, and Sweden south of the *limes norrlandicus,* form a cluster of relatively closely connected (and more or less mutually intelligible) varieties, to be referred to in the following as CENTRAL SCANDINAVIAN. The reason for the closeness of the Central Scandinavian varieties is then not so much common origin as intensive language contact over prolonged periods. On the other hand, the spoken varieties in the rest of Continental Scandinavia, that is, Jutland in Denmark, most of rural Norway and the Peripheral Swedish Area, together with "Insular North Germanic", i.e. Icelandic and Faroese, stand apart from Central Scandinavian; and, although there is great diversity among them, they tend to share many "conservative" traits inherited from Old Nordic which are no longer found in Central Scandinavian. In addition, there are also innovations that cover large parts of the peripheral areas which will be of particular interest to what follows.

2.3.2 Swedish

The area where varieties traditionally regarded as "Swedish dialects" are spoken includes all of Sweden (except the Saami-speaking and Finnish-speaking areas in the very north), the Åland islands (Finnish *Ahvenanmaa*), two separate areas

Figure 2.4: Swedish dialect areas according to Wessén (1966). Larger print: major areas, smaller print: minor areas. Grey dots indicate parishes within the traditional Swedish-speaking area. (This also gives a fairly adequate idea of the population density.) Notice that "East Swedish dialects" are called "Trans-Baltic" in this text.

along the Finnish coast, and a small area on the coast of Estonia. I shall refer to this as the SWEDISH DIALECT AREA. It is shown in Figure 2.4 together with the standard division into six dialect groupings following Wessén (1966: II:170):

- Southern dialects (*sydsvenska mål*)

- Göta dialects (*götamål*)

- Svea dialects (*sveamål*)

- Norrlandic dialects (*norrländska mål*)

- East Swedish dialects (*östsvenska mål*)

- Gotlandic dialects (*gotländska mål*)

Notice that "East Swedish" does not refer to dialects spoken in the eastern parts of Sweden but rather to those spoken east of the Baltic. For this reason the less confusing term "Trans-Baltic" was introduced in Rendahl (2001) and will be used here.

Wessén identifies a transitional belt between the Svea and Göta dialects in the area comprised of the western part of Södermanland, Närke, all of Östergötland except the south-western part, northeast Småland, and Öland (see Figure 2.5 for the provinces). For this reason, he says, the Svea dialects should be divided into two sub-areas: (i) the dialects in the transitional belt, referred to as "Central Swedish dialects" (*mellansvenska mål*), (ii) the rest, i.e. Uppland, Gästrikland, southern Hälsingland, south-eastern Dalarna, eastern Västmanland, and northern and eastern Södermanland, making up the "Upper Swedish" dialects (*uppsvenska mål*). He adds that the dialects of Upper Dalarna (*egentligt dalmål* 'Dalecarlian proper') "have a special position",[3] but does not specify if they should be counted as Upper Swedish or not.

The northern part of the Swedish-speaking area has been most controversial with respect to how it should be divided into dialect areas. Before the advent of modern dialectology in the 19th century, the traditional opinion seems to have been that there were two major Swedish dialects, "Svea" and "Göta". The former would then also include the vernaculars of Dalarna and Norrland (and presumably also the Trans-Baltic varieties). Another way of slicing the cake was proposed by the Swedish dialectologist Johan Lundell (1880, 1901) who united most

---

[3] "En särställning intar det egentliga dalmålet i Öster- och Västerdalarne, med sin mycket ålderdomliga prägel och sin starka splittring i underarter" (p. 30). (Wessén's map says simply *dalmål* 'Dalecarlian'.)

Figure 2.5: Swedish provinces (*landskap*).

Norwegian dialects together with those spoken in Norrland, Dalarna, Västman-land, Finland and Estonia into one area called "North Scandinavian", and lumped Svea and Göta dialects together with a "Central Swedish" group (thus a wider use of this term than Wessén's). Hesselman (1905), citing the older authors, stresses the links between the Upper Swedish dialects and those found in Northern Swe-den and east of the Baltic.

2.3.3 Norrlandic

It is hardly surprising that there is great variation among the vernaculars of Nor-rland in view of the size of the region. The different parts of Norrland also have rather different histories. Norrland was first populated more or less directly after the disappearance of the continental ice sheet, but agriculture arrived relatively late. The population were mainly hunters and fishers until permanent agricultural settlements were established, which took place in the early Iron Age in middle Norrland, but only in the 13th and 14th centuries in the northern provinces Västerbotten and Norrbotten. Saami-speaking and Finnish-speaking populations were found more widely in this period than today. The political status of large parts of Norrland was unclear in medieval times. For example, the border between Sweden and Russia became fixed only in 1323. The provinces of Jämtland and Härjedalen were officially part of Norway, although Jämtland's status was rather ambiguous: ecclesiastically, it belonged to the diocese of Uppsala, and in actual practice the province may have functioned more or less as an autonomous republic. This situation is reflected linguistically in that the vernaculars of Jämtland are in various ways transitional between Swedish and Norwegian, whereas Härjedalen, which was populated from Norway at a relatively late point in time, is usually seen as being Norwegian from the dialectological point of view.

If we look at the coastal Norrlandic provinces (see Figure 2.5), starting in the south, the vernaculars of Gästrikland, which historically did not belong to Norrland, do not differ much from those of northern Uppland. In fact, the same can be said to some extent about Hälsingland, where there appears to have been significant levelling of the vernaculars already in pre-modern times. Many phenomena that are characteristic of Northern Swedish vernaculars are found only in northern Hälsingland – for this reason Ågren & Dahlstedt (1954: 230) regard the southern part of the province as belonging to the "Upper Swedish" area and treat northern Hälsingland as a separate dialect area. Going further north, the vernaculars grow gradually more different from Standard Swedish. The most conservative ones are probably those found in northern Västerbotten, although the varieties in Norrbotten (notably the northernmost Swedish vernacular, Överkalixmål) are more distinctive, having undergone a number of specific innovations. The Swedish dialects of the landlocked province of Lappland – the so-called "settler dialects" (nybyggarmål) – are usually said to be closer to the standard language than the coastal vernaculars, since Swedish settlements there were generally quite late and were at least partly populated from the south. As we shall see later, however, some traits characteristic of the coastal vernaculars have also spread to the "settler dialects".

The dialectological map of Norrland is largely influenced by its physical geography: Norrland is crossed from west to east by a large set of rivers and since movement of people and goods has always tended to go along the rivers, there is a strong tendency for each river valley to make up a separate dialect area (see

Figure 2.3).[4] Some dialect areas are named after the provinces, but there is considerable mismatch between the borders of the provinces and those of the dialect areas.[5]

2.3.4 Dalecarlian

As noted in the quotation from Wessén (1966) on page 27 above, the vernaculars spoken in Upper Dalarna (Övre Dalarna), the northern part of the province of Dalarna (latinized name: Dalecarlia), have a "special position" in differing more radically from the standard languages than perhaps any Scandinavian variety and in also being extremely diverse internally. In Swedish dialectology, these vernaculars are usually referred to as *dalmål* or *egentligt dalmål* 'Dalecarlian proper'. Confusion arises from the fact that the word *dalmål* is for most Swedes associated with the characteristic accent of speakers from the southern part of the province, which belongs to the Central Swedish mining district referred to as Bergslagen. The traditional vernaculars of this part of Dalarna are referred to in the dialectological literature as *Dala-Bergslagsmål*. The term "Dalecarlian" will be used in this work to refer to "Dalecarlian proper", that is, the traditional vernaculars of the 21 parishes of Upper Dalarna. It should be borne in mind, however, that even though Dalecarlian as a whole was during a period assigned the status of a language in Ethnologue (www.ethnologue.com), the characterization given by the foremost expert on Dalecarlian, Levander (1928: 257), is more apt: "Dalecarlian is not one language...but rather a whole world of languages"[6] – the parish varieties are often not mutually understandable, and the differences between villages in one and the same parish can be quite significant.

Commonly, the Dalecarlian area is divided into three parts – Ovansiljan, Västerdalarna and Nedansiljan (see Figure 2.6), but the actual picture is somewhat

---

[4] Interestingly, the same goes also for the Saami varieties in Upper Norrland; this means that for several of the Swedish dialect areas, there is a Saami language with the same prefix to its name (Lulemål corresponds to Lule Saami etc.), although the Saami varieties are (or were) spoken in the upper parts of the river valleys and the Swedish varieties closer to the coast.

[5] I have tried to follow the map of the Norrlandic dialect areas in Ågren & Dahlstedt (1954: 230) (reproduced also in Dahlstedt 1971). However, the transitional Angermannian-Westrobothnian area is not quite clearly delineated in this map; the border cuts straight through the parishes of Fredrika and Örträsk. It is clear from the text in the book that Örträsk should belong to the area, while Fredrika, as belonging to "Åsele lappmark", should be counted as an Angermannian vernacular, although according to Ågren & Dahlstedt (1954: 289), what is spoken there is "almost standard language" ("nästan riksspråk").

[6] "Det bör ihågkommas, att dalmålet – trots den enhet, som kan anas bakom den nuvarande mångfalden – icke är ett språk utan en hel språkvärld."

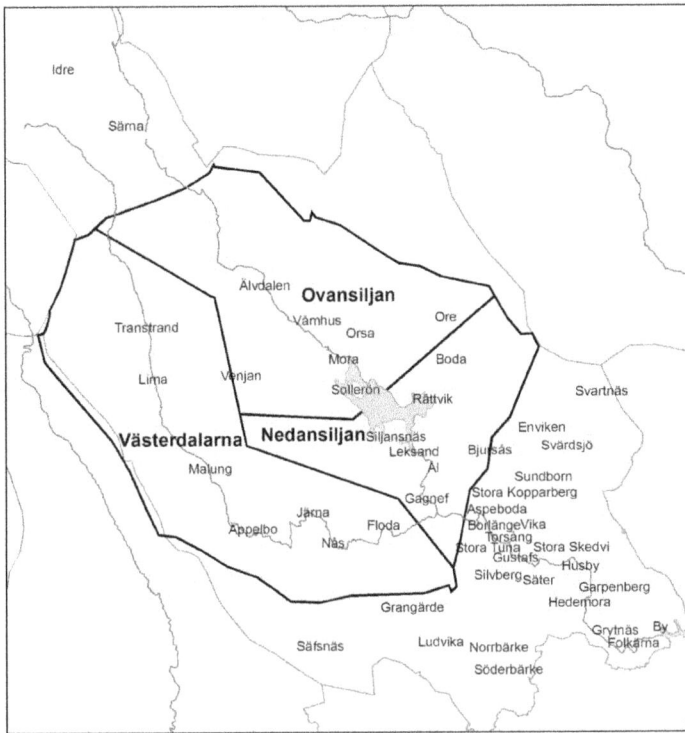

Figure 2.6: Dialect areas in Dalarna according to the traditional view.

more complex. Figure 2.7 is based on a lexical comparison between vernaculars in Dalarna described in more detail in Dahl (2005). It shows that the varieties that differ most from the others (and from Standard Swedish) are found in Ovansiljan (except Ore) and northern Västerdalarna (Transtrand and Lima), these forming two fairly well delineated areas. Within Ovansiljan, the vernaculars in Älvdalen and Våmhus form a highly distinctive subarea, and Orsa also stands out as having many specific traits. Within Nedansiljan, Boda and Rättvik make up an area of their own, although it differs less dramatically from the neighbours to the south. The rest of Dalarna, including the remaining parts of Västerdalarna and Nedansiljan, is most properly regarded as a dialect continuum without clear borders. The parishes of Särna and Idre in the northern tip of the province, however, belonged to Norway until 1645 and the vernaculars there are very different from Dalecarlian, being quite similar to the Norwegian vernaculars on the other side of the border.

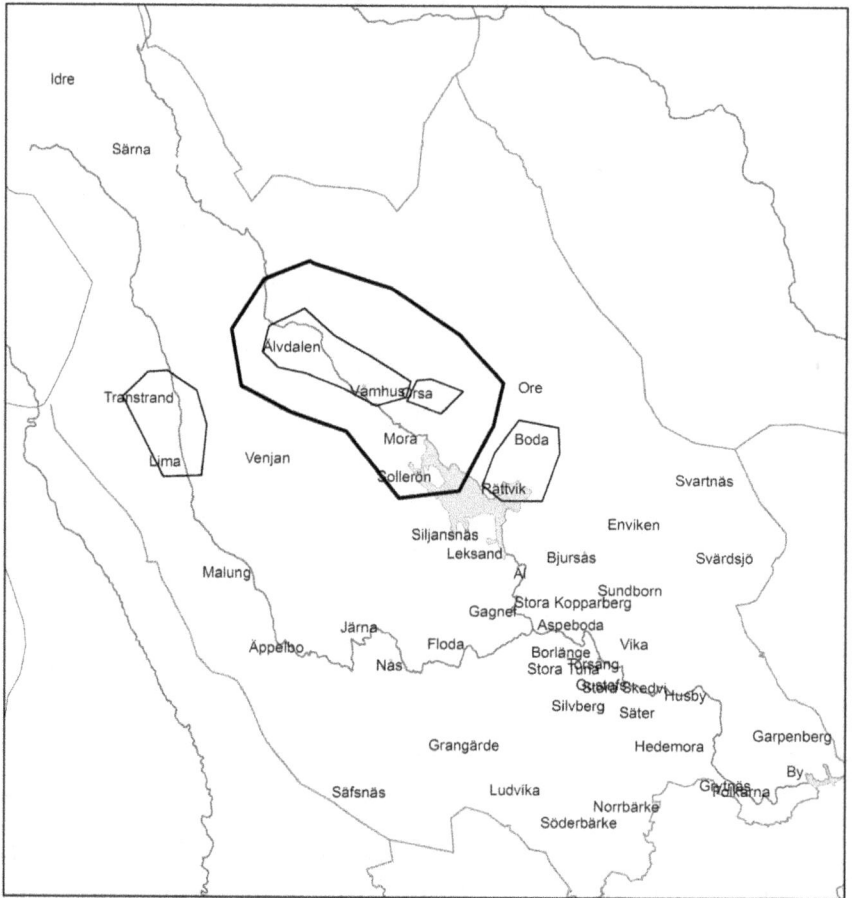

Figure 2.7: A more realistic view of Dalecarlian vernaculars.

2.3.5 Trans-Baltic Swedish

The Swedish-speaking minority in Finland is comprised of about 260,000 persons. While Standard Finland Swedish differs from "Sweden Swedish" mainly in pronunciation and to some extent in vocabulary, the spoken vernaculars often differ very much from the national standards.

Until the Second World War, Swedish was also spoken along the coast of Estonia by some 7,000 people, but most of them emigrated to Sweden during the war. During Soviet times, it was generally thought that there were no Swedish speakers left in Estonia but it is now known that a couple of hundred are still there.

In the 18th century, the Russian Empress Catherine the Great moved a number of Swedish-speaking peasants from Estonia to Ukraine, where they lived in a village called "Gammalsvenskby" in Swedish. The majority of the inhabitants of this village emigrated in the 1920s (mainly to Sweden and Canada), but again, there is still a handful of Swedish speakers there. (One of the texts in the Cat Corpus is in the Gammalsvenskby vernacular, which is confusingly called *gammalsvenska* 'Old Swedish'.)

The Swedish settlements on the east side of the Baltic derive from the Middle Ages, probably starting in the 12th century, while the Åland islands had a Scandinavian population much earlier. It may actually be misleading to think of the four geographically separate areas of Österbotten, southern Finland, coastal Estonia, and Åland as a dialectological unit, since contacts across the Baltic have been at least as important as contacts between the areas. From the point of view of the phenomena treated in this book, Ostrobothnian behaves much more like the Northern Swedish vernaculars than the other Trans-Baltic regions.

3 The expansion of the definite forms

3.1 Introduction

3.1.1 General

It is often pointed out in the dialectological literature that Peripheral Swedish vernaculars tend to use definite marking of noun phrases more than the standard language. An early mention (perhaps the first) of this is found in the description of the Närpes vernacular in Freudenthal (1878: 137), where it is said that this dialect, like the other Ostrobothnian vernaculars, has "a decided predilection"[1] for the definite form, which is often used "when the indefinite form would be appropriate". The examples given by Freudenthal are:

(1) Närpes (Southern Ostrobothnian)

  a. *Kva ha   et tjøft i stádin? – **Ättren** **o***
     what have.PRS you buy.SUP in town.DEF pea.DEF.PL and
     grýnen.
     grain.DEF.PL
     'What have you bought in town? – Peas and grains.'

  b. *Kva jer   he, som ligger op jólen?   – He je   gräse.*
     what be.PRS it REL lie.PRS on earth.DEF it be.PRS grass.DEF
     'What is it that is on the ground?' – 'It is grass.'

  c. *víne, som há   vuri **vattne***
     wine REL have.PRS be.SUP **water.DEF**
     'the wine, that has been water'

This feature of Peripheral Swedish area speech is also felt to be one of its salient characteristics by non-linguists, as witnessed by such facetious uses as the alleged translation of *filet mignon* into Westrobothnian: *stektjötte mä gulsåsn* 'the

---

[1] "Die Närpesmundart hat in Analogie mit den übrigen schwedischen Volksmundarten Österbottens eine entschiedene Vorliebe für die bestimmte Form des Substantivs, die daher häufig angewandt wird, wo eigentlich die unbestimmte Form am Platze wäre..."

fried meat with the yellow gravy' (this expression also exemplifies adjective incorporation, see §4.3.2). As is typical of the cursory treatment of grammatical
phenomena of this kind, however, few of the older works in the dialectological
tradition go beyond just pointing out the existence of such extended uses, and
even fewer try to treat it above the level of individual vernaculars. In more recent
work, there have been attempts to take a more theoretical and general approach,
but to this date nobody seems to have thought of it in terms of grammaticalization processes. This is unfortunate, since in fact it represents a development that
is not common typologically and that has not received any serious attention in
the literature on diachronic grammar and language typology.

3.1.2 Extended definites in the literature

In addition to the above-mentioned work on Ostrobothnian by Freudenthal, the
extended uses of definite articles in the Peripheral Swedish area are discussed
in the dialectological literature by Levander (1909) for Elfdalian and by Hummelstedt (1934) for Ostrobothnian. A relatively detailed discussion of the use of
the definite article in Upper Norrland and Ostrobothnian is found in Ågren &
Dahlstedt (1954: 281ff).

In recent years, the phenomenon has been treated by Nikula (1997), who restricts her discussion to Ostrobothnian, Delsing (1993), Delsing (2003a), and Holm
berg & Sandström (2003) [1996], among others.

Nikula (1997) gives a fairly detailed description of the extended use of definite
articles in the southern Ostrobothnian variety spoken in the town of Närpes. She
says that the general condition on the definite form in Närpesmål is that the noun
is used "referentially". "Referentially" is apparently used in a rather wide sense
here, more or less synonymous to "non-predicatively" (but see further discussion
under §3.6).

Delsing (1993: 50) proposes that "the special form with the suffixed article in
Northern Swedish is a partitive article", drawing parallels with French. He notes
that nouns with "partitive articles" are different from ordinary definite NPs since
they can occur in existential constructions, that is, with a dummy subject such
as *hä* in

(2)   "North Swedish" (unspecified location)
       Hä finns   ***vattne***   *däri*   *hinken.*
       it   exist.PRS water.DEF (there)in bucket.DEF

       'There is water in the bucket.'

Delsing (2003b: 15) says that the "partitive article" is used with uncountable nouns, plurals, and singulars that denote undelimited or arbitrary quantities. In addition, he postulates a separate use of definite articles in "predicative constructions" (see §3.7). Delsing is also the only scholar to my knowledge who has tried to map the areal distribution of the extended uses of definite articles in any detail. Thus, in Delsing (2003b: 18) there is a map of what he calls "partitive articles", divided into a northern and a southern area. The northern area, where "the partitive article is used when the standard language has a bare noun" (in our terms, mainly non-delimited uses, to be treated below in §3.4), includes the Swedish-speaking areas of Norrbotten, Västerbotten, Österbotten, and Ångermanland and parts of Jämtland. The southern part, where, according to Delsing, the "partitive article" has to receive a generic interpretation (see §3.3 below), basically comprises the rest of Norrland and the northern parts of Dalarna and Värmland. The basic picture provided by Delsing, with a greater use of definite articles in the north than in the south, is generally correct; but in particular the characterization and delimitation of the southern area has to be modified in various ways, as we shall see below.

3.1.3 Grammaticalization of definites from a typological perspective

How many languages have definite articles, and are they equally common in all parts of the world? Answers to these questions can be found in Dryer (2005), based on a world-wide sample of 566 languages.

In Dryer's sample, 337, or almost 60 per cent, were found to have definite articles, including 56 languages in which the definite article was formally identical to a demonstrative pronoun, and 84, or 15 per cent of the total sample, where the definite article was manifested as an affix. In other words, having a definite article may be more common among the world's languages than not having one; suffixed articles, like the ones we find in Scandinavian languages, on the other hand, are clearly a minority phenomenon.

Like most grammatical features, definite articles are not evenly spread geographically. As can be seen from Figure 3.1, which shows the distribution of definite articles in Dryer's sample, they are generally present in Western Europe and much of Africa north of the Equator but are rare for instance in most of Asia and South America.

Noun phrases with definite articles are used both anaphorically, that is, as picking up the reference of a noun phrase occurring earlier in the discourse, as in (3), or non-anaphorically. In the latter case, the referent of the noun phrase may be a unique object, as in (4), but more commonly it is something that is identifiable in the discourse situation, as in (5).

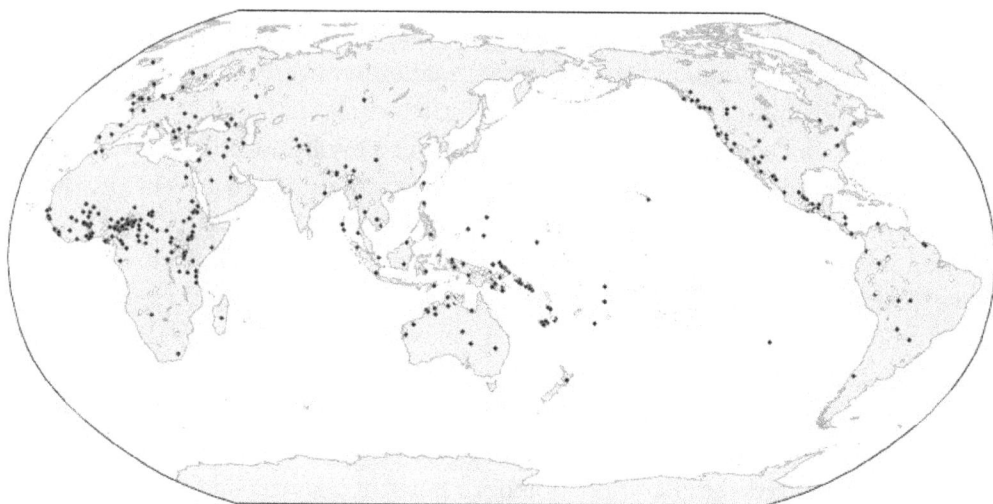

Figure 3.1: Distribution of definite articles (black symbols) in a sample of 566 languages (Dryer 2005)

(3) *In the street, I saw a cat and a dog. The dog was barking furiously.*[2]

(4) *I met the author of Syntactic Structures.*

(5) *Please close the door.*

A highly frequent phenomenon is the "anchoring" of a definite noun phrase to some other element, whether mentioned in the discourse or not (Fraurud 1992: 25). In (6), for instance, *the hard disk* is understood as the hard disk of the computer mentioned in the first clause – in other words, the computer serves as the anchor. This example illustrates what is often called "associative" or "bridging co-reference"[3] uses of definite noun phrases,

---

[2] It is perhaps symptomatic that examples of the anaphoric use of definite noun phrases in the literature tend to contain antecedents which are parts of a conjoined noun phrase: at least in natural speech, pronouns tend to be preferred to full noun phrases as straightforward anaphors in most contexts, and we need a structure such as a conjoined NP for there to be two equally possible antecedents, in which case a definite NP is motivated.

[3] Another term that is sometimes used is "bridging anaphora". Originally, the term "bridging" referred to the "bridging assumption" that provided the link between the definite noun phrase and its anchor. Thus, in (i) we have to make the assumption that the picnic supplies included beer (Clark & Haviland 1974):

(i) Mary got some picnic supplies out of the car. The beer was warm.

But the point that the interpretation of definite noun phrases sometimes involves inferencing

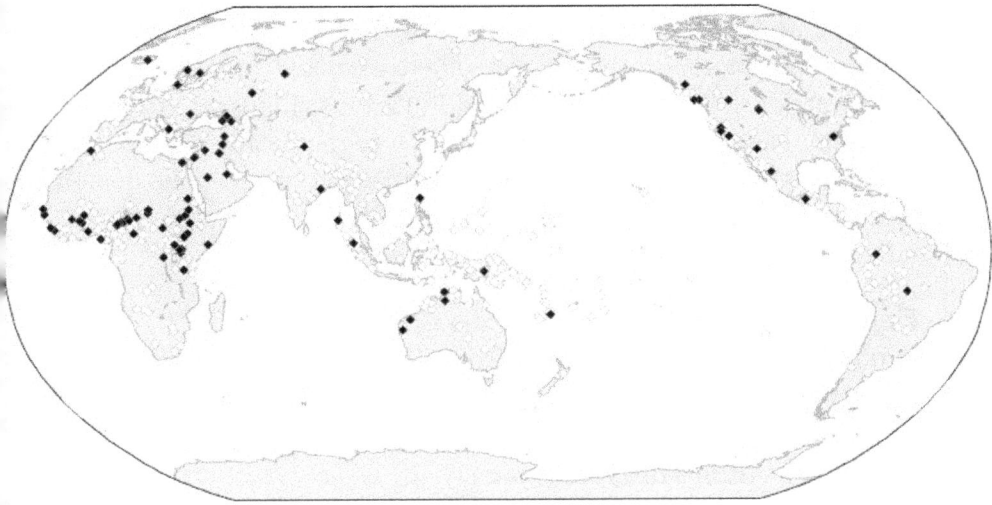

Figure 3.2: Distribution of definite affixes (black symbols) in a sample of 566 languages (Dryer 2005)

(6)   *I have to fix my computer: there is some problem with the hard disk.*

In addition to straightforward referential cases as the ones exemplified above, definite articles are also used in generic noun phrases, as in (7).

(7)   *The lion is a mammal.*

In English, this phenomenon is somewhat restricted, but as we shall see below, it plays a more salient role in other languages.

The most common diachronic source for definite articles is demonstrative pronouns, typically distal ones ('that'). As pointed out by Lyons (1999: 332), there is a substantial overlap between the domains of use of demonstratives and definite articles, notably in anaphoric function. For instance, in a context like the following, both *that* and *the* are acceptable:

(8)   *Last year, I saw a film by Ingmar Bergman. I would like to see that/the film again.*

---

gets lost if the term "bridging" is generalized to cases where the assumption in question is trivial or follows from the meaning of the noun phrases involved. In *In this group, the members work well together*, the only assumption necessary to link *the members* to *this group* is that a group has members.

The first stage in the development of definite articles from demonstratives, accordingly, consists in a more general use of a demonstrative in anaphoric function. Such "anaphoric articles" are attested in various languages – Lyons (1999: 53-54) mentions Hausa and Lakota as examples. Geographically closer to the area studied here is spoken Finnish, where at least in some varieties the demonstrative *se* tends to be used in ways suggestive of an "anaphoric article" (see Laury 1997 and, for a more sceptical view, Juvonen 2000):

(9) Finnish

...niin sit **se** *mies meni ja, osti* **ne** *kaikki ilmapallot*
so then **this** man go.PST and buy.PST **this.PL** all balloon.NOM.PL

ja anto ne **sille** *pojalle,*
and give.PST this.PL **this.ALL** boy.ALL

ja sit **se** *poika...*
and then **this** boy

'...so then the man went and bought all the balloons and gave them to the boy, and the boy...' (Juvonen 2000: 136)

For an erstwhile demonstrative to look more like the definite articles we are used to from languages such as English, it has to acquire also non-anaphoric uses. Finnish *se* is still unacceptable e.g. in a context as that exemplified in (6). The mechanism behind an expansion from an anaphoric to a more general definite article is not well understood, but we may note that it involves the elements usually associated with grammaticalization processes: a rise in frequency through the expansion to new contexts where the element becomes obligatory, combined with a loss of prosodic prominence and an ensuing reduction of phonetic weight (what is commonly but misleadingly referred to as "erosion").

A language can also have more than one definite article. One way in which such a situation can develop is through separate waves of grammaticalization that give rise to a "layered" system in which two (or more) elements of varying age compete with each other. The youngest element will then typically have the functions that are first to grammaticalize, such as anaphoric ones. This is exemplified by various West Germanic varieties, such as the Fering dialect of North Frisian described by Ebert (1971) (although the actual rules for choosing between the articles are a bit more complicated; for an accessible account see Lyons 1999: 162). Compare the following examples:

(10)   North Frisian (Fering dialect)

    a. *Hat kaam   me a   maan.*
       she come.PST with DEF man

       'She came with her husband, lit. the man.'

    b. *Hat kaam   me di maan.*
       she come.PST with DEF man

       'She came with the man.' (Lyons 1999: 163)

Among languages whose definite articles would seem to be of a "garden variety" kind, there is in fact considerable variation which is largely attributable to how far the grammaticalization process has gone and which routes it has taken. For example, the English definite article on the whole has a relatively restricted domain of use compared to definite articles in many other languages. Most saliently, as has already been noted, English has a restricted use of definite articles with generic noun phrases – this will be further discussed in section §3.3.1. But English also shows a reluctance to use articles with proper names, in contrast to many other languages, such as Greek and southern German vernaculars, but also many northern Scandinavian vernaculars, to be discussed in section §3.9. Even in English there are exceptions, such as some types of geographical names, e.g. names of rivers such as *the Thames*. Since proper names are usually seen as "inherently definite", the use of definite articles would seem to be wholly redundant from the communicative point of view. However, such apparently redundant uses of grammatical elements are typical of later stages of grammaticalization processes and show that the identification of the "function" of a grammatical element is not always easy (Dahl 2004: 81-86).

The story does not end here, however. A definite article may develop further, expanding its domain of use to a point where it is no longer possible to call it "definite" or even an "article". This process was described by Greenberg (1978), who argued that definite articles are the source of various grammatical morphemes. A particularly notable example of this process involves noun class markers, such as those found in Bantu languages wherein the affixes are obligatory with nouns irrespective of the context in which they appear. The details of the route to such a situation from "garden variety" definite articles are far from clear. One example of an intermediate stage suggested by Greenberg would be the "specific" articles found in many Oceanic languages which also cover many of the functions of the indefinite article of English, in particular that of introducing new, specific discourse referents. Compare the Samoan article *le* in the following example:

(11) Samoan (Austronesian)
'O **le** ulugāli'i, fānau l-a lā tama 'o **le** teine 'o Sina.
PRS ART couple give_birth ART-POSS 3DU child PRS ART girl PRS Sina
'There was a couple who had a child, a girl called Sina.' (Mosel &
Hovdhaugen 1992: 259)

What we find in Scandinavian vernaculars, however, is an expansion of the range
of uses of definite articles that goes in a different direction and cannot be described in terms of "specificity" in any sense. The Scandinavian development
therefore is of considerable interest for our understanding of the role of definite
articles in grammaticalization processes.

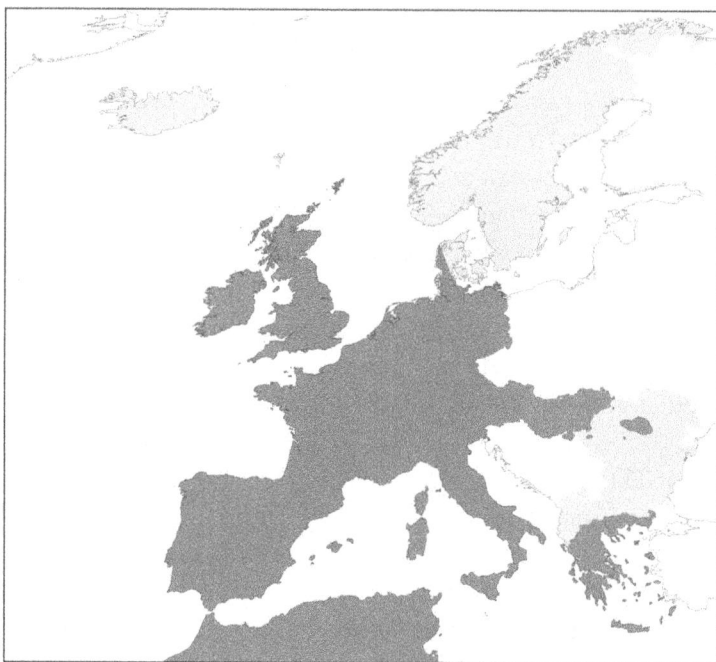

Figure 3.3: Definiteness marking of non-modified nouns in Europe west of 30°E
(dark grey: free article only, light grey: suffixal marking)

3.1.4 Definite marking in Scandinavian in general

As already noted, Western Europe is one of the areas in the world where definite articles are generally present. The distribution is determined by areal rather

than by genetic factors. Although definite articles would seem to be a general feature of the Germanic, Celtic and Romance families, this is a late phenomenon not found in the older historical stages of Indo-European. The presence of definite articles in these languages must therefore be attributed to a later spread rather than to inheritance from a parent language. In fact, there is a relatively neat diachronic progression in the appearance of definite articles from the Eastern Mediterranean to north-western Europe, basically in the order of Semitic → Greek → Romance → Germanic, suggesting a rather slow expansion wave which took about two thousand years to complete. The Fenno-Ugric and Slavic languages in Europe are split with respect to definiteness marking, and there is evidence that definite articles are latecomers in these languages also

If we focus on Europe west of 30°E (Figure 3.3), we find definite articles in one central and two relatively peripheral areas. In the large central area comprising most of Western Europe, definite articles are manifested as free morphemes occurring initially in noun phrases. However, in the two peripheral areas found in Scandinavia and the Balkans, definiteness is marked by suffixing. This marking occurs in the standard languages of Romanian, Bulgarian, Macedonian, and Albanian. These developments fit less straightforwardly into the general expansion pattern, although the general timing and the closeness to the preposed article area makes areal influence likely here, too. In Scandinavia, the situation is further complicated by the presence of both preposed and suffixed articles, with varying divisions of labour in the individual languages (see §4.3 for details). It should also be noted here that there are significant differences between the suffixed articles in Scandinavia and those found in the Balkans: the latter should probably be seen as movable clitics rather than suffixes – they typically show up on the first word in the noun phrase, more or less irrespective of its grammatical category (thus, in Macedonian and Bulgarian, definite articles can be cliticized even to possessive pronouns: *moja-ta kniga* 'my-DEF book').

The origins of definiteness marking in the Scandinavian languages are rather obscure. Definite articles seem to have been absent from the earliest stages of Old Nordic and there are only sporadic attestations from runic inscriptions. From Sweden, two attestations of what seems to be the same formulaic phrase *kuþ heabi onti-ni* or *kuþ hialbi *anti-ni* 'God help soul.DEF' i.e. 'may God help the soul' are cited. When written documents start to appear in the 13th and 14th centuries, both preposed and suffixed articles are still rare in many texts, in particular in laws and poetry (which happen to constitute the bulk of the preserved written material); such instances are possibly rarer in Denmark and Sweden than in the West Nordic area. Here are some statistics (Delsing 2002: 938), based on Larm (1936) and Skautrup (1944):

Table 3.1: Percentage of definite nouns among nouns in general

Older Västgöta Law	0.5
Uppland Law	5
Östgöta Law	7.5
Scanian Law	8
Jutland Law	10

The source of the suffixed article is commonly assumed to be an original demonstrative *inn* or *hinn*. The forms with an initial *h-*, which may be due to a reinforcement of *inn* in analogy with other 3rd person pronouns (Perridon 1989: 135), (Syrett 2002: 723), were only used in preposed position in East Nordic. According to a popular hypothesis (going back to Grimm (1822-40)), the suffixed article originated as an adjectival article in a construction such as *maþr inn gamli* 'man the old'. I think this hypothesis should be viewed with some scepticism. The low frequency in spoken language of the adjectival construction makes it unlikely as a general model for noun phrases (as is also noted by Saltveit & Seip (1971: 63). There also seems to be little concrete evidence of such a development anywhere. (In the Balkan languages the corresponding constructions would be expressed as 'man-the old' and the article would thus not be in the right place relative to the noun.) Thus, the alternative hypothesis that the suffixed article has developed out of an unstressed postposed demonstrative seems more plausible. In fact, this phenomenon is exemplified by the inscription *hali hino* '[flat] stone *this*' on the whet-stone of Strøm (Norway) from about 600 C.E.

With respect to the timetable for the development of the suffixed article, there seem to be two basic views. The first, which assumes that the genesis of the suffixed article in the spoken language is significantly earlier than its appearance in the written language, appears to originate with Neckel (1924). This position is also taken in recent works by both Perridon (1989: 142), who speaks of "a hidden life" of the article "before it starts its public written life", and Syrett (2002: 723), who says that "...it seems reasonable to suggest that" the suffixed article "was the end product of an unrelated series of morphological and syntactical developments within the progression from" Ancient Norse to Old Norse (the transitional period between these two being broadly defined as lasting from the 6th century until 1100).

The main representative of the other view is Delsing (2002: 938-939) who thinks that the suffixed article "developed as an innovation in the 13th century".

(He does not say explicitly what territory this claim is intended to cover, but it is given in the context of a treatment of Old Swedish and Old Danish.) He argues against the view that "the low frequency of articles in the oldest texts can be explained by style", pointing to the fact that not only legal and poetic texts but also texts which "are written in styles where we would expect an ample use of the articles", e.g. the Gutasaga (a text presumed to be from the 13th century and containing a description of the mythical origin of the island of Gotland) and the chronicles from Vidhem [S47], have a low frequency of definite marking.

Delsing's discussion of the style question seems to conflate two possible effects of style (or genre) on the use of definite articles: (i) a generally lower frequency of definite marking due to pragmatic reasons; (ii) the possible use of an archaizing language. Thus, he says: "Runic inscriptions, laws and poetry are not the kind of texts where we expect to find articles" (ibid.). There obviously are some text types where definite articles would be infrequent in any language due to a restricted need for definite reference, and runic inscriptions may be cases in point, but this would hardly hold for the other kinds of text mentioned by Delsing. Thus, in a language where definite articles are regularly used, such as English or Modern Swedish, they occur also in laws and poetry. Consider as an example Article 1:1 of the Swedish constitution (*Regeringsformen*), which contains two noun phrases with definite marking:

(12) Swedish
      Den offentliga makten *utövas*   *under **lagarna.***
      DEF public   power.DEF exert.PASS.PRS under law.PL.DEF
      '(The) public power is exerted under the laws.'

On the other hand, laws and poetry are genres which are often formulated in an archaizing language and which may thus differ significantly from other text types and in particular from informal spoken language. It may be noted that even contemporary legal Swedish exhibits patterns of article usage which most probably reflect an older stage of development. Thus, until the last decades of the 20th century, it was normal for singular generic noun phrases in legal texts to be used without any article, as in

(13) Swedish
      Hund *skall hållas*   *kopplad på **offentlig plats.***
      dog   shall keep.PASS.INF leash.PP on public   place
      'A dog shall be kept on a leash in public places (lit: Dog shall be kept leashed on public place)'

The absence of definite articles in medieval legal prose would thus be due to an archaizing language rather than to the general low frequency of definite articles in legal texts. The same goes for poetry, mutatis mutandis. But as Delsing points out, there are other texts which also exhibit a low incidence of definiteness marking. The first text mentioned by Delsing, the Gutasaga, may not be too relevant in this context, since the variety it is written in, Old Gutnish, is not necessarily representative of mainstream Old Swedish. On the other hand, the Vidhem chronicle (presumed to be written in Västergötland around 1250, although there seems to be no general agreement on this) may be evidence that the use of definite marking was generally restricted in the written language of the period. However, this text is an appendix to the Västergötland law, so one could perhaps expect the style to be close to that of legal language.

In my opinion, several things speak against the hypothesis that the suffixed article is a 13th century innovation. One is the geographical distribution of the suffixed article: in spite of its low frequency in some early texts, it is attested in the 13th century from all parts of the Scandinavian area: Iceland, Norway, Denmark, and Sweden. And even earlier, in the first half of the 12th century in Iceland (according to Perridon 2002: §1019), there is a consistent use in the First Grammatical Treatise. Moreover, although not frequent, even the very earliest texts in Sweden do contain quite a few definite articles. Thus, the Older Västgöta Law, assumed to be from around 1225, contains 23 instances of suffixed articles (Larm 1936: 24). This means that, already at this stage, the suffixed article was well enough entrenched to show up in written language all over Scandinavia, although it was still used in a restricted fashion.

Furthermore, if it were the case that the forms that we see in the oldest texts represent a recent innovation, we would expect them to behave in a way typical of early stages of a grammaticalization process. This is not the case, however. When we first meet the suffixed definite article, it has already reached a relatively advanced stage of grammaticalization. This goes both for form and function: even the earliest attestations are suffixed rather than separate words, and they display non-anaphoric uses (see §3.1.3), suggesting a full-fledged definite article. For instance, the earliest attestations from Sweden, *kuþ hialbi antini* 'God help the [i.e. his] soul' are clear examples of an associative use. The following example from the Vidhem chronicles is also clearly non-anaphoric:

(14)   Medieval Written Swedish
       *Han læt   gøræ   **kyrkiunæ**   i   agnistaðhum.*
       he   let.PST make.INF church.DEF.ACC in Agnestad
       'He had the church in Agnestad built.' [S47]

If the rise of definite articles was close in time to the creation of the documents in which they are common, we would expect to find more signs of the early stages of development, both with regard to form and to function.

What was just said about the earliest documented stages is paralleled in the modern forms of Scandinavian: there is no variety that reflects an earlier stage in the grammaticalization process. It should also be noted that the suffixed article has a virtually total coverage in Scandinavian, with the exception of the Jutish dialects in Denmark that use prefixed articles exclusively. Thus, the suffixed articles are also manifested in a remarkably uniform way in the most conservative and peripheral varieties. This is in contrast to the prefixed definite article, which is absent both in modern spoken Icelandic and in the Peripheral Swedish vernaculars, and the indefinite article, which is absent in Icelandic. It is also in contrast to most of the major phonological changes in medieval Scandinavian, which tended to be only partially implemented or not implemented at all in peripheral areas. An example is the monophthongization of the original diphthongs *ai* and *au* to *e* and *ö*, respectively, which according to the standard view spread from Denmark to south and central Sweden in the 11th century, but which a millennium later has still not yet been completed in some of the outlying areas, such as northern Norrland, western Dalarna, Österbotten and Gotland.

3.1.5 Neutralization of the definite-indefinite distinction

A fairly common phenomenon, which should be kept apart from the expansion of the definite forms discussed in this chapter, is the partial neutralization of the opposition between definite and indefinite forms: that is, the same form comes to represent both definite and indefinite. For instance, in Orsa (Ovansiljan), neuter nouns do not distinguish definite and indefinite forms. There is no vernacular in which the neutralization between indefinite and definite is total. Rather, as in Orsa, it tends to hit paradigms only partially. What forms are neutralized varies from place to place, but there are a few typical patterns.

Neutralization between indefinite and definite in the plural. This is probably the most common pattern, being found in relatively many places.

In Ovansiljan, this appears to be a relatively late development. Levander (1909) describes Elfdalian as still having a distinction for masculine nouns in the nominative plural, e.g. *kaller:kallär* (indefinite and definite nominative plurals of *kall* 'man'), and for some feminine nouns, e.g. *djieter:djietär* (from *djiet* 'goat'), but not for a feminine noun such as *flugu* 'fly' which has the only form *flugur* in the nominative plural. However, Levander notes that the distinction is not found in all villages in Älvdalen (with varying isoglosses for different types of nouns), and according to Levander (1928: 170), it is found in Orsa and Våmhus but not in Mora, Sollerön, Venjan and Ore. In the accusative plural, a distinction between forms such as *kalla:kallę*exist in all the varieties which retain the nasal vowels, that is, most of Älvdalen, Våmhus and Bonäs (Mora parish).

In Karleby[4] (Northern Ostrobothnian), the old indefinite plural forms have disappeared entirely in favour of the definite ones, e.g. *gåla* '(the) yards', *gatuna* '(the) streets' (Hagfors 1891: 93). Likewise, in Runö (Estonian Swedish vernaculars), there is no indefinite-definite distinction at all in the plural (cf. (78) below.)

Neutralization between indefinite and definite in neuter nouns, with zero endings in the nominative/accusative, is found in at least three geographically quite distinct areas: Orsa and northern Venjan in the Ovansiljan area (Levander 1928: 133) and parts of Värmland. In the Cat Corpus we thus find the following examples of cognates of Swedish *golv* 'floor' used as a definite noun with a zero ending:

(15) Orsa (Ovansiljan)
    Gow wa   *niskajrad.*
    floor be.PST new-clean.PP
    'The floor was newly cleaned.' (Cat Corpus)

(cf. Swedish *Golvet var nyskurat*)

(16) Västra Ämtervik (Värmland)
    Men nepå   **gôLv** *va*   *dä en*   *hög* *mä* *matt-traser.*
    But down_on **floor** be.PST it INDF heap with carpet_rag.PL
    'But on the floor there was a heap of rags.' (Cat Corpus)

---

[4] The previous town of Gamlakarleby and the parish of Karleby were merged into Karleby town in 1977. For simplicity, I use the name "Karleby" throughout.

(cf. Swedish *Men på golvet var det en hög mattrasor*) In Orsa and Venjan, where the dative case is still alive, there is also neutralization in the dative of these nouns.

Neutralization between indefinite and definite in the dative. This appears to be common or even normal in the dative-preserving vernaculars. Thus, according to Marklund (1976), nouns in Skelletmål have two rather than four dative forms – one for singular and one for plural, as in *pigen* 'the maid': *pigåm* 'the maids' (from *piig* 'maid'), or just one for both, as in *vaidjåm* 'the wall(s)'. There is thus no definite:indefinite distinction, and although Marklund does not say so explicitly, it appears that the normal interpretation of the dative forms is definite – the ending is also normally added to the definite stem (as in the case of *vaigg*:*vaidjåm*).

The developments are somewhat different in the singular and the plural. In the singular, the indefinite form tends to be marginal or absent, whereas the definite form is stronger; in the plural, it is the definite form that disappears. In Dalecarlian, the vernacular of Orsa appears to be the only exception in that there are separate forms for definite dative plurals ending in -*uma*, as in *revuma* 'fox.PL.DEF.DAT'. According to Levander (1909), at the time of his investigation in the first decade of the 20th century, elderly persons in Älvdalen sometimes used definite dative plurals in -*ume*. Otherwise, the indefinite dative plural ending -*um* has been generalized, e.g. Elfdalian *rövum* 'fox.PL.DEF.DAT'.

Neutralization of definiteness in individual lexemes. Individual lexemes or groups of lexemes sometimes have identical indefinite and definite forms. Thus, in Elfdalian, neuter nouns in -*ð* have a zero ending in the definite singular nominative and accusative, e.g. *broð* 'bread'. Many Elfdalian nouns are not inflected at all. The word for 'coffee' is perhaps most notable in this connection; *kaffi*, which like *broð* is highly frequent in contexts in what is below called non-delimited readings, would normally trigger a definite form.

Neutralization of the definiteness distinction means that the consequences of the changes discussed below are more restricted than they would otherwise be, since in many cases it will not make any difference if an indefinite or a definite form is chosen. It also means that direct comparisons between dialects are not always possible – if you translate an example from one dialect to another, the distinction between definite and indefinite may disappear on the way.

As I said above and as also argued by Hummelstedt (1934), neutralization of the definiteness distinction is in principle a different phenomenon from that of extensions of the domain of definite forms. One may of course also speculate whether there is any causal relationship between the processes by which definite forms acquire new uses and the processes by which definite and indefinite forms are neutralized. What could perhaps be expected is that if the definite forms expand too much, the indefinite forms will simply fall into oblivion. This is essentially what seems to happen in the final stages of the grammaticalization paths described by Greenberg. However, confusingly, it is not always the definite forms that win out in the neutralization process: for instance, in Orsa, as we have seen, neuter nouns have zero endings for both indefinite and definite. In other words, the neutralization process may well obliterate the results of the grammaticalization process. On the other hand, given that neutralization is so common, it is somewhat remarkable that speakers are still able to make the distinction when it is needed. Also, there is no consistency in the neutralizations: thus, Orsamål is "radical" in having no definiteness distinction in neuter nouns and "conservative" in being the only vernacular that preserves the same distinction in the dative plural.

It should also be noted that the systems described above often go against general assumptions about markedness relations in morphology (as when a distinction is upheld in oblique cases but not in the nominative) (Dahl & Koptjevskaja-Tamm 2006).

3.2 Some notes on the morphology of definiteness in Scandinavian

The recognition of definite forms of nouns in Scandinavian is not always straightforward, due to the interaction of definiteness marking with gender, number, case, and declension classes, and also phonological and other changes that have given rise to extensive variation between varieties and fusion of inflectional morphemes with each other and with the stem. Gender is important in that there are almost always separate definite suffixes for the different genders. While a two-gender system for nouns with an uter:neuter distinction is prevalent in Central Scandinavian (as defined in 2.3.1), most other North Germanic varieties and also many vernaculars preserve the original three-gender system with masculine, feminine, and neuter genders.

In two-gender Swedish varieties, uter nouns use the definite suffix *(e)n* and neuter nouns have the suffix *(-e)t*. In the plural, common gender nouns add *na* after the plural suffix, which varies between the declension classes, the most frequent ones being *-ar*, *-er*, and *-or*. Neuter gender nouns that end in a consonant have a zero plural ending and take the definite suffix *-en(a)*. If they end in a vowel the plural ending is *-n* and the definite suffix *-a*. Example paradigms are given in Table 3.2.

In three-gender systems, which are found in most varieties exemplified in this book, masculine nouns normally behave like uter nouns in Standard Swedish, but feminine nouns have a specific definite suffix in the singular, which can vary between *-a, -i, -in*, and *-ę*. The final consonant in the neuter definite suffix may be *-t, -d, -ð*. It may also have been lost through sound change, leaving only a vowel, usually *-e*. Another source of confusion is the marking in the plural, where many vernaculars have definite forms in all genders ending in *-an, -en* or *-a*, making them look very similar to singular nouns.

The most complex paradigms are found in the varieties which preserve case inflections in nouns. One such variety is Elfdalian. The example paradigms below are restricted to "strong" nouns and show part of the complexity only.

3.3 Generic and citation uses

3.3.1 Generic uses

Generic noun phrases are used to refer generally to a species (natural kind), class or type of entities.[5] There are actually at least two main kinds of generic uses of noun phrases (Krifka et al. 1995: 19). The first, and most well-known, is when the noun phrase occurs in a context in which a general, "law-like" or nomic statement is made about the species, class or type that the noun phrase denotes (Dahl 1973). The standard example in the linguistic literature is *Beavers build dams*, in which dam-building is described as a typical activity of beavers. This first type is called "characterizing sentences" by Krifka et al. (1995). In the second type, which they call "kind predications", the species or kind is referred to without there being a generalization over its members. For instance, in the sentence *The zoologist was studying the beaver*, the beaver species is referred to as the object of the zoologist's study, but no inference can be drawn about individual beavers.

An interesting typological generalization is that generic uses of noun phrases do not in general have a dedicated mode of expression; rather, several different types of noun phrases may be recruited for those uses. Thus, in English, bare plurals, singulars with indefinite articles, and singulars with definite articles can all be used generically. We may thus also say *A beaver builds dams* and *The beaver builds dams*. There are quite definite restrictions, however. Indefinite singulars can only be used for "characterizing sentences", not for "kind predications": *The zoologist was studying a beaver* must mean that he or she was studying a concrete

---

[5] In Swedish grammatical literature, the traditional term used is "allmän betydelse" 'general meaning'.

Table 3.2: Standard Swedish – uter and neuter nouns

	INDEF SG	DEF SG	INDEF PL	DEF PL
uter	*häst* 'horse'	*hästen*	*hästar*	*hästarna*
neuter	*hus* 'house'	*huset*	*hus*	*husen(a)*

Table 3.3: Elfdalian – strong masculine: *kall* 'man'

	INDEF SG	DEF SG	INDEF PL	DEF PL
nominative	*kall*	*kalln*	*kaller*	*kallär*
dative	*kalle*	*kallem*	*kallum*	*kallum*
accusative	*kall*	*kalln*	*kalla*	*kallą*

Table 3.4: Elfdalian – strong feminine: *nǫl* 'needle'

	INDEF SG	DEF SG	INDEF PL	DEF PL
nominative	*nǫl*	*nǫlę*	*nǫler*	*nǫlär*
dative	*nǫl*	*nǫln*	*nǫlum*	*nǫlum*
accusative	*nǫl*	*nǫlę*	*nǫler*	*nǫlär*

Table 3.5: Elfdalian – strong neuter: *buärd* 'table'

	INDEF SG	DEF SG	INDEF PL	DEF PL
nominative	*buärd*	*buärdeð*	*buärd*	*buärdę*
dative	*buärde*	*buärdę*	*buärdum*	*buärdum*
accusative	*buärd*	*buärdeð*	*buärd*	*buärdę*

individual (or, possibly, a specific sub-species). Also, in English, definite plurals and definite mass nouns cannot in general be used generically: *The beavers build dams* must refer to a specific group of beavers and *The gold is expensive* must refer to a specific mass of gold. In this respect, languages with definite articles vary quite considerably. To see this, it is sufficient to compare English to French, where in fact *Les castors construisent des barrages* is the standard way of saying that beavers build dams, and correspondingly, the articleless construction, which is typical of English, is generally ungrammatical. In fact, the French situation appears to be more common among languages with definite articles (at least in Europe). That is, plurals and mass nouns as a rule take a definite article when used generically. Behrens (2005) looked at five European languages – French, English, German, Greek, and Hungarian, and found that French, Greek and Hungarian all behave similarly in this regard, whereas German turned out to be somewhere in the middle. Compare the following example from Behrens' corpus, *The Little Prince*:

(17) a. *English: Flowers are weak creatures.*

    b. *German: Die Blumen sind schwach.*

    c. *French: Les fleurs sont faibles.*

    d. *Greek: Ta lulúdhja íne adhínama.*

    e. *Hungarian: A virágok gyengék.*

Swedish, like German, is an intermediate case in that it sometimes follows the French and sometimes the English pattern. Thus, Swedish uses a definite NP in *Livet är kort* 'Life is short' (cf. French *La vie est brève*) but like English prefers a bare noun in *Guld är dyrt* 'Gold is expensive'. Possibly, Swedish is slightly more restrictive than German in the use of definite generics: it would seem more natural to use an indefinite plural in the translation of (17) than a definite one:

(18) Swedish
    Blommor *är*   *veka*   *varelser.*
    flower.PL be.PRS weak.WK being.PL
    'Flowers are weak beings.'

However, many Peripheral Swedish varieties behave more like French in this respect, with an across-the-board use of definite forms in generics. We thus find examples such as the following:

(19)   Elfdalian (Ovansiljan)
Guldið ir   dyrt.
gold.DEF be.PRS.SG expensive.N
'Gold is expensive.' (questionnaire)

Generic uses of definites seem to be among the most widespread of the extended uses of definites found in the Peripheral Swedish area. They are thus characteristic not only of Upper Norrland and Upper Dalecarlian but also of regions such as Värmland, southern Finland, and Norway. Compare the following examples:

(20)   Östmark (Värmland)
Kaffen   ä   allt bätter än   ten.
coffee.DEF be.PRS sure better   than tea.DEF
'Coffee is sure better than tea.' (Broberg 1936)

(21)   Pernå (Nylandic)
Björčin, han ä   nⲱ   bäter ti möbler,   men han ä so hörder
birch.DEF it   be.PRS surely better for furniture.PL But it   is so hard
ti   arbita.
INFm work.INF
'Birch, it is better for furniture, but it is so hard-worked.' (Lundström (1939: 13-14))

(22)   Ingå (Nylandic)
*Va   hadde   man för tjö:rdo:n ti   de:? - **Tjärran.***
what have.PST one for vehicle for that cart.DEF
'What kind of vehicle did they use for that? – A [lit. the] cart.'
(Harling-Kranck & Mara 1998: 42)

(23)   Tromsø (Troms, Norway)

    a. *Det e   mer varme i **kola**   enn i **veden.***
       It   be.PRS more heat   in coal.DEF than in firewood.DEF
       'There is more heat in coal than in firewood.' (Iversen 1918: 19)

    b. **Ulvan**   e'   minder   som **bjørnan.**
       Wolf.DEF.PL be.PRS small.CMPR than bear.DEF.PL
       'Wolves are smaller than bears.' (Iversen 1918: 18)

The examples in (23) are the only ones that I have found in the literature from Norway, but reactions from Norwegian linguists suggest that such generic uses are in fact more widespread.

As noted above, Delsing's "tentative" map of the "partitive" uses of definites in Scandinavia shows all of Northern Sweden (and a strip in Norway along the Swedish border in Trøndelag) as having "partitive articles where the standard language has generic naked forms", the southern border coinciding more or less with the *limes norrlandicus.* More specifically, it passes through northern Värmland and southern Dalarna and cuts Gästrikland in two. As for Värmland, Delsing's line is roughly at the height of Torsby and Ekshärad, but the Cat Corpus examples – from Västra Ämtervik (Fryksdalen) and Mangskog – give evidence that the border goes at least 40-50 kilometers further south in Värmland:

(24)   a.   Västra Ämtervik (Värmland)
          FôggLân   *skâ*   *en*   *fôll*   *int*   *mat...*
          bird.PL.DEF shall.PRS one PRAG NEG feed

    b.   Mangskog (Värmland)
          Fugglane   *skâ*   *en*   *fôll*   *inte mate...*
          bird.PL.DEF shall.PRS one PRAG NEG feed

        'Birds, you should not feed...' (Cat Corpus)

The use is not consistent, however – in the following example the indefinite form is used:

(25)   Västra Ämtervik (Värmland)
      Sockerkak   *ä*   *dä*   *bäst Kâtt'n*   *vet.*
      Sponge_cake be.PRS DEF.N best cat.DEF know.PRS

      'Sponge cake is Cat's favourite.' (Cat Corpus)

(26)   Mangskog (Värmland)
      Sockerkake *ä*   *dä*   *bäste Katten*   *vet.*
      Sponge_cake be.PRS DEF.N best cat.DEF know.PRS

      'Sponge cake is Cat's favourite.' (Cat Corpus)

On the other hand, there is rather little evidence for generic uses of noun phrases in the rest of Delsing's southern area. Delsing does not himself provide any such examples, and the Cat Corpus evidence is rather negative, in the following sense: In the translations of (24)-(25), no definite forms show up in texts from Hälsingland (3 texts), Härjedalen (1 text), and Dalarna outside the Ovansiljan area (about ten texts). (The examples from Ovansiljan are sometimes ambiguous due to the neutralization of the definiteness distinction in the plural.) Consider, for example, the following three translations from Hälsingland:[6]

(27)   a. Färila (Helsingian)
           Fôgglâ skâ   mânn fäll   int   matâ,   häll!
           bird.PL shall.PRS one   PRAG NEG feed.INF either

       b. Forsa (Helsingian)
           Fuglar ska   man fell   int   mata   e.
           bird.PL shall.PRS one   PRAG NEG feed.INF NEG[7]

       c. Järvsö (Helsingian)
           Fôggla ska   man fell   int   mata,   e.
           bird.PL shall.PRS one   PRAG NEG feed.INF NEG

           'Birds, you should not feed...' (Cat Corpus)

Likewise Västerdalarna:

(28)   Transtrand (Västerdalarna)

       a. *Göll e   dirt.*
           gold be.PRS expensive

           'Gold is expensive.' (questionnaire)

       b. *Häster kut   fort.*
           horse.PL run.PRS fast

           'Horses run fast.' (questionnaire)

3.3.2 Citation uses

Among uses of definite nouns that are close to generics, one can mention meta-
linguistic uses or what is commonly called "citation forms". This kind of use
seems to be quite common in many parts of the peripheral area. Thus, speakers
who are asked to write down word lists often quote nouns in the definite form.
This use of definite forms is already reflected in the word lists of Pitemål compiled
by the philologist Johan Ihre in the 18th century (Reinhammar 2002).
   Some clear examples of citation uses are:

---

[6] The endings in the plural tend to be confusing – for instance, the *-a* ending is definite in some
vernaculars and indefinite in others. In the case of Färila and Järvsö the indefinite plural of
'bird' is *fôggla* and the definite plural is *fôgglan*.

[7] The morpheme *e* is a reinforcing element that co-occurs with negation often enough to warrant
talking of a double negation construction. It is common in vernacular texts from Uppland and
Hälsingland.

(29)   Ersmark (Northern Westrobothnian)
       He kall   ve fö sjanostn   för gammalt.
       it   call.PRS we for **sand_cheese**.DEF for old.N
       'This we call "sand cheese" of old.' [S43]

(30)   Svartlå, Överluleå (Lulemål)
       Jö tråo   dom kåles   skråkaran.
       I   think.PRS they call.PASS.PRS "**skråkar**".DEF.PL
       'I think they are called "skråkaran" ' [S45]

Definite forms in citation uses are occasionally mentioned in the literature. Thus, Ågren & Dahlstedt (1954: 282) say that if you ask a Norrlandic farmer what the berries that grow along the sides of the field are called, he answers *Åkerbära* 'the polar cloudberries'. According to Lagman (1979: 82), the definite form shows up "to a certain extent" as the "lexical form" in Estonian Swedish. Thus, he says, the answer to the question "What is 'white horse' in Nuckö Swedish?" would be *hoit aiken* 'white horse.DEF'. Steensland (1994: 8), in his book on Elfdalian plant names, says that he uses indefinite forms throughout, "although this can often appear unnatural to an Elfdalian". "In Elfdalian definite forms are most often used when a plant is named."[8]

3.4 Non-delimited uses

3.4.1 General

A major type of extended uses of definite forms in the Peripheral Swedish area are the ones I shall call NON-DELIMITED. Consider the following sentence from the Cat Corpus:

(31)   a. Swedish
          Ja, bara jag har   fått   in vedbördan,   så ska   jag
          yes only I   have.PRS get.SUP in wood_bundle.DEF so shall.PRS I
          värma   mjölk åt honom.
          warm.INF **milk** for him

---

[8] "Jag återger i regel de älvdalska växtnamnen i obestämd form, trots att detta många gånger kan te sig onaturligt för en älvdaling. I älvdalskan använder man nämligen oftast bestämd form, då man benämner en växt."

    b. Skelletmål (Northern Westrobothnian)

       Jå, bara I ha   börä   ein veabåla,   sä skå   I

       yes only I have.PRS get.SUP in wood_bundle.DEF so shall.PRS I

       *väärm   **mjölka** åt 'n.*

       warm.INF milk.DEF for him

    c. Orsa (Ovansiljan)

       Ja, bara i a   fendji in widn   sö skari   wärm

       yes only I have.PRS get.SUP in firewood.DEF so shall.PRS_I warm.INF

       ***mjötje**   a   num.*

       milk.DEF for him

    'As soon as I have got the wood bundle into the house, I'll warm some milk for him.' (Cat Corpus)

Here, both Skelletmål and the Orsa vernacular use the definite form of the noun *milk* in the second clause, although an indefinite form would be expected from the point of view of Standard Swedish, since there is no earlier mention of milk in the text.

Such uses have often been called "partitive" in the literature, which seems natural in view of the fact that they by and large correspond to the use of the the the "partitive articles" in French and Italian, and also are generally translatable by the partitive case in languages such as Finnish and Estonian. As pointed out in Koptjevskaja-Tamm (2001: 525), however, the term "partitive" is better reserved for constructions which express part-whole relationships in a narrower sense, such as *a piece of the cake*. For constructions that derive historically from partitive constructions but are synchronically used to express a non-specified quantity of something, such as noun phrases with partitive articles in Romance languages, Koptjevskaja-Tamm uses the term "pseudo-partitive". This term, however, is less suitable for patterns that have no direct link to partitive constructions in the proper sense, and I therefore prefer the term "non-delimited" here. "Non-delimited" means that the noun phrase contains no indication of a quantity such as *a cup of* in *a cup of tea* or *much* in *much beer*. The lexical heads of non-delimited NPs are either mass nouns or plural count nouns. In English and Central Scandinavian, they would typically be "bare NPs", e.g. beer in I am drinking beer.

Delsing (1993: 51) notes that the non-delimited uses of definite forms, or as he calls them, noun phrases with "partitive articles", can be used in existential constructions with a dummy subject, as in the following examples:

(32) "North Swedish" (unspecified location)
      Hä finns **vattne** *däri* *hinken.*
      it   exist.PRS **water.DEF** there_in bucket.DEF

      'There is water in the bucket.'

(33) *Hä väks* **granän** *överallt.*
      it   grow.DEF **fir.DEF.** everywhere

      'Fir trees grow all around.'

From this observation, Delsing draws the conclusion that these forms are not really definite, and that we are not dealing with "definite forms" or a "definite article" but rather with manifestations of a "partitive article" separate from the ordinary definite article or definite forms. He also includes generic uses of definite forms under this heading.

The definiteness constraint on NPs in the Swedish dummy subject construction (which is similar to the English one) makes it possible to use this construction as a test on definiteness in Swedish. The definiteness constraint is not universal, however; it does not hold for the corresponding constructions in German:

(34) German
      Es kommt **der** **Zug** *von* *Kiel.*
      it   come.PRS DEF.M.NOM train from Kiel

      'The train from Kiel comes/is coming.'

It follows that the definiteness constraint is not necessarily applicable to the varieties discussed here. Furthermore, it is not obvious that there is a unified notion of definiteness that can be applied at all levels of description. What is marked by a definite article may well be semantically or pragmatically indefinite, and vice versa. The postulation of two separate entities underlying the various uses of definite forms detracts attention from the fact that these forms are diachronically connected and may also be argued to form a continuum synchronically. We may of course decide that the distribution of definite forms in Peripheral Swedish vernaculars is too different from that of the entities we usually call definite articles to deserve that name. I think practical considerations speak in favour of not inventing a new term here. Delsing's proposal, "partitive article", could of course only cover the extended uses of definite forms. However, Delsing applies it not only to non-delimited uses but also to generic ones. Since there are dialects which

have generic but no non-delimited uses of definites, this has the rather peculiar
consequence that there would be partitive articles whose only reading is generic
Generic readings are not found with partitive articles in Romance. Instead, those
languages as a rule mark generic noun phrases by definite articles. Similarly,
with respect to case-marking in Fenno-Ugric, generic NPs pattern with NPs that
have definite reference. Furthermore, even in Swedish, the definite form is used
with generic noun phrases in various contexts (above all with singular nouns),
which, on Delsing's proposal, would make the borderline between the definite
and the partitive articles look a bit arbitrary. There is good reason, as we shall
see, to assume that generic readings of definites are diachronically prior to non-
delimited ones. We shall also see that there are various other extended uses of
definites for which "partitive" is not a natural label. In view of this, I find the term
"partitive article" rather inadequate for the extended uses of definites in Peripheral Swedish. (Bergholm, Linder & Yttergren (1999) take this line of reasoning
even further, labelling all extended uses of definite forms "generic".)

   As examples of extended uses of definite articles in the literature, one often
finds expressions such as 'pick berries'. In sentences such as (35) and (36) it is
natural to use a non-delimited noun phrase since it does not really make sense
to specify a quantity.

(35)   *I am picking berries.*

(36)   *I pick berries in summer.*

There are, however, other contexts where a quantity is at least implied:

(37)   *I picked berries today.*

In contradistinction to (35), where the activity is still going on and the result
is yet undetermined, (37) implies the existence of a specific quantity of berries
that I have picked. In similar contexts, English bare nouns are in competition
with nouns preceded by quantifiers, such as with the unstressed variant of *some*
sometimes denoted in the linguistic literature as *sm*):

(38)   *I picked some berries today.*

There may be some variation among languages as to the choice between constructions with and without quantifiers. It does appear that, in many Peripheral
Swedish vernaculars, cognates of Swedish *någon* 'some' have undergone a development which has led to a considerably wider use than in the standard language.
They thus show up both when Swedish has quantifiers such as *lite* 'a little' and

when it uses bare noun phrases. Levander (1909: 110) notes that Elfdalian *någär* is used in "indefinite individualization" in a way that differs from what is found in Swedish, as in

(39)   Åsen, Elfdalian (Ovansiljan)
       *Ig al   etter **nog   broðe**.*
       I   shall.PRS after **some bread**.DAT
       'I'll go and get some bread.'

Similarly, compare (31)(b) in Skelletmål, where a definite form *mjölka* is used, with the corresponding sentence in Ume-Sävarmål, from the southern part of the same province (Västerbotten):

(40)   Sävar (Southern Westrobothnian)
       Joo, barra ja ha   byre   in veabÖLa,   sä ska   ja
       yes only I have.PRS get.SUP in wood_bundle.DEF so shall.PRS I
       *väärm   **na   mjÖLk** ått 'n.*
       warm.INF **some milk**   for him
       'As soon as I have got the wood bundle into the house, I'll warm (some) milk for him.' (Cat Corpus)

The Skelletmål translator has here chosen to use a definite noun *mjölka*, whereas the Sävar translation contains *na* followed by an indefinite form of the noun *mjÖlk*. However, Skelletmål as described by Marklund (1976) is not alien to an extended use of *na*. Marklund (1976: 43) says that *na* is used often enough to "lose its character as a pronoun in the proper sense and may even sometimes lack a standard language counterpart", especially "with adjectives in negated and interrogative clauses", which sounds like a straightforward description of a grammaticalized item. Some examples are:

(41)   Skelletmål (Northern Westrobothnian)
       *Hæ   e kåmme   **na   måång?***
       have.PRS it come.SUP **some many**
       'Have many [people] arrived?' (Marklund 1976: 43)

(42)   Skelletmål (Northern Westrobothnian)
       *Eint vær I dâ   **na rädd**.*
       NEG be.PST I then **any afraid**
       'I wasn't afraid then at all.' (Marklund 1976: 43)

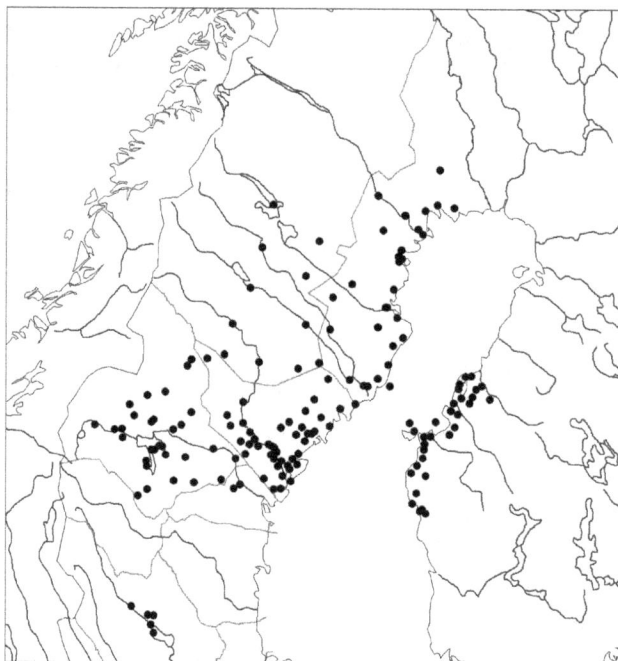

Figure 3.4: Present-day distribution of non-delimited uses of definite nouns

For Pitemål, Brännström (1993: 19) says: "In Pitemål, *na* is used as an indefinite article in the plural", quoting examples such as the following:

(43) Pitemål

    Hä kom   **na**   **fLi'ttjom** *ötät* *väjen.*

    it come.PST **some girl.DAT.PL** along road.DEF

    'There came some girls along the road.' (Brännström 1993: 19)

(44) *Dji´v*   *mä*   **na**   **kòrvom!**

    give.IMP PRO.1SG.OBL **some sausage.DAT.PL**

    'Give me some sausages!' (Brännström 1993: 19)

(For a discussion of the case marking, see §3.5.4 below.)

In other words, *na*-marked noun phrases have encroached on the territory of non-delimited definites in part of the Peripheral Swedish area.

3.4.2 Areal distribution of non-delimited uses

3.4.2.1 General

Although the map in Delsing (2003b) shows non-delimited uses of definite nouns as being restricted to the Swedish-speaking areas of Norrbotten, Västerbotten, Österbotten, Ångermanland and parts of Jämtland, the distribution is in fact wider. In addition to the northern area just mentioned, non-delimited definites are quite strongly represented in the Ovansiljan area, and more or less sporadic examples are found also elsewhere in the Peripheral Swedish area. We shall first look at the two core areas.

3.4.2.2 The northern core area

It appears that non-delimited definites are normal in all Westrobothnian, Norrbothnian, Angermannian, and Ostrobothnian vernaculars, and the usage is fairly stable. It is striking that non-delimited definites are even found in the so-called "settler dialects" (*nybyggarmål*) of the province of Lappland, which are usually said to be strongly influenced by Standard Swedish. Compare the following example from Arvidsjaur in the south-western Lappland:

(45) Arvidsjaur (Northern Settler dialect area)
Jaa, I ska   berätt för je   då   ji å   a   Karolina nåppe
yes I shall.PRS tell.INF for you when I and PDA.F Karolina pick.PST
snottren   i   höst.
cloudberries.DEF.PL in autumn

'Well, I'll tell you how Karolina and I picked cloudberries last autumn.' [S4]

In my opinion, Jämtland should also be included in the northern core area. Delsing is a bit vague here: he first mentions examples of definite forms after quantifiers from the Indal river valley, and then says that "partitive articles" (apparently in general) are "more frequent there than around Lake Storsjön and westward" (Delsing 2003b: 19). On the map, he draws the western border of the use of the partitive article in non-delimited uses at the parish of Lit – this seems to be based on the distribution of quantified uses. However, it is fairly clear that non-delimited uses can be found all over the province (Bo Oscarsson, personal communication). The following is an example from the parish of Kall in the western part of Jämtland (the informant was born around 1850, the text was written down in 1908):

(46) Kall (Jamtska)
En vakker 'n dag rest 'n åt skoga å skull skaff
one beautiful PIA day go.PST he to forest.DEF and will.PST get.INF
ven.
wood.DEF
'One day he went to the forest to get firewood.' [S11]

3.4.2.3 The southern core area (Ovansiljan)

This area is much smaller than the northern one, and the strength of non-delimited uses is also more variable, suggesting a general receding tendency. The most stable usage is found in the more conservative vernaculars of Älvdalen, Våmhus, and Orsa. Levander (1909: 95) quotes the following examples:

(47) Elfdalian (Ovansiljan)
Ulum fǫ stjyreð et middags.
shall.PRS.1PL have.INF **curdled_milk.DEF** to dinner.GEN[9]
'We'll have curdled milk for dinner.'

(48) *Will du fǫ snuseð min mig?*
want.PRS you have.INF **snuff.DEF** with PRO.1SG.OBL
'Do you want to have snuff from me?'

More recent attestations can be quoted from Bengt Åkerberg's translation of the novel *Hunden* by Kerstin Ekman:

(49) Elfdalian (Ovansiljan)

a. *Eð liep nið smeltwattneð i uälų.*
it run.PST down **melting_water.DEF** in hole.DEF.ACC
'Melting water was running down into the hole.' [S9]

b. *Måyre; war ikåv min wattnę.*
marsh.DEF be.PST pregnant with **water.DEF.DAT**
'The marsh was pregnant with water.' [S9]

(49a) demonstrates the possibility of using a definite form in the dummy subject construction, showing that this is indeed possible also in the Ovansiljan area.

---

[9] This is a fossilized "old" genitive, see §5.4.2.

Also in Mora, which has always been the centre of the Ovansiljan region, non-delimited uses of definite forms are relatively strong. Thus, the translation of (31) in the Mormål version in the Cat Corpus is:

(50) Mora (Ovansiljan)
      Ja, bar I a   feir-in   wiråbördu,   så ska   I werm
      yes only I have.PRS get_in.SUP wood_bundle.DEF so shall.PRS I warm.INF
      mjotse   a   onum.
      milk.DEF for PRO.3SG.M.DAT
      'As soon as I have got the wood bundle into the house, I'll warm some milk for him.' (Cat Corpus)

An example from the Bible texts in [S20]:

(51) Östnor-seljamål (Ovansiljan)
      Finns   ä nån   ...   såm   djäv   dem jen   wårm när   dem
      exist.PRS it somebody that give.PRS 3PL.OBL   INDF snake when they
      fråg   ettär fistjen?
      ask.PRS after fish.DEF
      'Is there anybody ... who gives them a snake when they ask for fish?' (Matt. 7:10) [S20]

In an older text we find the following:

(52) Mora (Ovansiljan)
      Ä   wa   je   keLing frammä, so   add   selt   brendunä.
      there be.PST INDF woman out_there REL have.PST sell.SUP aquavit.DEF
      'There was a woman out there, who had sold aquavit.' [S46]

(It may be noted that both (51) and (52) contain dummy subjects.)
   However, the use of definite forms may be receding in Mormål. Compare the following parallel examples from the Elfdalian translation of the Gospel of John (*Juanneswaundsjilq*) and *Mormålsbibeln*:

(53) a. Elfdalian (Ovansiljan)
         Ed so   ar   kumid   til åv tjyötį,   ed ir   tjyöted...
         it REL have.PRS come.SUP to of flesh.DEF.DAT it be.PRS flesh.DEF
         'That which is born of flesh is flesh...' (John 3:6) [S37]

    b. Önamål (Ovansiljan)

        Er så   a   kem-til   åv tjöt e   tjöt...

        it REL have.PRS come_about.SUP of **flesh** be.PRS **flesh**

        'That which is born of flesh is flesh...' [S20]

    c. Elfdalian (Ovansiljan)

        *...ig ar   kumid   og döper   min **wattnę**.*

        I   have.PRS come.SUP and baptize.PRS with **water.DEF.DAT**

        '...I have come to baptize with water.' [S37]

    d. Önamål (Ovansiljan)

        *...ar   I kem   å   döpär   min **wattn**.*

        have.PRS I come.SUP and baptize.PRS with **water**

        '...I have come to baptize with water.' [S20]

Among the other parishes in Ovansiljan, non-delimited definites are used fairly systematically in the Cat Corpus texts from Orsa and Våmhus:

(54)   a. Orsa (Ovansiljan)

        Ja, bara i a   fendji in widn   så skari   wärm

        yes only I have.PRS get.SUP in firewood.DEF so shall.PRS_I warm.INF

        mjötje   a   num.

        milk.DEF for PRO.3SG.M.DAT

    b. Våmhus (Ovansiljan)

        Ja, bara i a   faið   in wi:ðn,   so ska   i werm

        yes only I have.PRS get.SUP in firewood.DEF so shall.PRS I warm.INF

        miö:tsī   a   na.

        milk.DEF for PRO.3SG.F.DAT

        'As soon as I have got the wood bundle into the house, I'll warm some milk for him.' (Cat Corpus)

Similarly, in the extensive questionnaire materials from Orsa collected by Eva Olander, the overwhelming majority of the informants used definite forms in examples such as the following:

(55)   Orsa (Ovansiljan)

        An drick   mjötji.

        he drink.PRS milk.DEF

        'He drinks milk.'

In Sollerön, the use of non-delimited definites appears to be weaker. Thus, according to informants, it would be most natural to use an indefinite form in the following example:

(56) Sollerön (Ovansiljan)
      An drikk   mjok.
      he drink.PRS milk
      'He is drinking milk.' (questionnaire)

However, according to Margit Andersson (personal communication), it might be possible to use the definite form if a habitual interpretation is intended:

(57) Sollerön (Ovansiljan)
      An drikk   mjotji.
      he drink.PRS milk.DEF
      'He drinks milk.'

Similarly, Andersson & Danielsson (1999) quote examples such as the following, with bare nouns where e.g. Elfdalian, for example, would clearly use definite forms:

(58) Sollerön (Ovansiljan)
      I åt   bermos   ata mjotjän.
      I eat.PST lingonberry_jam with milk.DEF.DAT
      'I ate lingonberry jam with the milk.' (Andersson & Danielsson 1999: 373)

(59) *Ä e   mjok   i putällim.*
      it be.PRS milk.DEF in bottle.DEF.DAT
      'There is milk in the bottle.' (Andersson & Danielsson 1999: 373)

However, the same book also lists expressions such as *res päroni* 'peel potatoes.DEF.PL' (Andersson & Danielsson 1999: 176). In the Cat Corpus, there is at least one clear case of a definite form:

(60) Sollerön (Ovansiljan)
      ... å ä add   vurti   skårån   upå snjom.
      and it have.PST become.SUP hard_crust.DEF on snow.DEF
      '... and there was a hard crust on the snow.' (Cat Corpus)

In the translation from Ore, which is regarded as a transitional variety between Ovansiljan and Nedansiljan, we find an indefinite form even in this sentence:

(61) Ore (Ovansiljan)

> ... ô ä add *wurte* **skare** *på snjon.*
> and it have.PST become.SUP **hard_crust** on snow.DEF

'... and there was a hard crust on the snow.' (Cat Corpus)

3.4.2.4 Attestations outside the core areas

The areas where non-delimited uses are more sporadically represented include most of the rest of Norrland, and also the central province of Uppland, and possibly also Estonia. We shall look at each province in turn.

Medelpad. This province is situated along the coast immediately south of Ångermanland. As in the case of Jämtland, Delsing (2003b: 19) is a bit vague here. He quotes Vestlund (1923: 21) as saying that an example such as *de väks granen*[10], registered in Häggdånger in southern Ångermanland and labeled an "existential construction" by Delsing, would be "completely impossible" in Medelpad. Somewhat later, Delsing says that for southern Norrland in general (and, as is clear from the map, including Medelpad) it seems that partitive articles have to be generic, which "among other things excludes existential constructions". However, Vestlund has more to say on this issue in the work referred to by Delsing. In his comparison of Angermannian and Medelpadian, he says that in both vernaculars the definite form is used "to a considerably greater extent" than in the standard language[11] and that it is easy enough to hear expressions in Medelpad such as the following:

(62) Selånger (Medelpadian)
> *nôppä* **bära**
> pick.INF berry.DEF.PL

'pick berries'

(63) *sälä* **vön**
> sell.INF firewood.DEF

'sell firewood'

(64) *Vi ha* *fåt* **möN** *ti väjän.*
> we have.PRS get.SUP ant.DEF in wall.DEF

'We have got ants in the wall.'

---

[10] "Vestlund (ibid.) nämner också att ångermanländska exempel med existentialkonstruktion, som hä väks granän [sic], är omöjliga i Medelpad."

[11] "I såväl mp. som åm. användes best. form hos substantivet i betydligt större utsträckning än i riksspråket." (Vestlund 1923: 20)

(65) *Hä bli   vakkär-värä   i   môra.*
      it   become.PRS **nice_weather.DEF** in morning
      'The weather will be nice tomorrow.'

Similarly, Bogren (1921: 140) says that the vernacular of Torp, a parish in the western part of Medelpad, "uses the definite form in some phrases where the standard language has indefinite forms".[12] He gives additional examples such as:

(66) Torp (Medelpadian)
      ha   tin
      have.INF **time.DEF**
      'have time'

(67) *fara   t8ge*
      travel.INF **train.DEF**
      'go by train'

It is therefore unclear what to make of Vestlund's claim about the impossibility of sentences such as *de väks granen.* Curiously enough, it seems to be contradicted by the following example from one text that Vestlund himself edited, where there is a fairly clear case of a dummy subject construction:

(68) Liden (Medelpadian)
      [Då han fick si bjȮ(r)n-dænn, sa vart-n sa ivri hætt han gLömde tell å slättje elen, å då han hadde sätt å(v) mæ bjȮ(r)n, sa fek-n si hætt]
      *hæ hôlle   på brann   **skogelen**   efrån dær   han hadde*
      it   keep.PRET on burn.PST **forest_fire.DEF** from where he   have.PST
      lega,
      lie.SUP
      '[When he saw that bear, he got so excited that he forgot to put out the fire, so he saw that] there was a forest fire burning where he had been lying.' [S38]

Admittedly, the text originates from Liden, the northernmost parish of Medelpad, and may not be representative of the province in general.

Hälsingland. Going further south along the coast, we find that the vernaculars of Hälsingland do not in general seem to employ definite forms of nouns in non-delimited uses. Compare

---

[12] "Torpm. använder i en del fraser best. form där rspr har obest"

(69) Färila (Helsingian)
*De hadde   vôrsste   **skåre** på snön.*
it   have.PST become.SUP **crust** on snow.DEF
'There was a hard crust on the snow.' (Cat Corpus)

(70) Järvsö (Helsingian)
*Momma va   på väg ut   ätte **ve**.*
Granny be.PST on way out after **firewood**
'Granny was on her way out to get firewood.' (Cat Corpus)

In a text originating from the parish of Bergsjö in the 1870's, however, there are several examples that suggest that non-delimited uses were possible in earlier times in Hälsingland, e.g. the following (notice the dummy subject):

(71) Bergsjö (Helsingian)
*Hæ tʊg   te   bĺåsæ   **sönnaväre**.*
it take.PST INFm blow.INF **southerly_wind**.DEF
'It started blowing from the south.' [S28]

(72) *...o jɷLə   *opp* **elən**   för å   rəsta   sə   en   kaffədrəpa.*
and make.PST up **fire**.DEF for INFm roast.INF REFL INDF coffee_drop
'...and made a fire to roast themselves a drop of coffee.' [S28]

We shall see that the use of a definite form of the noun 'fire' in lexical expressions such as 'make a fire' is particularly widespread.

Härjedalen. Between the northern and southern core areas, we find the small province of Härjedalen, the vernaculars of which are traditionally regarded as "Norwegian". Reinhammar (1973: 28), quoted by Delsing (2003b: 19), says rather cautiously that definite forms in general are "possibly less common" here than in other Norrlandic dialects. Delsing quotes some cases from Härjedalen texts where definite forms would be expected but do not occur. This is also in accordance with my findings, at least for non-delimited uses. Compare

(73) Ljusnedal (Härjedalian)
*Dä kommer **snö**   uppepå.*
it come.PRS **snow** on_top
'There will be snow on top.' (Cat Corpus)

Uppland. Non-delimited uses of definites are in general not found in the vernaculars of the Mälar provinces. The only clear example mentioned in the literature is the following from Alunda in Uppland, in a transcription of the speech of a man born in 1880:

(74) Alunda (Uppland)
[*Ann(â)rs sô brênde-râm âpp rörn ibʟann,*]
*mênn dôm tord   (i)nt sêttâ   **jêll'n**   på dê*
but   they dare.PST NEG put.INF fire.DEF on that
[*för ê sjenâ âpp i skogen.*]
'[Otherwise they burnt the reeds sometimes,] but they did not dare to put fire to it, [since then it [the fire] would spread into the woods].'
(Västerlund 1988: 60)

Here, we recognize the use of a definite form of the word for 'fire' in a lexicalized expression meaning 'make fire' or 'put fire to' that we also saw in (71)(b) from Hälsingland. Västerlund (1988: 40) comments that the use of the definite form of *jell* 'fire' is surprising in view of the fact that this "syntactic peculiarity", i.e. an extended use of definite forms, "has earlier only been attested from Norrland, Dalarna and Värmland".[13] I shall return to this kind of example below (§3.4.3).

Nedansiljan. In the Nedansiljan vernaculars in Dalarna, non-delimited uses of definite forms do not in general seem possible, to judge from the written sources. Consider for instance the following example from Häradsbygden (Leksand):

(75) Häradsbygden, Leksand (Nedansiljan)
*Fôrst skâ   o   körna,   gör   **ust**   å   kok   **missmör.***
first shall.PRS she churn.INF make.INF **cheese** and cook.INF **whey-cheese**

'First she'll churn, make cheese and cook whey-cheese.' [S48]

However, in Levander, Nyström & Björklund (1961) I have found a couple of examples of what seems to be non-delimited uses:

(76) Leksand (Nedansiljan)
*tännd   **jelln**   ti nävra*
light.INF **fire.DEF** in birch-bark

'put fire to the birch-bark'

---

[13] "...ägnat att förvåna, eftersom denna syntaktiska egenhet tidigare endast tycks vara känd från Norrland, Dalarna och Värmland." (Västerlund 1988: 60)

(77) Rättvik (Nedansiljan)

*Vi hallom-å   fåm   smått om   **mjôltjä.***
we PROG.PRS.1PL get.PRS.1PL little about **milk.DEF**

'We're getting short of milk.'

These may be taken as suggesting that definite forms have been used earlier in these contexts. Notice again the use of definite forms in the expression *tännd jelln* 'put fire to'.

Estonia. I have found a single plausible example of a non-delimited use of a definite form in an Estonian Swedish text. Interestingly, it comes from the very south-east end of the Swedish dialect area in the Baltics, from the small island of Runö (Estonian: Ruhnu) in the Bay of Riga, and is taken from Vendell (1882), thus representing a rather old variety. In the following example, there are several non-delimited nouns. Some of them are clearly indefinite, such as *brämin* 'aquavit' (definite form *brämini*); others could be both indefinite and definite, since the distinction is neutralized in plural forms, e.g. the plurale tantum *käta* '(the) meat', but the word *kLimskin* appears to be an indisputable definite form (Vendell lists the base form of this word as *kLimsk*).

(78) Runö (Estonian Swedish vernaculars)
[*Hesto ska bullupi kuma.*]

Tua ska   vi dans,   ita   käta,   drikk   brämin,
then shall.PRS we dance.INF eat.INF meat.PL drink.INF aquavit

kLimskin,   *ita*   *kLing upa hoitbre,*   *kakubre, setsurt*
dumpling.DEF eat.INF butter on wheat bread cake   bread

breγu,   *kouk   hurs brufolki*   *kuma*   *uter*
sweet-sour bread.PL look.INF how bride-people.DEF come.PRS.PL out

kirki.
of   church.DEF

'[In autumn we'll have the wedding.] Then we shall dance, eat meat, drink aquavit, (eat) dumplings,[14] eat butter on wheat bread, cake bread, sweet-sour bread, watch how the newlyweds come out of church.' (Vendell 1882: 76)

Norway. Delsing (2003b: 16) says that it is not clear to what extent "partitive articles" are used in Norway. "Some Norwegians associate the use with Trøndelag" [my transl.]. He quotes Iversen as "giving a few examples"; the ones he

---

[14] *kLimsk* is used in the singular. It is somewhat unclear if it is a mass or a count noun – the corresponding Swedish word *klimp* seems to be rather indifferent to the distinction.

seems to have in mind (quoted above) are clearly generic, however. He says that he has found a few examples in texts that resemble North Swedish "partitive articles", but mentions only one perhaps not too convincing example:

(79)   Ytre Vikna (Nord-Trøndelag, Norway)
       *...der   vi låog   å   drog   **garna.***
       ...where we lay.PST and pull.PST **net.PL.DEF**
       '...where we were pulling the fishing-nets.' (Delsing 2003b: 16)

Several Norwegian linguists whom I have asked have denied any knowledge of non-delimited uses of definites in Norwegian.

3.4.3 Attestations of non-delimited uses from earlier periods

Probably the oldest attested example of a non-delimited use of a definite form from the Dalecarlian area, although not a particularly clear one, is in the oldest known wedding poem in a Swedish dialect, written in 1646 by a student at the university of Dorpat (present-day Tartu, Estonia, at the time one of the two universities on Swedish territory), who originated from Mora. The text is quoted in Björklund (1994: 166). The passage contains many obscure terms and rather than trying to translate it into English I quote it in the Appendix together with Björklund's incomplete translation into Swedish. It consists of an enumeration of different kinds of food. Most of them are denoted by bare nouns, with one exception, *lunssfiskren*, translated by Björklund as *surfisk(en)* '(the) sour fish', supposedly referring to fish preserved by salting. This is apparently a definite form, although the ending *-ren* is unexpected (the definite form of *fisk* 'fish' is *fistjen* in the modern vernacular, cf. ex. (51)). Such inconsistent usage of definite forms is common in older sources, and might be taken as an indication that the use of the definite form was optional, but it may also be interpreted as an influence from the standard language, or to the extent that the examples are from poetry, as a result of exigencies of the bound form.

   From the 18th century, there are several clear examples, such as the following from 1716:

(80)   Dalecarlian (18th century)
       *Färdas   um   näter,   og   **tobaken**   räkia,   og   såfwå   å*
       travel.INF about night.PL and **tobacco.DEF** smoke.INF and sleep.INF on
       marcki.
       ground.DEF.DAT
       'Travel by night, smoke tobacco, and sleep on the ground' [S25]

A similar example is found in Näsman (1733). It contains a definite form *Snus-tobakin* 'snuff-tobacco.DEF' which corresponds to an indefinite form in the accompanying Swedish translation (b), making the intended interpretation fairly clear:

(81) a. Mora (Ovansiljan)(1733)

[*Dug ir jen mann dug Ilof, soss satt mig i stukkin,*]

fær ig soup **Snustobakin** *mæss Præstn* *hiælt*

for I inhale.PST snuff-tobacco.DEF when clergyman.DEF keep.PST

â pridikâ.

on preach.INF

b. Swedish1733 Swedish (1733)

[*Du är en mann du Elof, som satt mig i stocken,*]

för jag söp **Snustobak** *medan Præstn* *hölt* *på*

for I inhale.PST snuff-tobacco while clergyman.DEF keep.PST on

at predika.

INFm preach.INF

'[You're some man you Elof, who put me in the stocks], because I was using snuff tobacco when the vicar was preaching.'

From the northern area, the oldest attested example is from an 18th century wedding poem from Nederluleå in the Lulemål area in Norrbotten, which contains the following passage with several definite forms mixed with indefinite ones:

(82) Nederluleå (Lulemål)

[*Gud hån bewåra dåm wel fra ou-aro*
Gifwi dåm Hwäite å Råg nou i laro]

Drick uti tonnen kjött/ fläske å kökin / Neda

drink.IMP in barrels.DEF.PL meat pork.DEF and cake.DEF.PL down

fra gålfwen å åltt up dill tökin Kouen å

from floor.DEF.DAT and all up to ceiling.DEF.DAT cow.DEF.PL and

ouxan å gjeitren å faara

ox.DEF.PL and goat.DEF.PL and sheep.DEF.PL

'[God may save them from the bad years
Give them wheat and rye enough in the cases]
Drink in the barrels, meat, pork and cakes,
All the way from the floor to the ceiling
Cows and oxen and goats and sheep' [S10]

From the same time and area we also find multiple attestations of extended uses of definite forms in the word lists from Pitemål compiled by the 18th century Swedish philologist Johan Ihre, e.g. the typical expression *nåpp bera* 'to pick berries' (Reinhammar 2002).

Non-delimited uses of definite forms are thus attested as early as the 17th century for Dalarna and the 18th century for Upper Norrland, that is, more or less as early as we can get using written sources emanating from these areas.

Going further back, it is quite clear that non-delimited uses of definite forms are not characteristic of Written Medieval Swedish. On the other hand, it is possible to find a few indications of such uses. We saw that the use of a definite form of the noun *eld/jell* 'fire' seems to be, or have been, possible in an area which is rather much wider than the one where non-delimited definites are commonly found (exs. (71)(b), (74), (76) above). This inspired me to do a search for such examples in medieval texts. I thus excerpted all occurrences of the word *eld(h)* 'fire' in the Old Swedish corpus *Källtext*, focusing on the use of this word in more or less lexicalized collocations as the object of verbs such as *tända* 'light up' and *göra* 'make'. In the majority of all cases, a bare noun was used, but there were a few examples of definite forms, such as (83):

(83) Medieval Written Swedish
    Misther falken   klöffwana, tha tak   paper oc tänth
    lose.PRS falcon.DEF claw.DEF.PL then take.IMP paper and light.IMP
    ***elden**   thär j* [oc bren the thaana som klöffwen wil aff falla, oc smör
    fire.DEF there in
    sidhan äffther mädh honagh oc bint bombas thär wm j nyo dagha]
    'Should the falcon lose its claws, then take paper and make fire therein
    [and burn the toes from which the claw is falling off, and rub afterwards
    with honey and tie a bandage around it for nine days].' [S7]

The quoted text is a complete and independent section of the manuscript in which it occurs; the possibility of an anaphoric interpretation is precluded because there is no mention of fire earlier in the text that *elden* 'fire.DEF' could refer back to. The manuscript, "Bondakonst" from around 1500, was written by Peder Månsson (Petrus Magni), who was the last Catholic bishop of Västerås and the translator or author of several books. According to the 16th century chronicle of Peder Swart, Peder Månsson was born in the parish of Tillberga in Västmanland, fairly close to the border with Uppland; he would thus have been a speaker of an Upper Swedish variety. However, in her monograph on Peder Månsson's language, Nordling (2001: 51) rejects this claim as not being trustworthy; thus, unfortunately, it does not seem possible to locate Peder Månsson linguistically. (More examples of this type from Written Medieval Swedish are found in the Appendix.)

3.4.4 Typological parallels

Although the extension of definite marking to non-delimited noun phrase usage that we find in the Peripheral Swedish area is typologically rather uncommon, and the possibility is not discussed at all in recent works such as Himmelmann (1997) and Lyons (1999), it is not unique. One language where a parallel use is found is Spoken Moroccan Arabic.[15] Thus, Caubet (1983: 235) quotes the following example:

(84)   Moroccan Arabic
       Kāin   əl-ḫobz.
       there-is DEF-bread
       'There is bread.'

While the definite article in other modern Arabic vernaculars does have a comparatively wide range of uses, it is not in general used in non-delimited noun phrases (Elie Wardini, personal communication). A detailed investigation of the use of definite articles in Arabic varieties could shed further light on the evolution of articles in general.

3.5 Uses with quantifiers

3.5.1 General

A defining criterion of non-delimited uses was said in §3.4.1 to be the absence of any expression that indicates individuation or a measure. However, in a part of the geographical area where non-delimited uses of definites are found, definite forms can also be used after quantifying expressions such as numerals or words meaning 'many', 'few' and the like. Delsing (2003b) quotes examples such as (85).

(85)   Överkalix (Kalixmål)
       mitsi fålke
       much **people.DEF**
       'many people' (Delsing 2003b: 17)

---

[15] I am indebted to my former student Rashid El-Maaroufi who first made me aware of the Moroccan facts.

He says that the use is well attested in Norrbotten, Västerbotten and Ångerman-land, and is also found along the river valley of Indalsälven in Jämtland. However, Delsing does not distinguish between cases like (85) and constructions where the quantifier and the noun are linked by a preposition, as in (86).

(86) Ragunda (Jamtska)
      gott   om   fistjevattna
      plenty about **fishing-water.DEF**
      'plenty of fishing-water' (Delsing 2003b: 18)

It appears that in the latter construction, where the noun has a more independent syntactic status, definite forms tend to be used more widely. In what follows, I shall be looking mainly at constructions of the first type, where the quantifier is immediately followed by a noun.

3.5.2 Areal distribution of uses with quantifiers

Westrobothnian. In this dialect area, the patterns seem different for numerals and other quantifiers such as 'much' and 'many'. Bergholm, Linder & Yttergren (1999) studied three parishes representing different parts of the Westrobothnian dialect area: Bjurholm (transitional Angermannian-Westrobothnian), Burträsk (northern Westrobothnian), and Sorsele (southern Westrobothnian in the province of Lapland). For quantifiers other than numerals, it was only in Sorsele that the use of definite forms after quantifiers was predominant, most consistently after 'much', 'many' and 'not any':

(87) Sorsele (Southern Westrobothnian)
      Heä   mycke snön   dära   backen.
      it_be.PRS much snow.DEF there_on hill.DEF
      'There is much snow on the hill.' (Bergholm, Linder & Yttergren 1999: 24)

(88) *Han drack   mycke öle.*
      he drink.PST much beer.DEF
      'He drank a lot of beer.' (Bergholm, Linder & Yttergren 1999: 24)

(89) *Han ha   int na peninga.*
      he have.PRS NEG any money.PL.DEF
      'He hasn't got any money.' (Bergholm, Linder & Yttergren 1999: 24)

In Burträsk and Bjurholm, definite forms with these quantifiers were uncommon or even "exceptions", according to Bergholm et al. Curiously, the pattern with numerals was almost the opposite – here the Sorsele informants showed considerable variation and only the older informants tended to use definite forms consistently:

(90) Sorsele (Southern Westrobothnian)
      *Han ha   **tre brödr**   **en.***
      he   have.PRS **three brother.DEF.PL**

      'He has three brothers.' (Bergholm, Linder & Yttergren 1999: 24)

In both Burträsk and Bjurholm, however, definite forms were used with numerals '2' and '3' by most informants:

(91) Bjurholm (Angermannian-Westrobothnian transitional)
      ***Han** ha   tre   brören.*
      He   have.PRS three brother.DEF.PL

      'He has three brothers.' (Bergholm, Linder & Yttergren 1999: 24)

A similar example is also reported from Vilhelmina (Southern Westrobothnian) by Wälchli, Parkvall & Shokri (1998). In a questionnaire from Arvidsjaur, definite forms are given as the only alternative after *mycke* 'much'.

According to Ågren & Dahlstedt (1954: 282), presenting examples from Åsele (Angermannian) and Vilhelmina (Angermannian), the definite plural form in Laplandic vernaculars has "often totally ousted"[16] the indefinite form "even after numerals". Delsing (2003b: 17) also quotes examples from these locations as well as from Örträsk (Angermannian-Westrobothnian transitional).

Norrbothnian. In Pitemål, judging from the examples given in Brännström (1993) and Berglund & Lidström (1991), plural quantifiers are followed by the dative (see below), but definite forms without case marking are possible with *mö'tje* 'much', both in the singular and the plural:

(92) Pitemål
      *Hä var   **mö'tje foLKe**   krö'gom 'en.*
      it be.PST **much people.DEF** around he.OBL

      'There were a lot of people around him.' (Brännström 1993: 52)

---

[16] "I de svenska målen i Lappland har däremot den bestämda flertalsformen ofta totalt trängt ut den obestämda, t.o.m. efter räkneord..." (Ågren & Dahlstedt 1954: 282)

(93) *E fjŏłomsómmarn   var   -e mŏtje djätinga.*
      ? last_summer.DEF be.PST it **much wasp.DEF.PL**

      'Last summer there were a lot of wasps.' (Berglund & Lidström 1991: 93)

In Lulemål, the use of the definite form seems relatively consistent after *mitji* – there are more than 30 examples in Nyström (1993), all except one with the definite form.

(94) Lulemål
      He vär   so åomitji   pojkan   o fLikken   ini gämeLstän
      it be.PST so **very_much boy.DEF.PL** and girl.DEF.PL i old_town.DEF
      dil häLjen.
      to holiday.DEF

      'There were so terribly many boys and girls in the church town[17] during the holiday.'

Similarly, from the Cat Corpus:

(95) Lulemål
      O   åt   tordes jö gä   främ ati gålan   heler, för der vär   so
      and NEG dare.PST I go.INF up to farm.DEF.PL either for there be.PST so
      mitji heondan.
      much dog.DEF.PL

      'And I didn't dare go close to the farms either, for there were so many dogs.' (Cat Corpus)

From Råneå in the Lulemål area, Delsing (2003b: 17) quotes *mitsi bröde* 'much bread.DEF'.

However, with most other quantifiers, including *meir* 'more', negative quantifiers such as *öyngar* 'none' and *ånt na* 'not any', and numerals, only indefinite forms show up:

(96) Lulemål
      Ho hä   öynge förhål.
      she have.PRS **no   restraint**

      'She has no restraint, i.e. she cannot restrain herself.' (Nyström 1993)

---

[17] This refers to the "Gammelstad church town" (included in the UNESCO World Heritage List), comprising more than 400 cottages serving as an overnight stop for parishioners coming from far-away. See http://www.lulea.se/gammelstad/.

(97) *Ini skapen   fännsch e bara **tvo kålper**,   in   litn*
in cupboard.DEF exist.PST it only **two cold_potato** One small
*korvbuyt   o   **in hålv lök**.*
sausage_piece and **one half** onion

'In the cupboard there were only two cold potatoes, one small piece of
sausage and half an onion.' (Cat Corpus)

Delsing quotes the example *nå döfolke* from Lulemål, with the intended interpretation 'some dead people'. This would be the only such example from Norrbotten. However, since other sources give the form *nä* for 'some' in Lulemål, which
should according to Nordström (1925) be followed by an indefinite form in the
singular and a dative form in the plural, some checking of the source seems to
be warranted. The texts Delsing refers to for Lulemål do not as far as I can see
contain any such phrase, but there is a passage in the text [S31] which might
have been misinterpreted. It contains the phrase *spadd upa nꝏ döfolke*, where
the first three words are translated in a footnote as 'put on him by evil magic'
["trollade på honom"], where *nꝏ* is the dative form of 'him'; 'some dead people'
would rather be *nä döfolk*.

From the Kalix area, we find examples both with 'much' and with numerals:

(98) Nederkalix (Kalixmål)
Wå   söynda skå   dö vä   så myttji sopan?
What sin.DEF shall.PRS you with so much milk.DEF

'What the hell are you going to do with so **much milk**?' (Cat Corpus)

(99) *A tåo   fram to   kålpotåtisan , in*
she take.PST out   two cold_potato.DEF.PL   one
kårvbäit   å   in hålv lök.
sausage-piece and one half onion

'She took out two cold potatoes, a piece of sausage, and half an onion.'
(Cat Corpus)

(100) Siknäs, Nederkalix (Kalixmål)
*så forskrätseli **mytji smöre***
so terribly   **much butter**.DEF

'so terribly **much butter**' (Stenberg 1971)

For Överkalix, cf. (76) above, with 'much'. Definites with numerals are not attested from Överkalix, however.

Northern Settler Area. In a questionnaire from Arvidsjaur, definite forms are given as the only alternative after *mycke* 'much', *nå* 'some', and alternating with indefinites after numerals.

Ostrobothnian. For Karleby, Hagfors (1891: 94) quotes the examples *mytji järne* 'much iron.DEF' and *na lite tjöte* 'some little meat.DEF'. For the same vernacular, as described by Vangsnes (2003), the use of definite forms is obligatory after *mytji* 'much' and *somt* 'some, certain':

(101)   Karleby (Northern Ostrobothnian)
   mytji öle
   much beer.DEF
   'much beer'

This is only visible in the singular since the Karleby vernacular has neutralization of definiteness in the plural. To make things more complex, other quantifiers, such as *mang* 'many', *noga* 'some' and numerals, require the indefinite singular of the following noun (possibly under Finnish influence):

(102)   Karleby (Northern Ostrobothnian)
   tri   hest
   three horse.SG.INDF
   'three horses'

Eriksson & Rendahl (1999: 26), in their questionnaire investigation of Ostrobothnian, report that, in general, their informants did not use definite forms after quantifiers. One exception was a person from Pedersöre, a neighbour parish of Karleby. Even this informant showed variation (e.g. *mytchi öli* 'much beer.DEF' but *mytchi snö* 'much snow'.) Two informants from Malax in their material used a definite form after *itt na* 'not any' in the following example:

(103)   Malax (Southern Ostrobothnian)
   *He je   itt **na snön**   på martje.*
   it be.PRS NEG any snow.DEF on ground.DEF
   'There is not any snow on the ground.' (questionnaire)

It does seem that the use of definite forms after quantifiers in Österbotten is basically restricted to the northernmost part.

Jämtland. Delsing quotes three examples from written texts, but two of them are prepositional constructions, so the only remaining one would be *nå brännvine* 'some vodka' from Lit. I have not been able to find any other attestations from Jämtland.

Ångermanland. Delsing reports four examples from written texts, two with *myttje* (Tåsjö, Anundsjö) and two with *na* (Säbrå, Stigsjö). Wälchli, Parkvall & Shokri (1998) quote the following examples from Edsele:

(104) Edsele (Angermannian)
  Där vax -e mötje gräse.
  there grow.PST it much grass.DEF
  'There was much grass.' [S5]

(105) *Män hon fann inge ägga utan sto där utan ägg*
  but she find.PST no.PL egg.DEF.PL but stand.PST there without egg.PL
  o utan höne
  and without hen
  'But she did not find any eggs but stood there without eggs and without a hen.' [S5]

In the Cat Corpus, we find the following examples:

(106) Junsele (Angermannian)
  Momma hadd bodd eschammen häri stugern mang e
  Granny have.PST live.SUP alone in hut.DEF many PIA
  åra nu.
  year.DEF.PL now
  'Granny had lived alone in the cabin for many years now.' (Cat Corpus)

(107) *Momma titte åt sia, steg opp å geck hit tell fönstre*
  Granny look.PST at side, rise.PST up and go.PST here to window.DEF
  å gnôp tå na gulblaa tå blomma däri
  and pinch.PST off some yellow_leave.DEF.PL from flower.DEF in
  fönstre.
  window.DEF
  'Granny looked aside, got up and went up to the window, and pinched off some yellow leaves from the plant in the window.' (Cat Corpus)

No examples with numerals are attested from this area, to my knowledge.

Dalecarlian. Definite forms are not in general used with quantifiers in any Dalecarlian variety. In the literature, counterinstances to this are found in two places, both from Älvdalen. One is discussed below under the heading "Earlier periods", the other is a brief mention in Levander (1909: 95), where it is said that definite forms are "occasionally" found with *någär* 'some', as in *nå grandeð* 'a little bit' – which looks like a set expression, although it is hard to tell, since no details are given.

3.5.3 Attestations from earlier periods

In Written Medieval Swedish, quantifiers and interrogative pronouns were sometimes followed by a definite noun. At least two different types can be distinguished (Wessén (1956: 36-37)). One can be labeled "true partitive" – the noun refers to a specific superset, that is, a larger set from which a member or a subset is picked out by the quantifier or interrogative pronoun:

(108) Written Medieval Swedish
       somlikin *sädhin*
       some   grain.DEF
       'some of the grain'

(109) *Han sporde,* **hulkom**   **gudhenom**   *thet*   *teknit*
       he   ask.PST which.DAT.SG.M god.DEF.DAT.SG that.N sign.DEF
       tilhörde.
       belong.PST
       'He asked which of the gods the sign belonged to.' [S36]

This type of definite, then, is different from what we find in quantifier phrases in modern vernaculars where there is no specific superset involved. The construction was probably a general feature of older forms of Scandinavian and survives in Modern Icelandic. The Icelandic use is mentioned by Rießler (2002) as a typological parallel to the "partitive" uses of definite forms in northern Scandinavian, but there is no overlap between the two types. Although this fact does not exclude a diachronic relationship, there is to my knowledge no historical evidence to suggest such a connection.

The second medieval Swedish type at first seems more like the modern Peripheral Swedish area one. Compare:

(110) Written Medieval Swedish
       Tha war   om siidher **engin födhan** *i* *stadhenom.*
       then be.PST finally   no   food.DEF in town.DEF.DAT
       'Eventually, there wasn't any food in the town.' [S32]

However, it turns out that the distribution of definite forms after quantifiers is different in medieval Swedish than in the modern vernaculars. Wessén notes that the definite form is most common with the inherently negative *ängin* 'no, none'. Among the rather numerous examples he lists, there are only two that contain another quantifier, and in one of these, the quantifier is clearly within the scope of a negation:

(111) Written Medieval Swedish
...*medhan the orkadho*   *ekke bära*   ***mykin matin***   *mz*
...while   they be_able_to.PST.3PL   NEG carry.INF **much**   **food.**DEF with
sik.
REFL
'...while they did not manage to carry much food.' [S6]

The only example that is neither inherently negative nor within the scope of a negation is the following:

(112) Written Medieval Swedish
...*æn hans*   *discipuli*   *gingo in i*   *stadhin*   *at faa*   *them*
...but he.GEN disciple.PL go.PST in in town.DEF   to get.INF them
nakan   ***matin.***
some.ACC.SG.M food.DEF
'... but his disciples went into the town to get some food.' [S6]

The pattern represented by (110)–(112) does not appear to have been a general one in Written Medieval Swedish. In the Källtext corpus, most occurrences of *ängin* 'no, none' are followed by indefinite nouns. Most of Wessén's examples come from a few texts (the Pentateuch, Bonaventura), and even in those texts the pattern appears exceptional. On the other hand, the use still survived in some 16th century texts, notably the New Testament translation of 1526:

(113) Early Modern Swedish
Wij haffuom   ***intit brödith.***
we have.PRS.1PL no.N bread.DEF
'We have no bread.' [S30]

There is an intriguing example from an early text in what purports to be Elfdalian (Näsman 1733):

(114)   Elfdalian (Ovansiljan)(18th century)
    ...ingan uidn   *klufin...*
    ...**no**   firewood.DEF hew.PP...
    '...no firewood hewn...'

When Lars Levander transcribed this text in Lundell (1936: T117), "normalizing" it according to early 20th century usage, he changed this phrase into *inggan wi kluvnan*.[18] It is impossible to tell whether (114) really represents 18th century Elfdalian or not.

A fairly similar pattern is found in Norwegian, both the standard varieties and the dialects. The following sentence is quoted by Faarlund, Lie & Vannebo (1997: 302) as one of several examples where "individual predicative expressions in negated sentences" take a definite suffix on the noun.

(115)   Bokmål Norwegian
    Mange kronene *var*   *det ikke.*
    many crown.PL be.PST it NEG
    'Many crowns it wasn't.'

However, with quantifiers this pattern is not restricted to predicative positions. Examples like the following are quite common:[19]

(116)   Bokmål Norwegian
    *De snakket ikke **mange ordene**.*
    they talk.PST NEG **many word.PL.DEF**
    'They didn't speak many words.' (Internet)

(117)   *Det tok*   *ikke **mange sekundene***   *før*   *døren*   *var*   *åpen.*
    it take.PST NEG **many second.PL.DEF** before door.DEF be.PST open
    'It didn't take many seconds before the door was open.' (Internet)

Compare also examples such as the following, in which a definite noun with indefinite meaning is used in the scope of negation:

(118)   Tromsø (Troms, Norway)
    Han eide   ***ikkje nåla***   *i* *væggen.*
    he own.PST NEG nail.DEF in wall.DEF
    'He did not own a nail (lit. the nail) in the wall.' (Iversen 1918: 18)

---

[18] Or rather, using the Swedish dialect alphabet (landsmålsalfabetet): *ɪggąn wɪ klˊůvnąn.*

[19] A Google search for the string "tok ikke mange" yielded 1360 hits, and of the first 50 examples more than 80 per cent were followed by a definite noun.

3.5.4 Datives after quantifiers

This is a topic that I have treated in another paper (Dahl 2008), and although it is related to the question of definite marking, it is strictly speaking separate from it, so I will only briefly state the facts here. In the dialect areas Northern Westrobothnian, Pitemål and Lulemål[20], a quantifier may be followed by a form which is diachronically (and at least in some varieties also synchronically) a definite dative plural form. In Pitemål and Lulemål, this is obligatory after *na* 'some':

(119)   Pitemål
    Hä kom   ***na***   ***fLi'ttjom*** *ötät* *väjen.*
    it   come.PST **some girl.DAT.PL** along road.DEF
    'There came some girls along the road.' (Brännström 1993: 19)

In a curious development restricted to the southern Norrbothnian varieties – Pitemål and Lulemål – this pattern has spread in such a way that the erstwhile dative plural form is also used in contexts where there is no quantifier, notably when some modifier such as an adjective or a possessive pronoun precedes the noun. Examples from Råneå (Lulemål) are *truy swårta faro* 'three black sheep', *våder bano å dåmers aongo* 'our children and their [other people's] brats', *nuya kLedo* 'new clothes' (Wikberg 2004). An unexpected property of these constructions is that they contain a non-apocopated form of the plural adjectives, with the weak ending *-a* (Dahlstedt 1956: 36). In fact, such combinations of non-apocopated adjectives and dative-marked nouns are in competition with the construction that would be expected in such contexts, viz. definite nouns with incorporated adjectives. Compare the following examples which illustrate the two possibilities:

(120)   Lulemål
    Hån hä   *fo*   *fLugo, hån hä*   *låga*   *se*   ***wita***
    he   have.PRS get.SUP fly   he   have.PRS make.DEF REFL white
    bökso
    trouser.DAT.PL
    'He's got crazy, he has got himself white trousers.'

(121)   *Hån kåm*   *o*   *lovere*   *ini* ***witböxen.***
    he   come.PST and brag.PST in **white_trouser.DEF.DAT.PL**
    'He came bragging in white trousers.' (Nyström 1993: 105)

---

[20] As I was later informed by Oskar Rönnberg, the phenomena described here for Pitemål and Lulemål are also found in Kalixmål as spoken in Kalix.

In Dahl (2008), I suggest as a possible scenario that the construction with an adjective in -*a* and a noun in the historical dative form has arisen as an attempt to fill what seemed like a gap in the paradigm, namely an analogue to Swedish premodified indefinite noun phrase. It should be noted in this context that the original indefinite plurals in these vernaculars have by and large lost their endings while retaining the grave pitch accent, at the same time as they have become restricted in their use to combinations with numerals. The following example illustrates how such endingless forms alternate with historical dative forms:

(122) Pitemål

      Hä stå:r   **åått àasp**   *dēna båårt, å*   *hä jär*   **sto:ra**

      it   stand.PRS **eight aspen.PL** there away   and it be.PRS **big.PL**

      àspom.

      aspen.DAT.PL

      'There are eight aspens over there, and they are big aspens.' (Berglund & Lidström 1991: 20)

Such plural forms are used also in premodified noun phrases. Thus, according to the suggested scenario, -a ending was directly imported from Swedish, while the original dative forms -om/-o, which were used with quantifiers such as na, were apparently seen as more natural alternatives to Swedish plural nouns than the endingless historical indefinites. Some nouns, however, retain plural forms that are also distinct from the singular forms at the segmental level, e.g. Pitemål *ha´nd: hénder* 'hand:hand.PL'. Such plural forms are also used in pre-modified noun phrases rather than the historical datives, the reason presumably being that these forms were more directly analogous to Swedish plurals than the endingless ones.

3.5.5 Definites after quantifiers: Summing up

The use of definite forms after quantifiers in the Swedish dialect area is more restricted than the non-delimited use. The dialectal areas involved are Norrbothnian, the Northern Settler Area, Westrobothnian, Jämtland, Angermannian, and Ostrobothnian, that is, in principle corresponding to the whole northern "core area" of non-delimited uses, while the southern "core area" (Ovansiljan) lacks attestations except for the marginal examples from Älvdalen. But even within the northern area, there is considerable variation. What is most striking is that the geographical distribution of the attestations differs quite considerably between the various quantifiers involved, as can be seen in Figure 3.5–Figure 3.8.

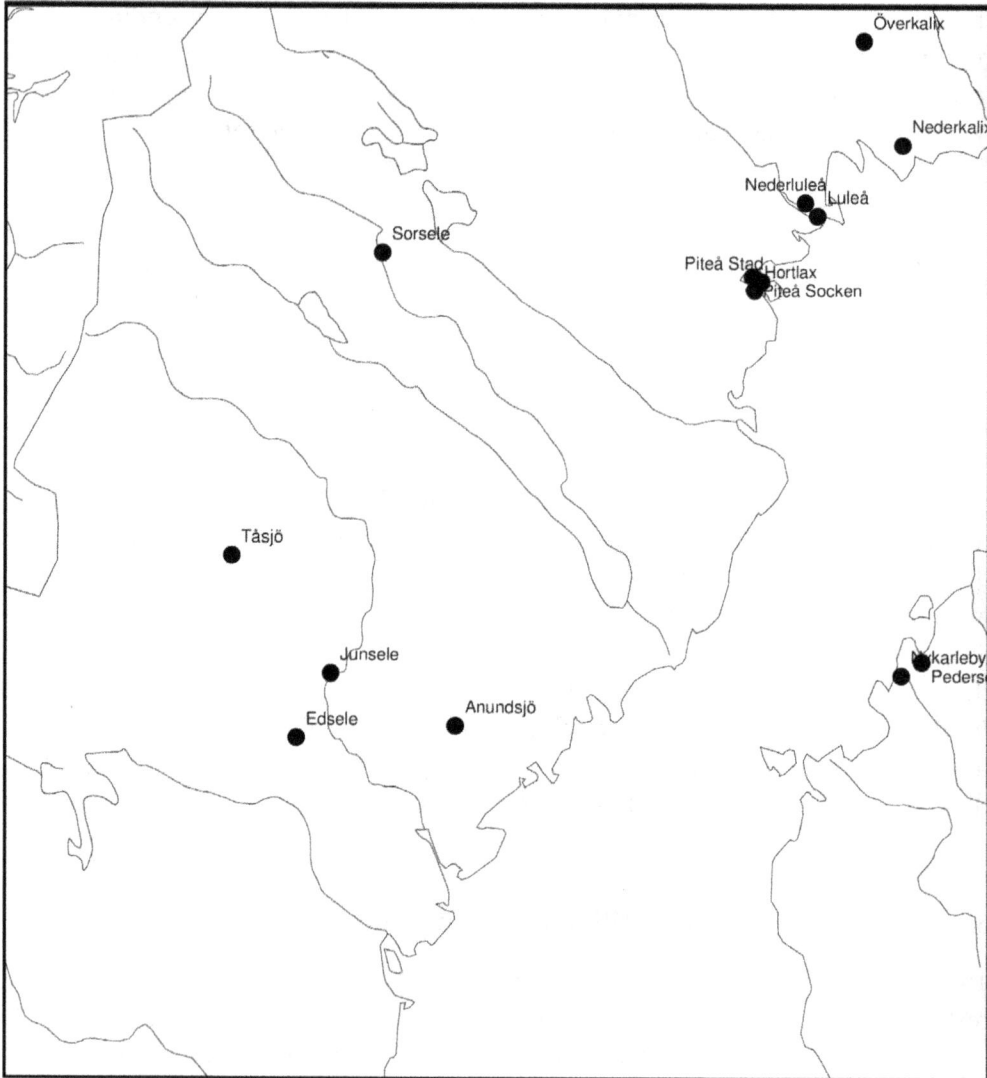

Figure 3.5: Attestations of definites after 'much'

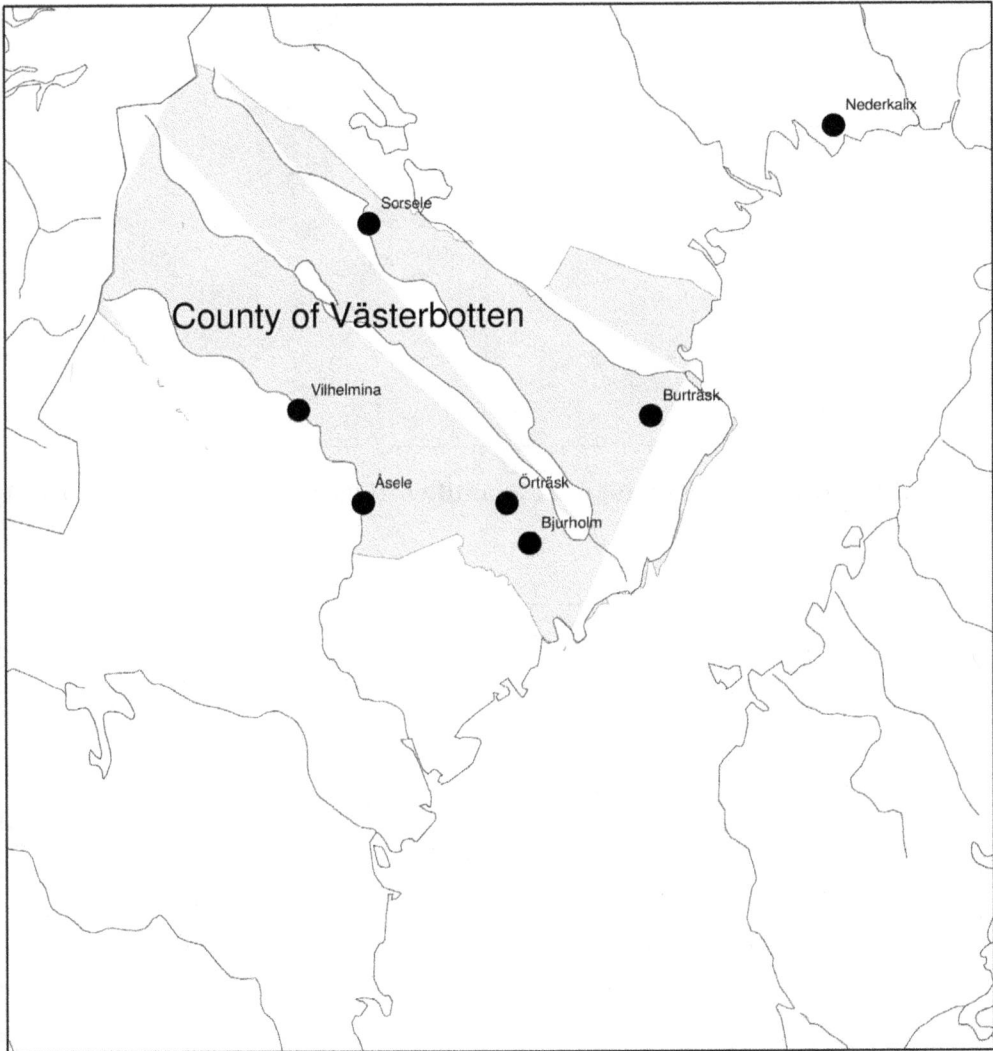

Figure 3.6: Attestations of definites after numerals

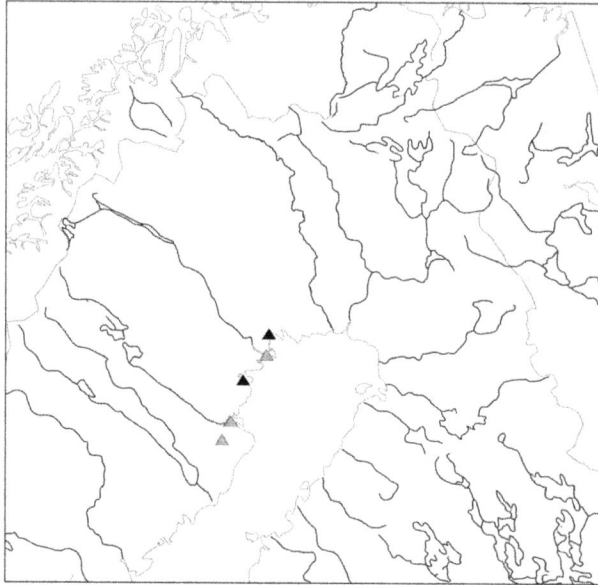

Figure 3.7: Attestations of dative after quantifiers (black symbols: extended uses)

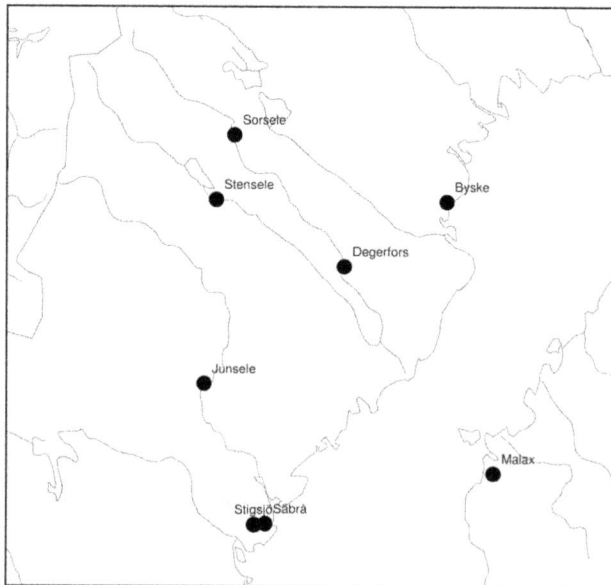

Figure 3.8: Attestations of definites after *na*

Since attestations tend to be somewhat sporadic, one should be somewhat cautious with conclusions, but there seem to be some fairly clear tendencies. Thus, the use of definite forms after numerals is almost exclusively attested in the county (not the province!) of Västerbotten – which is not an entity according to the dialectological tradition, but rather consists of parts of four different dialect areas in Dahlstedt's maps. The use of dative after quantifiers is also a geographically restricted phenomenon, found in Northern Westrobothnian, Pitemål and Lulemål.

The historical relationships between the uses of definite nouns after quantifiers in Scandinavian are not clear. Disregarding the true partitive uses, the definite forms in older Swedish, Norwegian, and the singular example from 18th century Dalecarlian, seem to be "negative polarity items", that is, they occur basically only within the scope of negation (with (112) as the only attested exception). In the Peripheral Swedish vernaculars where definite nouns show up after quantifiers, there is no such limitation – on the contrary, in some varieties the definite forms are used primarily with 'much'. I would therefore submit that we are dealing with two separate developments.

3.6 Singular count uses

3.6.1 General

In the peripheral area, there are also some unexpected uses of suffixed articles with singular count nouns, such as the following:

(123) Elfdalian (Ovansiljan)
   Am   est-n.
   have.1PL **horse-DEF**
   'We have a horse, i.e. we are horse-owners.' (questionnaire)

Such examples, which would normally take an indefinite article in English, by and large correspond to "bare nouns" in the Central Scandinavian languages e.g.

(124) Swedish
   Vi har   häst.
   we have.PRS **horse**
   'We have a horse, i.e. we are horse-owners.'

I shall call such cases "low referentiality uses" (Teleman, Hellberg & Andersson (1999: 3:56) "svagt referentiell betydelse"), since they share the trait that the identity of the referent is not highlighted; what is important in (123)-(124) is rather the property of owning a horse. Correspondingly, the bare noun construction in Swedish is normally used when speaking of something that it is normal to have exactly one exemplar of, including cars[21] and telephones (at least until recently!), but excluding spaceships (because you are not expected to have one) or books (because you are expected to have several). However, the corresponding sentences with indefinite articles are also grammatical, and in fact preferred in certain contexts, e.g. if the referent is going to be important in the ensuing discourse. The articleless variant is however felt to be ungrammatical in Elfdalian (I have not been able to systematically check on other vernaculars), but conversely, the definite article is not possible in Central Scandinavian.

From the diachronic point of view, the article-less cases of Central Scandinavian could be seen as due to an incomplete grammaticalization of the indefinite article, whereas the use of the definite article in Peripheral Swedish vernaculars is a case of grammaticalization that goes further than we would perhaps expect. Typologically, it is not wholly unique, however. While (123) could not be translated into French using a definite article, there are similar examples such as (125), where a definite article is normal:

(125)   French
        Nous avons   **le   téléphone.**
        we   have.PRS.1PL   DEF telephone
        'We have a (lit. the) telephone.'

Cases like this are mentioned in standard grammars of French, but they tend to be subsumed under generic uses of the article (I'll return to this question in §3.13).

With respect to the peripheral Swedish dialect area, the low referentiality uses of definite forms are not well documented in the literature, and when examples are provided they are usually not seen as a type of their own, distinct from non-delimited uses. For instance, Ågren & Dahlstedt (1954: 282), after discussing uses of definite forms for "indefinite quantities" and saying that Norrlandic dialects "are very consistent in this use of the definite forms", cite the following as "maybe particularly striking to a Standard Swedish ear":[22]

---

[21] A Google search suggests that the bare noun phrase *har bil* 'has car' is about ten times as common as *har en bil* 'has a car' in Swedish, and of the latter the overwhelming majority were followed by a relative clause.

[22] "De norrländska bygdemålen är mycket konsekventa i detta bruk av bestämd form. Särskilt påfallande för ett rikssvenskt öra är måhända..."

(126) Vilhelmina (Southern Westrobothnian)
*Sä vi mâka   ôss **kâmmarn**.*
so we clear.PST us chamber.DEF
'so we cleared us a chamber.' [i.e. we made a shelter by clearing some snow]'

This example, like the following ones, shows that the phenomenon may include cases that do not correspond to bare-noun constructions in Swedish:

(127) Elfdalian (Ovansiljan)
*E wa   **swaindjin** å   weem.*
it be.PST bend.DEF   on road.DEF.DAT
'There was a bend in the road.' [S12]

(128) *Ig ar   gart   **stark-äln**   ig.*
I have.PRS make.SUP strong_heel.DEF.ACC I
'I have made a strong heel' (Levander 1909: 95)

Due to restricted documentation and a rather low text-frequency, it is not so easy to establish the precise geographical distribution for the extended use of definite forms of singular count nouns, but I have found a number of examples from various ends of the Peripheral Swedish area, to be listed in the following:
   Norrbothnian. Starting from the north, the following two translations of the same sentence from the Cat Corpus can be cited from the Kalix area:

(129) Överkalix (Kalixmål)
Ji skå   taLa   om   föR di   mamm aT ji ållti   hä
I shall.PRS speak.INF about for you.OBL mother that I always have.PRS
önske   mi   i   kätt, men he gär   jåo   äint änn aT
want.SUP me.OBL INDF cat   but it go.PRS PRAG NEG well INFm
ha   kätta   da´n   båo   ini in   höires-häos.
have.INF cat.DEF when_one live.PRS in one.DAT.N apartment house
'I want to tell you, Mother, that I have always wanted to have a cat – but it isn't possible to have a cat (lit. the cat) when you live in an apartment house.' (Cat Corpus)

(130) Nederkalix (Kalixmål)
    Jä skå   tåla   åom för dä,   måmme åt jä ållti
    I shall.PRS speak.INF about for you.OBL mother that I always
    veillt   hå   i   kjaatt män hä gja jo   ät   håå
    want.SUP have.INF INDF cat   but it go.PRS PRAG NEG have.INF
    kjatta når man båo ini i   *höreshöus.*
    cat.DEF when one live.PRS in INDF apartment house
    (same translation as above)

In Stenberg (1971), we find the following examples:

(131) Siknäs, Nederkalix (Kalixmål)
    He *fanns   jo   separatoN.*
    it   exist.PST PRAG separator.DEF
    'There was a milk separator.'

(132) **Jåå,** *hästn   har   ve jo.*
    yes horse.DEF have.PRS we PRAG
    'Yes, we do have a horse.'

A transcribed text on the DAUM website contains a couple of clear examples from the Lulemål area (female speaker born in 1895):

(133) Edefors (Lulemål)
    *Vi hadd   ju   åt **jänspisn**   så en kodd ju   åt*
    we have.PST PRAG NEG iron_stove.DEF so one can.PST PRAG NEG
    *baka   bulla....   Da   ve fikk **jänspisn**   da baka   ja*
    bake.INF bun.DEF.PL when we get.PST iron_stove.DEF then bake.PST I
    ju   wettbulla   å   peparkakun   men strakks
    PRAG wheat_bun.DEF.PL and ginger-bread.DEF.PL but right_away
    *hadd   ve barra **öppenspisn.***
    have.PST we only open_stove.DEF
    'As you know, we didn't have an iron stove so we couldn't bake buns...
    When we got an iron stove I used to bake wheat buns and gingerbreads,
    but in the beginning we had only an open fireplace.' [S33]

Westrobothnian. In Västerbotten, there seems to be more variation in the use of singular count uses of definites than is found for non-delimited uses. Thus, Bergholm, Linder & Yttergren (1999) report that mainly older speakers used definite forms in (134). Wälchli, Parkvall & Shokri (1998), on the other hand, did not find any examples of definites at all in this sentence when using the same questionnaire.

(134) Burträsk (Northern Westrobothnian)
*Vi hadd   **hästn**   menn ja vor   litn.*
we have.PST **horse.DEF** when I be.PST small
'We had a horse when I was a kid.' (questionnaire)

In transcribed texts from Västerbotten, a few examples are found, e.g.:

(135) Norsjö (Northern Westrobothnian)
*...å   för-ḷa'aịŋ se´nn där-ḍäm   inte ha'add   **tjö'ttkwa'ŋa**   se*
and for long ago   where they NEG have.PST **meat-grinder.DEF** so
*a'nnvä'nnde däm **kḷe'sta'ịt'n.***
use.PST   they **"clothes-poker".DEF**
'...and long ago where they didn't have a meat-grinder they used a *klädstöt*.[23] (Westerberg 2004: 303)

(136) Skelletmål (Northern Westrobothnian)
*Hänna dug   äint för ajn som ha   **julpän.***
this   do.PRS NEG for one that have.PRS **fly.DEF**
'This won't do for someone with a fly.' (Westerlund 1978: 94)

Middle Norrland. There seem to be no clear examples from the provinces of Jämtland, Ångermanland, and Medelpad. Although it is hard to argue from the absence of evidence, something could certainly be expected to show up in the extensive text materials, so it would appear that singular count uses are not found here. This impression is strengthened by the fact that definite forms are also not found with instrumental prepositional phrases (see below).

Ostrobothnian. Nikula (1997: 207) quotes the following examples from Närpes, exemplifying the bare noun pattern:

(137) Närpes (Southern Ostrobothnian)
*Vi ha: **häst** därhäim.*
we have.PRS.PL **horse** at_home
'We have a horse at home.'

---

[23] Tool used when washing clothes.

(138) *Ja ha:r   no: **moånanslyö:n.***
      I   have.PRS certainly **monthly_salary**
      'Sure, I have a monthly salary.'

She seems to imply that this is the only possibility in this vernacular and explains this by the "non-referential function" of the noun phrases in question, which do not introduce a referent but rather contribute to the characterization of the subject as horse-owners and salaried employees respectively.

    Eriksson & Rendahl (1999), in their questionnaire investigation of Ostrobothnian, also found that the bare noun pattern was predominating. However, one informant from Munsala in northern Österbotten did produce a definite variant, together with one with an indefinite article:

(139) Munsala (Northern Ostrobothnian)

    a. *Vi had   **hästin,**   tå   ja va   lill.*
        we have.PST **horse.DEF** when I be.PST small

    b. *Vi had   **in   häst,** tå   ja va   lill.*
        we have.PST **INDF horse** when I   be.PST small

        'We had a horse when I was a kid.' (questionnaire)

Eriksson & Rendahl (1999) also quote a number of examples of definite-marked countable singulars from published texts:

(140) Sideby (Southern Ostrobothnian)
    *Så kviila   vi **middain.***
    SO rest.PST we **noon.DEF**
    'Then we took a nap.' (Standard Swedish *vila middag*) [S19]

(141) Sideby (Southern Ostrobothnian)
    *Å   dåm hav   **öitjon.***
    and they have.PRS **dinghy.DEF**
    'And they have a dinghy.' [S19]

Ivars (2005) presents at least one fairly clear example from Närpes:

(142) Närpes (Southern Ostrobothnian)
    *Han ha: ju   **brännvinsbo:den** han.*
    he   have.PST PRAG **liquor-shop.DEF**   he
    'He had a liquor shop, he.'

Thus, the use of definite forms with singular countables is fairly well documented also in Ostrobothnian, although the article-less pattern is more common in present-day usage.

Ovansiljan. Examples from Elfdalian have already been quoted above. Questionnaires from Orsa and Sollerön give a result which is similar to the one reported above for non-delimited uses. Thus, the majority of the informants from Orsa used the definite form in (143), whereas none from Sollerön did:

(143)   Orsa (Ovansiljan)
    Wi addum   ***äst'n***   *dö*   *i wa*   *lit'n.*
    we have.PST.1PL **horse.DEF** when I be.PST small

    'We had a horse when I was a kid.' (questionnaire)

Summing up. Like the use of definite forms after quantifiers, the extended use of definite forms with count nouns display is less well entrenched in the Peripheral Swedish area than the non-delimited type. Their absence from the Middle Norrland area is conspicuous. (Compare also the more questionable example (219) from Hållnäs in Uppland below.)

3.6.2 Instrumental prepositional phrases

Himmelmann (1998) claims that articles "are generally used less frequently, and with regard to semantic and pragmatic generalisations, less consistently in adpositional phrases than in other syntactic environments (such as subject or object position)". Manner and instrumental adverbial phrases would be a case in point, and indeed, in English, certain types of manner-characterizing prepositional phrases tend to involve bare nouns, particularly those that indicate manner of locomotion, such as *by train, by foot, by car*. In Central Scandinavian, the use of such bare nouns is considerably wider. Thus, in Swedish, the phrase *med kniv* '[lit.] with knife' is much more common[24] than *med en kniv* 'with a knife', and in the following sentence, the use of an indefinite article sounds definitely strange:

(144)   Swedish
    Hon äter   *soppa med* ***(?en) sked.***
    she eat.PRS soup with INDF **spoon**

    'She eats soup with a spoon.'

---

[24] A Google count: *med kniv*: 14300, *med en kniv*: 2820. In English, there is a parallel in the phrase *by knife*, appearing in phrases such as *homicide by knife*.

In the light of these observations and Himmelmann's claim, it is rather unexpected to find languages where in fact (144) would be translated using a definite article in the phrase 'with a spoon', even when it is evident that no specific spoon is being referred to. Nevertheless, in French, if the preposition *à* is chosen, it is regularly followed by the definite rather than by the indefinite article:

(145) French
      *Elle mange la   soupe à   **la cuillière.***
      she eat.PRS DEF soup with DEF **spoon**
      'She eats soup with a spoon.'

where a definite NP is used after the preposition *à*. With this preposition, the definite article seems more or less obligatory. (Compare captions of paintings such as *Jeune fille au chèvre* 'Young girl with a goat'). With the synonymous preposition *avec* the definite article is possible but the preferred variant appears to be with an indefinite NP:

(146) French
      *Elle mange la   soupe avec **une cuillière.***
      she eat.PRS DEF soup with INDF **spoon**
      'She eats soup with a spoon.'

Similarly, in the Peripheral Swedish vernaculars, instrumental phrases of this type often show up with a definite head noun. Thus, Levander (1909: 126) quotes the following Elfdalian example, which he translates into Swedish using a bare noun construction (*med kniv* 'with a knife')

(147) Elfdalian (Ovansiljan)
      *Sjo ur   dier ovo   skrievað **min knaivem!***
      see how they have.PRS.3PL write.SUP **with knife.DEF.DAT**
      'Look what they have written with a knife!' (Levander 1909: 125)

A modern Elfdalian example elicited by questionnaire is (148).

(148) Elfdalian (Ovansiljan)
      *An jät   suppy̨   **min stjiedn.***
      he eat.PRS soup.DEF.ACC **with spoon.DEF.DAT**
      'He eats soup with a spoon.' (questionnaire)

However, the informant indicated that the indefinite form was also possible:

(149) Elfdalian (Ovansiljan)
    *An jät   suppų   **min stjied.***
    he eat.PRS soup.DEF.ACC with **spoon.DAT**
    'He eats soup with a spoon.' (questionnaire)

From Orsa, where there were several questionnaire responses, the majority used a definite form, either in the dative or non-case marked:

(150) Orsa (Ovansiljan)
    *An jat   suppo   **mi   stjed'n/stjedi.***
    he eat.PRS soup.DEF.ACC with **spoon.DEF**
    'He eats soup with a spoon.' (questionnaire)

Out of four questionnaire responses from Sollerön, a definite form was given by all three informants born before 1940:

(151) Sollerön (Ovansiljan)
    *An jät   såppo   **minn stjedn.***
    he eat.PRS soup.DEF.ACC with **spoon.DEF**
    'He eats soup with a spoon.' (questionnaire)

For Upper Norrland, we find definite forms throughout, as evidenced in questionnaires from Bjurholm, Burträsk, Norsjö, and Glommersträsk:

(152) Bjurholm (Angermannian-Westrobothnian transitional)
    *Han ät   soppa **ve   skea.***
    he   eat.PRS soup.DEF with **spoon.DEF**
    'He eats soup with a spoon.' (questionnaire)

In an early text from Överkalix, the following example is found:

(153) Överkalix (Kalixmål)
    *...fistsen fik   di   takkɷ åys   ɷpp **ve   slaiven bårti***
    fish.DEF get.PST they almost scoop.INF up   with **ladle.DEF** from
    anɷ...
    river.DEF
    '...as for the fish, they almost had to scoop it up with a ladle from the river...' [S17]

Similar examples are found in other transcribed texts from Överkalix.

Middle Norrland. No examples have been found in texts from Ångermanland, Jämtland, and Medelpad. For Jämtland, informants from Lit indicate that definite forms are not possible in examples of this type.

Ostrobothnian. Hummelstedt (1934) enumerates quite a few examples of the type from Närpes.

(154)   Närpes (Southern Ostrobothnian)

    a. *Vi skār   a me štjeron.*
       we cut.PST it **with sickle.DEF**
       'We cut it with a sickle.'

    b. *Vi λōw   me lijjan.*
       we cut.PST **with scythe.DEF**
       'We cut [grass] with a scythe.'

    c. *Ja tjuŏp   me tjärron.*
       I   drive.PST **with cart.DEF**
       'I drove [with] a cart.'

    d. *He jiēg   me λedan.*
       it go.PRET **with sledge.DEF**
       'We went [lit. it went] by sledge.' (Hummelstedt 1934: 135)

Ivars (2005) gives examples such as *me kni:vin* 'with knife.DEF', *me li:an* 'with scythe.DEF' from South Ostrobothnian. (Nikula (1997), who also discusses Närpesmål, does not mention instrumental phrases at all.)

In the translation of the sentence 'He eats soup with a spoon', Eriksson & Rendahl (1999) obtained four definite-marked responses among a total of 11 Ostrobothnian informants:

(155)   a. Malax (Southern Ostrobothnian)
      Ha jeter   soppu   me skeide.
      he eat.PRS soup.DEF? **with spoon.DEF**

    b. Närpes (Southern Ostrobothnian)
      An jäter   soppon   me sjöiden.
      he eat.PRS soup.DEF **with spoon.DEF**

    c. Tjöck (Southern Ostrobothnian)
      Han jiter   sopon   me skeiden.
      he   eat.PRS soup.DEF **with spoon.DEF**
      'He eats soup with a spoon.'

They also quote the phrase *sloo me liian* 'cut with a scythe' from [S19].

Examples are also found in Southern Finland and Estonia, where extended uses of definites are in general quite restricted. Thus, Lundström (1939) quotes examples from Nyland:

(156) Snappertuna (Nylandic)
      *Man slōr   gräse   **me līan.***
      one cut.PRS grass.DEF **with scythe.DEF**
      'One cuts the grass with a scythe.' (Lundström 1939: 15)

(157) *Nꙍ blīr   e brā dehäran, bara man tar   innoger tāg*
      sure become.PRS it good this   just one take.PRS a_few take.PL
      me hyviln.
      with plane.DEF
      'This will surely be good, if you take a few shavings with a plane.'
      (Lundström 1939: 15)

In a text from Ormsö in Estonia, we find the following example:

(158) Ormsö (Estonian Swedish vernaculars)
      *Nu   kond   ve bere   hlå   rågen **mä lian**   å*
      now can.PST we begin.INF cut.INF rye.DEF **with scythe.DEF** and
      triske   bLai   nu   mike leta.
      threshing become.PST now much easy.CMPR
      'Now we could begin to cut the rye with a scythe and the threshing
      became much easier.' [S24]

Summing up. The use of definite forms in instrumental prepositional phrases can be considered a special case of uses with singular count nouns. The distribution of the instrumental use also is somewhat similar to that of definite forms in constructions such as 'We have a horse', discussed in §3.6.1. In particular, we may note that no attestations are found from Middle Norrland. On the other hand, the instrumental use extends to some areas where the other types of definite singular count nouns are not found, viz. southern Finland and Estonia.

A possible objection (Ulrika Kvist Darnell, personal communication) is that the intended interpretation in the examples in this section is not indefinite but instead closer to something like 'the X that I have'. It is true that if the examples had occurred in a text corpus, it would have been difficult to know exactly how they should be understood. However, the use of definites in such contexts has been noted as striking from the point of view of the standard language by several scholars who are well acquainted with the vernaculars in question. Many examples were also given as translations of Swedish sentences with indefinite noun phrases. But the fact that such examples have a somewhat fluid interpretation may be relevant in a diachronic context – see further the discussion in §3.13.

3.7 "Det var kvällen"

Delsing (2003b: 16) subsumes two different cases under "predicative constructions": one exemplified by examples such as *hä ä sommarn* 'it is summer', which he calls "impersonal", and another exemplified by "identifying constructions" such as

(159)   (no location)
    De här ä   körpen.
    this here be.PRS pick.DEF
    'This is a pick.'

It appears, though, that these two patterns have rather different geographic distributions. Examples like (159), which are rather close to citation uses (see §3.3.1), are not to my knowledge attested outside the area where extended uses of definites are normally found, but "impersonal" constructions characterized by the pattern

(160)   *impersonal subject 'it' + copular verb 'be' or 'become' +* *noun denoting a temporal interval*

are quite widespread in Scandinavia. In the Swedish dialect area, examples can thus not only be found in Härjedalen, Västerdalarna, Dalabergslagen and Åboland, all close to the extended definite area, but also in south-western Sweden (the provinces of Halland and Bohuslän):

(161)   Träslövsläge (Halland)
    *Nu borja   här a   bli   **kwälen,**   a   sola   gick*
    now begin.PST here INFm become.INF **evening.DEF**   and sun.DEF go.PST
    nair i   sjön.
    down in lake.DEF

    'Now evening was coming (lit. it started to become the evening), and the sun set in the lake.' (Cat Corpus)

(162) Sotenäs (Bohuslän)
Dä hôllte   pô ô   bli   vårn   no,   dä   kjännte
it   hold.PST on INFm become.INF spring.DEF now that feel.PST
Pissen.
pussycat.DEF

'Spring was coming (lit. it was becoming spring), Cat felt that.' (Cat Corpus)

(163) Östmark (Värmland)
Nu   ä   dä snart sommarn.
now be.PRS it soon summer.DEF

'Now it will soon be summer.' (Broberg 1936)

(164) Transtrand (Västerdalarna)
Hä vaL   snart vintern.
it become.PRS soon winter.DEF

'It will soon be winter.' (questionnaire)

(165) Houtskär (Åbolandic)
Nōr   he bḷei   kvēldinj   o   in kōm   heim me
when it become.PST evening.DEF and he come.PST home with
fōrenj...
sheep.DEF.PL

'When evening came and he came home with the sheep...' (Lundell 1936: 38)

Delsing mentions a Norwegian informant from Trøndelag who accepts examples of this type, giving the impression that it is locally restricted in Norwegian. In fact, the construction is well represented in written Norwegian, both Bokmål and Nynorsk. The following example is from the Nynorsk part of the "Norsk Tekstarkiv":

(166) Nynorsk Norwegian
Det vart   kvelden   og det vart   natta   på nytt.
it   become.PST evening.DEF and it   become.PST night.DEF on new

'Evening came and it became night again.' [S29]

An Internet example in Bokmål:

(167) Bokmål Norwegian
*Da   det ble   **kvelden**   hadde   bortimot 250 shaman'er*
when it become.PST **evening.DEF** have.PST around 250 shaman.PL
samlet   seg   rundt slangen   og kvinnen...
collect.PP REFL.3PL around snake.DEF and woman.DEF

'When evening came, around 250 shamans had collected around the snake and the woman...' (Internet)

The pattern does not seem to be possible in Danish or in the southernmost Swedish provinces (although it goes as far south as Halland). Its wide distribution makes it somewhat unlikely that it has spread together with the other extended uses of definite forms, which are less widespread.

3.8 Various minor patterns

3.8.1 Illnesses

In the literature, names of illnesses are sometimes provided as examples where definite forms are used in vernaculars more extensively than in Swedish. Thus:

(168) Pyttis (Nylandic)
*Bꞷonen   har   jꞷ   **čikhꜷston.***
child.DEF.PL have.PRS PRAG whooping-cough.DEF

'The children have got whooping-cough.' (Lundström 1939: 11)

(169) Östmark (Värmland)
*Han ä   ill   kommen ta **jekta.***   'He is suffering badly from gout'
he be.PRS badly come.PP of **gout.DEF**
(Broberg 1936)

(170) Sollerön (Ovansiljan)
*I a   fänndji **ålldi.***
I have.PRS get.SUP stitch.DEF

'I have got a stitch in my side.' (Andersson & Danielsson 1999: 285)

It seems hard to generalize here, though, since names of illnesses tend to behave idiosyncratically in many languages, including English – thus, *flu* is preferably used with the article but the synonymous *influenza* without.

3.8.2 Measure phrases

Definite forms also sometimes show up in phrases denoting measurements of time, weight, etc. Lundström (1939: 9) provides a number of examples from Nyland:

(171) a. Pojo (Nylandic)
           [Hur länge räcker det till Lovisa?]
           Timmen* o *femton.
           hour.DEF and fifteen

           '[How far is it to Lovisa?] - One hour fifteen.'

       b. Borgå (Nylandic)
           *Han čŏrd   **på tīman.***
           he drive.PST **on hour.DEF**

           'He drove [the distance] in an hour.'

In the Cat Corpus, I have only found one clear example from Överkalix (all the other vernaculars have an indefinite NP in the corresponding sentence):

(172) Överkalix (Kalixmål)
       *He dråo   nestan **haL(e)v-täimen** enan fressn   tåoRs*
       it take.PST almost **half-hour.DEF**   before tomcat.DEF dare.PST
       koma   främm.
       come.INF fore

       'It took almost half an hour before Cat dared come out.' (Cat Corpus)

3.9 Preproprial articles

What is most appropriately called preproprial articles are used widely in Scandinavia. Preproprial articles are identical in form to third person pronouns – either full forms, which is common in Norway, or reduced (clitic) forms, as is the normal case in Sweden: *a Brita* 'Brita', *n Erik* 'Erik'.

In most colloquial varieties of Swedish, third person pronouns can be used in front of proper names but then with a rather clear pragmatic effect: *han Erik* 'that person Erik you know'. No such effect is found in the vernaculars where preproprial articles in the proper sense are used, rather they are normally obligatory with persons' given names and with name-like uses of kin terms. They normally do not occur with surnames (which may instead have "postproprial" articles, see below). They do not appear when names are used metalinguistically ('His name is...') or as vocatives.

Delsing (2003b: 21) claims that in many vernaculars, preproprial articles are normally used only to refer to persons with whom the speaker is acquainted. It is not clear how this claim should be reconciled with the obligatory character of the articles, which he also mentions. In her study of the use of preproprial articles, Törnqvist (2002) quotes several earlier works on Norwegian dialects in which the use is said to be unrestricted, and also a wide range of examples from Swedish vernaculars of the use of preproprial articles to refer to unacquainted referents. The reluctance that Delsing has found in some dialects against using preproprial articles with names such as *Jesus* and *Elvis* should perhaps be explained by their cultural foreignness rather than by the relationship between the speaker and their referents.

According to Delsing (2003b: 21), preproprial articles are used generally in Norrland excluding Hälsingland and Gästrikland, in Västerdalarna and northern Värmland, and in most of Norway, excluding an area in the south and bilingual areas in the north. This is in full accordance with other statements in other sources and with the usage reflected in texts that I have seen, in particular the Cat Corpus. Delsing also says that they are used "sometimes" in Faroese and "optionally" in Icelandic spoken language. It can be seen that the distribution of preproprial articles overlaps significantly with that of extended uses of definite forms, but there are also some striking differences. Thus, if we compare the area where preproprial articles are obligatory with the area where non-delimited uses of definite forms are common, we can see that they overlap in Upper and Middle Norrland, that is, in the provinces of Jämtland and Ångermanland and the Westrobothnian and Norrbothnian dialect areas. Outside this zone, however, there is no location where the two phenomena co-exist. Thus, preproprial articles are found in most of Norway and along the Norwegian border all the way from northern Värmland and northwards except in Ovansiljan – the southern stronghold of non-delimited uses of definite forms. On the other side of the Baltic, Ostrobothnian behaves like the Ovansiljan vernaculars in these two regards. These facts suggest that preproprial articles and extended uses of definite forms have separate histories of origin.

Looking back in time, I do not know of any very old attestations of preproprial articles from Swedish vernaculars, but I have found several older texts in the Norwegian Diplomatarium with uses of pronouns that look very much like preproprial articles. One such text, consisting of one long sentence with no less than five occurrences of the pattern Pronoun+Proper Name, is rendered in the

Appendix. It dates from 1430 – unfortunately, the location is not known. It thus appears that the usage was already fairly firmly established in at least some Norwegian varieties in medieval times. This, together with the geographical distribution in the Swedish dialectal area, suggests a spread from Norway, perhaps most probably from Trøndelag.

Proper names also sometimes show up with definite suffixes (called "postproprial articles" by Delsing 2003b: 23). This usage appears to be less systematic and is most common with surnames (occasionally even in more standard varieties of Swedish). With kin terms, definite suffixes are found in Upper Norrlandic vernaculars where Standard Swedish has a bare form and many other vernaculars have preproprial articles. Compare the following examples:

(173) Sävar (Southern Westrobothnian)
     Mormora   *vart*   *alldess rö oppi öga.*
     Granny.DEF become.PST quite   red   in   eye.DEF.PL

     'Granny's eyes became quite red.' (Cat Corpus)

(174) Malung (Västerdalarna)
     O   *Mormor* *vaṭ*   *âlldeles rö i   ögon.*
     PDA.F Granny become.PST quite   red in eye.DEF.PL

     'Granny's eyes became quite red.' (Cat Corpus)

(175) Swedish
     Mormor *blev*   *alldeles röd i   ögonen.*
     Granny become.PST quite   red in eye.DEF.PL

     'Granny's face became quite red.'

The fourth logical possibility – both a preproprial article and a definite suffix on the same noun – is so far unattested in any variety (Törnqvist 2002).

3.10 Postadjectival articles

Some Scandinavian dialects feature indefinite NPs according to the pattern exemplified by *en stor en bil* 'a big car', where there is, in addition to the usual preposed indefinite article, another one between the adjective and the noun. According to Delsing (2003b: 46), the construction is found in Norway from southern Trøndelag and northwards, and in Sweden in Västerbotten, Ångermanland, Medelpad, and Jämtland. There is evidence to suggest, however, that the phenomenon had a wider distribution in earlier times. Thus, Delsing himself mentions an example from 18th century Norrbothnian, and I have found a couple of attestations also in 18th century Dalecarlian texts, such as the following from 1730:

(176)   Dalecarlian (18th century)
        Kullur der   giärå   'n   jen   snoggan jen krantz um
        girl.PL there make.PRS.3PL him.DAT INDF neat.ACC PIA laurel   about
        missommors   nåti
        midsummer.GEN night.DAT
        'Girls there make a neat laurel for him in the midsummer night' [S26]

Delsing notes that it is sometimes hard to tell postadjectival articles from inflectional suffixes on the adjective. He claims that a suffixal analysis is more adequate in most provinces further south, as well as east of the Baltic.

3.11 Summary of geographical distribution of extended uses

We have seen that there are several different types of extended uses of definite forms in the Peripheral Swedish area, which vary to some extent in their geographical distribution. Some of the types, notably the pattern *Det är sommaren* 'It is the summer' and (to a somewhat lesser extent) generic uses of definites, go beyond the Peripheral Swedish area, being found also in Norway and/or southern Sweden. For the geographically more restricted uses, we can identify a few core areas: a large northern one, comprised of the provinces of Norrbotten, Västerbotten, Ångermanland, Jämtland, and Österbotten, and a smaller southern one, basically restricted to the Ovansiljan region in Dalarna. Sporadic attestations elsewhere suggest that the core areas were earlier more extensive.

3.12 Some earlier attempts to explain the extended uses of definite forms

3.12.1 Holmberg & Sandström

In a paper written in Swedish, Holmberg & Sandström (2003) try to give a unified generative treatment of many of the phenomena discussed in this book. The title of their contribution is, in translation, "What is particular with Northern Swedish noun phrases?". By "Northern Swedish" (*nordsvenska*), they are actually referring to a not precisely specified group of dialects in Västerbotten and the parts of Ångermanland and Norrbotten that border on the former province, said to have the following properties: 1) preproprial articles, 2) postposed possessives, 3) preposed possessives with definite head nouns, 4) postposed demonstratives, 5) adjectival incorporation, 6) suffixed definite articles on adjectives in noun phrases without a lexical head, 7) definite forms of generic nouns, 8) definite forms of "partitive" plurals and mass nouns.

Holmberg & Sandström admit that these features do not always occur together, and that some of them also occur outside the "Northern Swedish" area. "However, there are a number of Westrobothnian dialects which display all the features, and we shall show that their combination is not accidental but on the contrary, a consistent language variety" (Holmberg & Sandström 2003: 87, my translation).

Holmberg & Sandström adhere to the analysis of noun phrases in which they are projections of a functional category D or "determiner", which has the consequence that in a noun phrase such as *the house*, it is *the* rather than *house* that is the head. They suggest that a major difference between Northern Swedish and other Scandinavian varieties, such as Standard Swedish, lies in the status of definite articles: the postposed article in "Northern Swedish" is a clitic, "base-generated in D [determiner position]", whereas in Standard Swedish it is an inflectional suffix, "base-generated on [the] N[oun]". Another difference, relating to the first, is that Northern Swedish, like the Romance languages, requires that the D-position always be filled (that is, it is realized overtly).

Let us see how these properties are used to explain the eight phenomena enumerated above.

The D-position can essentially be filled in two ways: either by a base-generated determiner, or by moving the head noun (as in the figure above). The first way is seen in preproprial articles, the second in postposed demonstratives and possessives, where the head noun supposedly moves across the postposed element in order to fill the D-position. Definite adjectives in "Northern Swedish" have to be incorporated because if they appeared separately from the noun they would have to agree with it – and they don't.

In the case of adjectives in noun phrases without a lexical head, it is assumed that the empty element *pro* [which is the head of the NP] moves to D and the adjective is incorporated into it.

Definite suffixes on generic nouns and "partitive" plurals and mass nouns are explained by the requirement that the D-position be filled, in the relevant cases by a definite suffix that attracts the head noun of the noun phrase.

Holmberg & Sandström suggest that the properties of North Swedish have developed in two steps. In the first step, the definite article is reinterpreted as a

Romance-style clitic in D (the determiner position) to which a noun has to move – a clitic needs a host. This gives rise to movement of all definite nouns to D. In the second step, language-acquiring children choose to interpret this movement as depending on a requirement that D must always be filled, which gives rise to "generic and partitive articles".

One major problem with Holmberg & Sandström's theory is how to apply it to dialects in which not all properties enumerated above are present. We can note that Norwegian vernaculars tend to have preproprial articles and postposed possessives but in general lack the extended uses of definite forms found in Northern Sweden. Conversely, the Ovansiljan vernaculars lack preproprial articles and postposed demonstratives, although they display most of the other properties. This means that the evidence for movement of nouns to D is considerably weaker in those vernaculars. Moreover, the differences in geographical distribution between e.g. preproprial articles and extended uses of definites suggest that they also have different historical origins).

Notice further that nouns preceded by demonstratives generally take definite suffixes in all Swedish spoken varieties, e.g.

(177) Elfdalian (Ovansiljan)
       an   dar   kalln
       that there man.DEF
       'that man'

If the definite suffix originates in the D position, it is not clear how it could end up on the noun in such noun phrases. The same can be said of noun phrases with definite nouns following quantifiers, as described in §3.5, which are common in the area focused on by Holmberg & Sandström, although they do not mention them. It would appear that those noun phrases have both an unfilled D and a definite suffix in an unexpected position where it cannot be accounted for by the demand for a filled D. (One could probably say more or less the same of possessives with definite head nouns which are listed as one of the interesting properties by Holmberg & Sandström but are not further commented upon in the paper.)

Consider also the explanation of the preproprial articles, where the condition on filled D's is also invoked. Holmberg & Sandström, quoting Longobardi (1994, 1995), note that in Romance languages, which are also supposed to have the filled-D condition, some varieties (e.g. Standard Italian) do and others (e.g. some Italian vernaculars) do not have preproprial articles. It thus has to be assumed that, in a language with the filled-D condition, there are two possibilities: either there s a preproprial article or the proper name moves to D. What is excluded, they say, is for a proper name that remains in situ to lack an article. The problem here is that the movement of proper names to D is in general "invisible" since the proper name is in initial position in the NP anyway. Thus, the filled-D condition could be said to be vacuously fulfilled for proper names even in languages such as Elfdalian and Swedish. This fact raises some doubt about the motivation for the introduction of preproprial articles. If the filled-D condition is fulfilled anyway, why should a language bother to introduce them? Indeed, since there is more than one solution compatible with the filled-D condition, it may be said that this parameter underdetermines the behaviour of proper noun phrases. Notice that apparently one and the same language can choose different solutions: it is generally only with first names that preproprial articles are obligatory.

With respect to the claim that definite suffixes are clitics in Peripheral Swedish vernacular, it may be noted that clitics generally represent less advanced stages in grammaticalization processes, and the development from inflectional ending to clitic is rather uncommon. It is generally assumed that the Scandinavian definite articles have passed through a clitic stage, and later been fused with their head nouns – that is, the opposite direction. The wider range of uses of definite forms in Peripheral Swedish vernaculars compared to Central Scandinavian rather suggests that the Peripheral Swedish forms have advanced further in the grammaticalization process. There is little indication of synchronic clitic-like behaviour. One may for instance compare the definite suffixes to the marker of the *s*-genitive, which in Central Scandinavian may be added to the last constituent of the noun phrase even if that is not the head noun. The same holds for the possessive marker *es* in Elfdalian (see §5.4.2). No such thing is possible with definite suffixes in Peripheral Swedish vernaculars. Also, phenomena such as portmanteau expression of definiteness, number and case, neutralization of the definiteness distinction (see §3.1.5), and variation between different declension classes are not typical of clitics. The fact that indeclinable nouns such as *kaffi* 'coffee' take zero definite endings is also unexpected if the definite suffix is a clitic. Admittedly, it is true that the fact that headless adjectives can take definite suffixes can be interpreted as a deviation from what could be expected from a well-behaved noun suffix.

3.12.2 Extended uses of definite forms – a Fenno-Ugric substrate?

In Finnish, non-delimited subjects and objects take the partitive case in situations where other noun phrases would take the nominative or accusative, respectively, as in the following examples:

(178)   Finnish
     Ostin   **olutta.**
     buy.PRET.1SG **beer.PART**
     'I bought beer.'

(179)   *Ostin*   **oluen.**
     buy.PRET.1SG **beer.ACC**
     'I bought the beer.'

There would seem to be an analogy here with Peripheral Swedish vernaculars, in particular if we choose to describe them, as e.g. Delsing does, as having a "partitive article". Given the fact that the Peripheral Swedish area borders on Fenno-Ugric speaking territory, could there be a historical connection between the two phenomena: the partitive case in Finnish and the "partitive article" in Peripheral Swedish vernaculars? The idea of such a connection pops up now and then in the discussion and has recently been articulated by Rießler (2002). It does have some initial plausibility, but I shall argue that the analogy is superficial and that there is little empirical evidence to support the hypothesis.

It is fairly easy to see that the analogy is not very direct. After all, the partitive case in Finnish is a case, not an article, and as such it has rather many different uses, which tend to correlate with indefiniteness rather than definiteness, and often these uses have no counterpart in definite forms in the Peripheral Swedish vernaculars. Thus, the Finnish partitive is used with negated objects, with objects of non-resultative verbs, and in predicative uses such as

(180)   Finnish
     Opiskelijat   *ovat*   **suomalaisia.**
     student.NOM.PL be.PRS.3PL **Finn.PART.PL**
     'The students are Finns.'

where Peripheral Swedish vernaculars would have indefinite forms. Conversely, not all the extended uses of definite forms in those varieties correspond to Finnish partitives. Thus, generic noun phrases as subjects or objects are consistently in the nominative or accusative in Finnish. Likewise, countable nouns in the singular take the nominative or accusative if the syntactic conditions are the right ones, even in the cases where Swedish has a bare noun and Peripheral Swedish vernaculars use definite forms. Thus, we get

(181) Finnish
   *Meillä on   **hevonen.***
   we.ALL be.PRS.3SG **horse.NOM**
   'We have a horse'

rather than **meillä on hevosta*, with the partitive.

In his discussion of the issue, Rießler does acknowledge many of these circumstances. Actually, he maintains that one of the reasons why a Finnish learner of Scandinavian could be inspired to use definite forms in contexts where Finnish has the partitive is because the latter cannot be generally associated with indefiniteness or partitivity, and because it is syntactically the unmarked case for native speakers of Finnish. Rießler suggests that the extended definite forms in the vernaculars might be explained as resulting from second-language learners' filling of a morphologically empty position. After all, Rießler says, there is no "naked form" of uncountable nouns ("nicht zählbare Substantive") in Finnish. The German term is probably intended to include also plurals; on the other hand, the statement is not quite true as it stands, as uncountable nouns such as *olut* 'beer' certainly do have a zero-marked form, the nominative, which appears in definite and generic uses such as

(182) Finnish
   Olut on kylmää.
   beer be.PRS.3SG cold.PART.SG
   '**The beer** is cold.'

(183) ***Olut**   on   virvoitusjuoma.*
   beer.NOM.SG be.PRS.3SG beverage.NOM.SG
   '**Beer** is a beverage.'

The unmarked status of the partitive is thus less obvious than Rießler makes it.

Another relevant issue is whether the kind of interference suggested can be attested in second-language learning. Rießler quotes some cases of overuse of definite forms in the Norwegian of Saami speakers taken from Bull (1995). Indeed, second-language learners of Scandinavian languages often over-generalize definite forms, but the question is whether it happens more often with speakers of Uralic languages than with others. We find some data relevant to this question in Axelsson (1994), who studied how speakers of Finnish, Polish, and Spanish handled Swedish noun phrases at different stages of second-language acquisition. The subjects were 60 adults attending a Swedish course for immigrants and were in the investigation divided into a "low-level" and a "high-level" group depending on their initial proficiency in Swedish.

Among other things, Axelsson provides some statistics on the use of definite nouns when the norms of the target language require bare nouns. Such overuse of definite marking turns out to occur in the speech of all three groups, and both with "low-level" and "high-level" speakers. Out of 2599 noun phrases in the total material that should show up as "bare nouns" according to target-language norms, 126 (4.8 %) had a definite suffix. The Finnish group had the largest percentage – 57 occurrences or 7.4 % – and the Spanish the lowest – 30 occurrences or 3.3 %. The Polish group was in between with 39 occurrences or 4.3 %. This seems to indicate that Finnish speakers may have a larger propensity than the others to overuse definite forms. However, the variation in the material is fairly large— on one occasion, when "low-level" learners were tested for the second time, the Polish group had actually more occurrences (17) than the Finnish one. Also, as it turns out, even the Spanish speakers, who make the fewest mistakes of this kind, and who have a relatively "standard" kind of definiteness marking in their native language, sometimes produce sentences which look as if they were from a Peripheral Swedish area vernacular:

(184) Swedish L2 (Spanish speakers)
*Därför   kan   man inte ta   **salvan**   varje dag.*
therefore can.PRS one   NEG take.INF **ointment.DEF** every day
'Therefore one could not take ointment every day.'

(185) *Ja vill   **skilsmässan.***
I   want.PRS **divorce.DEF**
'I want a divorce.'

(186) *när   man har   **tiden**   att   läsa*
when   one have.PRS **time.DEF** INFm read
'when one has time to read.'

Conversely, the examples Axelsson provides of inappropriate uses of definite forms by Finnish speakers do not at all fall under the heading of non-delimited uses:

(187) Swedish L2 (Finnish speakers)
Ja vill   jobba   på sjukhuset.
I   want.PRS work.INF on hospital.DEF
'I want to work at a hospital.'

(188) *kanske kontoret   eller nånting*
       maybe office.DEF or   something
       'maybe an office or something'

Axelsson notes that "In some of these isolated examples it might also seem possible to use a definite noun, but with regard to the larger context this has been assessed as impossible." For (187)(b), no context is given but presumably it is uttered as a response to a question like "What kind of job would you like to have?")

It should also be noted that for all the groups, it is much more common not to use a definite article when it should be there than to use it when it should not be there. Thus, out of the 1266 noun phrases (without modifiers) in the material where the target language norms would require a definite head noun, the learners used a bare noun in 429 (33.8%). Interestingly, however, the Finnish speakers did so more seldom: their error rate was only 21 per cent here. Thus, compared to other groups, Finnish L2 learners of Swedish are more prone to overuse than to underuse definite forms – however, in absolute terms, omissions are more frequent than inappropriate uses, even for Finnish speakers.

If we grant that, judging from available data, there is a slightly higher tendency for Finnish speakers to overuse definite suffixes than for some other groups, two questions remain: whether this tendency has anything to do with the existence of a partitive case in Finnish, and whether the tendency is strong enough to give support to the idea that Fenno-Ugric speakers could be behind the expansion of the definite forms in various Scandinavian vernaculars. In my opinion, the evidence for a positive answer is in both cases rather dubious. Also, I shall now argue that in spite of the fact that Peripheral Swedish vernaculars tend to have Fenno-Ugric neighbours, the historical and geographic picture does not fit the idea of a Fenno-Ugric source for the extended definites.

That Finnish influences could be expected in the Swedish varieties in Finland is fairly obvious, although it may be noted that such influence is likely to be stronger in urbanized areas, where language contact is bound to be intensive, than in monolingual rural areas. If the extended uses of definites are the result of Finnish influence, we would not expect them to be strongest in Österbotten but rather in southern Finland. As for Sweden, Finnish influence could be expected in Norrbotten and Västerbotten, where there are fairly large groups of Finnish (or Fennic) speakers, and the area of Finnish settlement was even larger in medieval times (Wallerström 1995). However, further south in the Peripheral Swedish area, contacts with Finnish speakers have been more restricted. Rießler says that the use of the partitive article in "dialects in North and Central Scandinavia" is not unexpected as the shift from Finnish to Scandinavian among the "Forest Finns" in Eastern Norway, Värmland, and Dalarna "is a fact".[25] This would imply that the developments in the south are separate from those in the north, since the "Forest Finns" came relatively late (starting in the late 16th century) and the language shift to Swedish is even later (it was completed only in the 20th century). This is perhaps not necessarily an obstacle to the hypothesis, but what is more serious is that the "Forest Finns" and the non-delimited uses of definite forms turn out to have an almost complementary distribution – that is, the Ovansiljan area, which makes up the southern core area is almost the only place in Svealand and southern Norrland where the "Forest Finns" did not settle,[26] as can be seen from Figure 3.9.

Now, Finnish, or Fennic, speakers are not the only representative of the Fenno-Ugric family in Scandinavia: there are also the Saami, who speak a number of fairly divergent varieties traditionally referred to as the Saami language. Rießler says that "probably both Finnish and Saami interferences have triggered the change in North Scandinavian morphosyntax". Referring to papers by himself and Jurij Kusmenko, he points to various phenomena that have to be explained by a Saami substrate, mainly in the area of phonology.

Postulating Saami influence could possibly help explain why the extended definites are found in areas where there have been few Finns. Unfortunately for the Saami substrate hypothesis, however, there is no very good reason to assume the existence of a Finnish-style partitive in Saami as spoken in the areas in question. As Rießler notes, present-day Saami varieties in Sweden and Norway do not have a partitive case at all – he submits, however, that this may not be a problem since a partitive is attested in older forms of Ume and Lule Saami, spoken in the immediate vicinity of the regions where the extended uses of definites are strong. But this partitive was apparently not like its present-day Finnish counterpart, in spite of Rießler's claims to the contrary. His evidence for a parallel between Finnish and Saami in this respect is that the Saami partitive was used with the objects of verbs like 'seek'. But this is most probably a use which is indepen-

---

[25] "Der Gebrauch des partitiven Artikels ist nicht nur über die schwedischen Dialekte in Finnland sondern auch über Dialekte in Nord- und Mittelskandinavien verbreitet. Das verwundert nicht, da die Skandinavisierung und der damit verbundene Sprachwechsel der skogsfinnar in Ostnorwegen, Värmland und Dalarna ein Fakt ist." (Rießler 2002: 57).

[26] A possible exception would be the area called "Orsa Finnmark", which is, as the name indicates, technically part of Orsa parish. In Figure 3.9, these are the dots immediately north of the grey circles. As the map suggests, however, Orsa Finnmark is quite separate from the main settlements in Orsa. In Älvdalen, the name "Finnmarken" is used to refer to some peripheral, relatively recently settled villages; there seems to be no evidence that there were ever any Finns there.

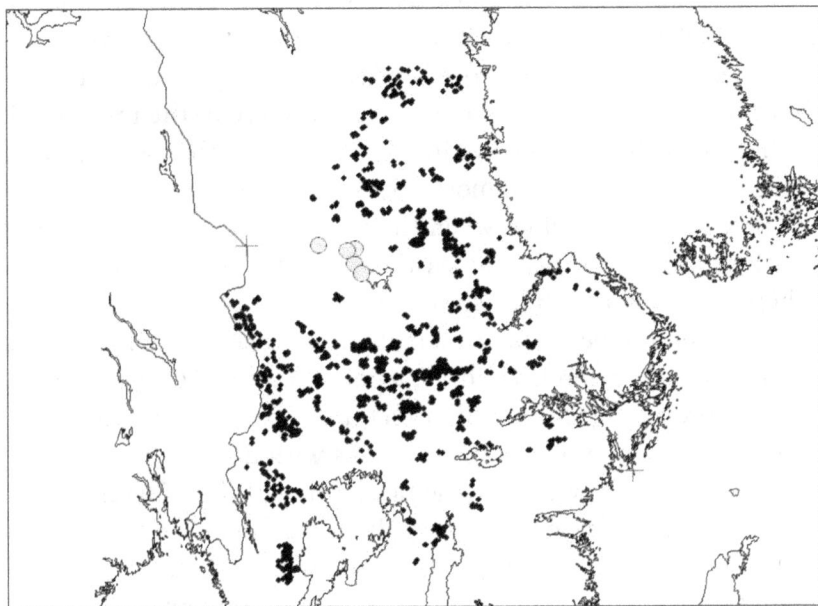

Figure 3.9: Distribution of "Forest Finns" (black dots) compared to that of non-delimited uses of definite forms (grey circles). Sources: Tarkiainen (1990), Broberg (1980).

dent of the general use of the partitive with non-delimited objects and reflects an earlier stage in the development of Fenno-Ugric languages, whereas the non-delimited use is most plausibly explained as an areal phenomenon in the Baltic region, and there seems to be no basis for assuming that it ever spread to Saami (Lars-Gunnar Larsson, personal communication). What all this means is that it is not possible to construct a plausible scenario where the extended definites in Peripheral Swedish vernaculars would arise through influence from a partitive case in the neighbouring Fenno-Ugric languages.

3.13 Reconstructing the grammaticalization path

The extended uses of definite forms that we see in the Peripheral Swedish area represent a kind of development that has not been studied from a typological or diachronic point of view, although, as was noted above, it is not without parallels outside Scandinavia. In historical linguistics, like in evolutionary biology, it is often the case that researchers look in vain for the "missing link", that is, the crucial intermediate stages in a process of change – instead, the details of the process have to be inferred from what we can observe in the present. This also holds here. From written documentation, we know that the patterns in question go back at least to the 18th and almost certainly to the 17th century, but we can only guess at what happened between the introduction of the suffixed definite article, which probably took place at least half a millennium earlier, and the point in time when the first attestations show up.

Our guesses need not be totally unqualified, however. Among the uses of the definite forms that are "extended" from the point of view of Central Scandinavian (and for that matter, English), not all are equally exotic – on the contrary, as I have noted above, many if not most languages with definite articles tend to use them more systematically with generic noun phrases than English and Central Scandinavian. We can also observe that the area where we find more generic definites than in the standard languages is larger than that, for example, of the non-delimited uses and the low-referentiality singular count uses. Given these observations, it seems natural to look closer at the possibility that generic uses are the stepping-stone to the latter ones.

This idea indeed seems to make sense also from the semantic point of view. In fact, genericity has sometimes been used as a collective label for the extended uses: thus, Hummelstedt (1934: 134), speaks of "allmän eller generell betydelse",[27] Marklund (1976: 29) of "totality meaning" [totalitetsbetydelse] and Bergholm, Linder & Yttergren (1999) suggest the term "generic article" as a replacement for Delsing's "partitive article". Calling something like *beer* in a sentence such as *He's drinking beer* "generic" certainly presupposes a rather generous definition of that term, but it has to be admitted that the notion of genericity does not lend itself to an easy delimitation. In the section on generic noun phrases above, I distinguished two basic kinds of generic uses of noun phrases. One of the two basic uses of generic noun phrases discussed in §3.3.1 was "kind predications", meaning that something is said about a kind or species rather than about its members, e.g.

(189)   *The northern hairy-nosed wombat is an endangered species.*

The question that arises is whether it is not possible to say that almost any mention of a species constitutes such a "kind predication". Indeed, one of the major

---

[27] This quotation is difficult to translate since *allmän* and *generell* both mean 'general' in Swedish.

claims in the influential paper by Carlson (1977) was that "existential" uses of bare nouns in English (as in *There are wolves in the forest*) are really kind-referring. In most contexts, there is in fact no ambiguity between generic and existential readings due to restrictions on the syntactic positions in which these readings can occur. However, there are some seemingly genuine cases of ambiguity, such as (190), which has one clearly kind-referring reading, which is synonymous to (191), and one existential, which might occur in a context such as (192).

(190)   *John studies cats.*

(191)   *John studies the species Felis catus.*

(192)   *John studies cats, because he is not allowed to use humans for his experiments.*

In a language such as French, the two readings of (190) would be distinguished formally, the generic reading taking a definite article and the existential one taking a partitive article. Consider the following quotation from a theological discussion site:

(193)   French
        Peut-on, par exemple, étudier l' **Homme** *sans*   *étudier*   ***des***
        can-one for example study DEF man   without study.INF PART
        hommes?
        man.PL
        'Can one for instance study man without studying human beings?'
        (Internet)

These observations notwithstanding, the borderline of genericity is rather fuzzy. I said above that it seems that it is often the construction in which a noun phrase appears that determines whether we understand it as generic or not. But another side of the matter is that one and the same content can often be expressed by alternative constructions, only one of which involves a generic noun phrase. For instance, plain existential statements can be paraphrased as statements involving singular definite generics, e.g.:

(194)   *There are not many wombats left.*

(195)   *The wombat is rare these days.*

(196)   *There are lions in Kenya and Tanzania.*

(197)   *The lion is represented in both Kenya and Tanzania.*

These alternative ways of expressing what is basically the same proposition have parallels in cases such as

(198)   *I suddenly became dizzy.*

(199)   *A sudden dizziness came upon me.*

where the difference is in whether the state of dizziness is expressed via an adjective or highlighted as an abstract noun *dizziness,* which obtains the role of the subject of the sentence. Semantically, this means that the state is "reified" or "hypostasized", that is, treated as an abstract object.

As it turns out, there is considerable cross-linguistic variation in how propositions such as those expressed in (198)-(199) are constructed grammatically, and some languages may well choose standard ways of expression that are more similar to (199). Sympathizers of Whorfianism will see this as evidence of differences in how we structure the world. I am personally somewhat skeptical to such hypotheses, at least as far as fully grammaticalized constructions go. That is, if there is just one standard way of expressing some particular content, more substantial evidence is needed to show that this influences the ways people think. But interesting phenomena are observable when different patterns compete. Consider the following Italian sentence:

(200)   Italian
        Papa beve   il caffè ogni mattina.
        father drink.PRS.3SG DEF coffee every morning
        'Father drinks coffee every morning.' (Internet)

In English or Swedish, using definite marking on 'coffee' to express the corresponding content results in a rather weird interpretation (the natural reaction is "what coffee?"). In Italian, on the other hand, it is the article-less alternative that is felt to be weird: Father drinks (an unspecified, and thus unusual amount of) coffee every morning (Pier Marco Bertinetto, personal communication). Thus, the definite article seems to be induced by the fact that coffee is drunk regularly, in more or less specified quantities.

Similarly, in the following Sicilian sentence (quoted from Bertinetto & Squartini (2000: 413), original source: Skubic (1973–1974: 231), and its translation into Italian, the swordfish is, it seems, focused enough to be worth "reifying" by the use of a definite article:

(201)   a. Sicilian
    Aju   *manciatu tanti voti*   ***u piscispata, e   m'***
    have.PRS.1SG eat.PP   many time.PL DEF swordfish and me.DAT
    ha   *fattu sempri beni.*
    have.PRS.3SG do.PP always good

    b. Italian
    Ho   *mangiato tante volte*   ***il   pesce spada, e   mi***
    have.PRS.1SG eat.PP   many time.PL DEF fish sword and me.DAT
    ha   *fatto sempre bene.*
    have.PRS.3SG do.PP always good

    'I have eaten swordfish many times, and it has always done me well.'

The competition between different grammatical patterns makes it possible for subtle nuances in interpretation to arise (see for further discussion Dahl 2004: 128-134). If, on the other hand, the use of the definite article in a similar context becomes obligatory, as in the Peripheral Swedish vernaculars, such nuances are lost. Another point to be made in this connection is that usage is often regulated in specific constructions but the way it is regulated may vary from one language to another. Consider, as an example, complements of verbs like *smell*, as in

(202)   *He smells of vodka.*

In most Germanic languages, it is simply impossible to use definite marking here, and from this point of view, it may seem more plausible to construe such sentences as talking of a restricted quantity of vodka, rather than as involving a kind predication in the sense of Krifka et al. (1995). Nevertheless, in many Peripheral Swedish varieties as well as in French, the normal construction is with a definite article:

(203)   a. Elfdalian (Ovansiljan)
    *An lupter   **brendwineð***
    he smell.PRS vodka.DEF

    b. French
    Il sent   la   vodka
    he smell.PRS.3SG DEF vodka

    'He smells of vodka.'

This could be interpreted as evidence that Elfdalian and French construe the predicate 'smell' as holding between a perceiver and a kind, and that other languages construe it as holding between a perceiver and an indefinite quantity of something. On the other hand, since there is no evidence for such a cognitive difference, it could be argued that it is equally plausible that languages are indifferent to the distinction between these two possible construals.

The Romance languages, which on the whole seem more generous than Germanic in allowing definite articles in the fuzzy border area of genericity, exhibit some interesting cross-linguistic patterns of variation. Zamparelli (2002) discusses various examples of what looks like extended uses of definite articles in Italian and other Romance languages. According to him, the following cases "force us to conclude that, in Italian, some definites can ... have a purely indefinite meaning". (The glosses in (204)-(209) and (213)-(215) are Zamparelli's. The boldface is mine.)

(204) Italian
Ogni settimana, il mio sito web viene attaccato
every week, DEF.M.SG my.M.SG site web come.PRES.3SG attack.PP
dagli hacker.
by.DEF.PL hacker

'Every week, my web site is attacked by **the hackers**.'

(205) Italian
*Nel 1986 i **ladri** hanno svuotato il*
In_DEF.M.SG 1986 DEF.M.PL thief.PL have.PRS.3PL empty.PP DEF.M.SG
mio appartamento.
my.M.SG apartment.

'In 1986 the thieves emptied my apartment.'

(206) Italian
La casa è sporchissima. In cantina ci sono
DEF.F.SG house be.PRS.3SG filthy.SUPERL.F.SG In basement there are
*i **topi** e sotto il lavello vivono **gli***
DEF.M.PL mouse.PL and under DEF.M.SG sink live.PRS.3PL DEF.M.PL
***scarafaggi**.*
cockroach.PL

'The house is filthy. In the basement there are the mice and under the sink live the cockroaches.'

(207) Italian
*Che fai   per mestiere? Fotografo   **gli   uccelli**.*
What do.PRS.2SG for living?   photograph.PRS.1SG DEF.M.PL bird.PL
'What do you do for a living? I photograph the birds.'

(208) Italian
*Con questi disturbi   ho dovuto   smettere   di   bere **il***
with this   problem.PL have.PRS.1SG have_to.PP stop.INF from drink
caffè.   Il   tè invece mi facilita   la   digestione.
DEF   coffee DEF.M.SG tea instead me help.PRS.3SG DEF digestion
'With this condition I had to stop drinking the coffee. The tea instead
helps my digestion.'

(209) Italian
Gianni è   così pallido che sembra   abbia
Gianni be.PRS.3SG so   pale.M.SG that seem.PRS.3SG have.PRS.SBJV.3SG
*visto **i   fantasmi**.*
see.PP DEF.M.PL ghost.PL
'Gianni is so pale that it seems he has seen the ghosts.'

Zamparelli's examples have in common that it is not natural to preserve the definite article when translating into English. They differ from each other in various ways, however. Consider, to start with, (204). It is not generic in the sense that it is a general statement about hackers. Rather, what it says is that every week, some hackers visit my site. Whether it is the same persons every week or not is not said, and probably the speaker does not know. What could be argued here is that in (204), the hackers who visit my site are seen as representatives of the world-wide community of hackers, as it were. Similarly, the mice in the basement in (205) could be thought of as representing the mouse species in general. This would make (204) and (205) a bit similar to sentences such as the following:

(210) *The Americans have visited the moon.*

(211) Swedish
***Räven** har   varit i hönshuset   igen.*
fox.DEF have.PRS be.SUP in hen-house.DEF again
'The fox has been in the hen-house again.'

There are clear differences here though. In English, the conditions for using the definite article in a "representative" sense are stricter than in Italian. It appears that the reason one can say something like (210) is that the American visitors to the moon were representatives of the American nation not only in some extended or metaphorical sense but also quite concretely, since they acted on behalf of the US government. When it becomes possible to go to the moon as a tourist, it clearly will not be sufficient for me and some of my friends to go there for (212) to be true.

(212)   *The Swedes have visited the moon.*

(211) is different from Zamparelli's example in that the noun phrase is in the singular. Zamparelli notes that if *il topo* 'the mouse' is substituted for *i topi* in (205), the interpretation has to be specific. A prerequisite for the use of a singular in (211) is that foxes tend to operate one by one, in such a way that we can think of the fox that visited the hen-house last night as a representative of the fox species

Zamparelli notes that the three Romance languages Italian, Spanish and French differ in how readily they accept definite noun phrases in contexts of this kind Thus, in the French translation of (205), only partitive articles are possible. In Spanish, definite articles are possible, but not with the existential verb *hay* 'there is', only with verbs such as *estar* 'be' and *vivir* 'live':

(213)   French
    Dans la   cave,   il y   a   ?les / des   souris, et
    in   DEF.F.SG basement it there have DEF.PL PARTART.PL mouse.PL and
    dans l'   évier vivent   ?les / des   cafards.
    in   DEF.M.SG sink live.PRS.3PL DEF.PL PARTART.PL cockroach.PL
    'In the basement there are the mice and under the sink live the cockroaches.'

(214)   Spanish
    En el   sótano   hay (*los)   ratones, y   bajo la
    In   DEF.M.SG basement exist (DEF.M.PL) mice   and under DEF.F.SG
    fregadera hay   (*las)   cucarachas.
    fridge   exist.PRS (DEF.F.PL) cockroach.PL
    'In the basement there are mice and under the fridge there are cockroaches.'

(215)   Spanish
    En el   sótano   están   *(los)   ratones, y   bajo
    In   DEF.M.SG basement be.PRS.3PL (DEF.M.PL) mouse.PL and under

la	fregadera	vivon	*(las)	cucarachas.

DEF.F.SG fridge   live.PRS.3SG (DEF.F.PL) cockroach.PL

'In the basement are mice and under the fridge live cockroaches.'

What we see here, then, is a cline of acceptability for definite noun phrases in uses that can be seen as non-delimited, with French being most restrictive and Italian being most liberal. This then suggests a way by which definite noun phrases may expand their domain of use into the indefinite territory with the situation in the Peripheral Swedish vernaculars or Moroccan Arabic (see §3.4.4 above) as the eventual result. In the absence of historical data, it is of course impossible to verify whether the route has been exactly the same, but given the other circumstances mentioned in the beginning of this section, generic uses must be regarded as a highly probable diachronic source for the extended uses of definite forms.

For singular count nouns, there are also non-generic uses of definite-marked noun phrases than generic ones that could serve as bridging cases. Consider the following sentences in English:

(216) *Did you bring **the knife**?*

(217) *Did you bring **a knife**?*

In many situations, both (216) and (217) would be acceptable. (Imagine, for instance, a picnic.) It is often rather irrelevant if a specific knife is held in mind or not. In Swedish, one could use any of the following three variants:

(218) Swedish
       *Tog   du med dig **kniven/en kniv/kniv?***
       take.PST you with you **knife.DEF/INDF knife/knife**
       'Did you bring a knife?'

It thus seems plausible that the fluidity of the use of articles here could set the scene for the expansion of the definite forms. In fact, this fluidity sometimes makes it difficult to evaluate uses of definite markings in written sources. Consider the following excerpt from a recording of a speaker born in 1881 and coming from Hållnäs, one of the linguistically most conservative parishes in Uppland:

(219) Hållnäs (Uppland)
       [The speaker is describing how sheep were collected from their summer-pasture in the autumn.]

> *Å   den såm hadde   nô   förstånd då   se   feck   han ju*
> and he   who have.PST some sense   then see.IMP get.PST he   PRAG
> *ha   bröy-sättjin,   helle bröy-kôrjin,   å   le't   åpp*
> have.INF **bread-sack**.DEF or   **bread-basket**.DEF and search.INF up
> *en   ta´ckå såm fåLd   etter.*
> INDF ewe   who follow.PST after
>
> 'And he who had some sense got to have the bread sack, or the bread basket, to find a ewe who was lagging behind.' (Källskog et al. 1993: 33)

Speakers of standard Swedish do not react to the use of definite forms here, but if (219) had occurred in a Peripheral Swedish area vernacular, it could relatively easily be seen as parallel to the examples discussed in §3.6.

Many of the extended uses of definite forms seem rather eccentric from the point of view of standard definitions of definiteness. As was mentioned above, it is a general characteristic of advanced stages of the evolution of definite articles that the semantic element of definiteness is weakened or gets lost entirely, as when articles develop into general affixes on nouns. Such a loss of the semantic essence of a morpheme may appear paradoxical, in that the motivation for having a definite article in the first place ought to be to express definiteness. In the words of Hawkins (2004: 91), "why should the definite article be recruited for more and more NPs in performance and grammar and gradually jettison the semantic-pragmatic conditions of its deictic source?" Hawkins suggests that the answer has to be found in the processing of grammar: the functions of definite articles that become dominant at later stages of its evolution are to "construct a (case-marked) NP" and to "attach specified categories to the (case-marked) NP that it constructs". It is not clear from Hawkins' text if "construct" means anything but "unambiguously signal", but the consequence is in any case that the function of a definite article is syntactic rather than semantic. Hawkins notes (quoting Lyons 1999: 64) that the cross-linguistic tendency for definite articles to occur early in noun phrases can be explained through the necessity to signal the NP-hood of an expression early on. Notice that the principle "Signal NP-hood as early as possible" would have much of the same effect as the principle "The D-position must be filled" suggested by Holmberg & Sandström. However, Hawkins' principle makes most sense in complex NP's, where an article preposed to or cliticized to the first word would function much as a labeled left bracket. It is less clear what the point of having a definite article on a bare noun would be. Perhaps we should see the function of definite articles whose use is extended beyond what is warranted by semantic definiteness as enhancing the general level of redundancy in grammar and thus making the transmission of the message safer (see Dahl 2004: 9-11). It should be added that any theory which attributes too essential a role to definite suffixes in varieties like the Peripheral Swedish ones will have problems explaining the tendency in the same varieties towards extensive neutralization of the distinction between definite and indefinite forms.

4 Attributive constructions

4.1 Introduction

One area of grammar where Scandinavian languages show some well-known peculiarities is in the expression of definite noun phrases which contain preposed attributes. In all varieties of Central Scandinavian, a preposed definite article is employed in such noun phrases; however, whereas this article in Danish has a complementary distribution to the ordinary suffixed article, as illustrated by *det store hus* 'the big house' (as opposed to *huset* 'the house'), Swedish (and also normally Norwegian) uses both articles, as in *det stora huset* 'the big house'. However, in northern Scandinavia, there is a radically different way of combining an adjective and a noun: the normal translation of 'the big house' would be something like *stor-hus-et* 'big-house-DEF', where the adjective is incorporated into the noun and there is no preposed article. In this chapter, I shall discuss this construction and a number of additional variations on the general theme that contribute to a quite variegated picture. However, one challenge in doing so is the tight interaction of several different parameters with different histories and geographical distribution. Another problem is the low frequency of adjectival modifiers in definite noun phrases (noted by Thompson 1988). In the corpus *Samtal i Göteborg* (Löfström 1988), comprising half a million words of spoken Swedish – corresponding to 1250 printed pages, there were only 253 examples of the pattern

(1)   *den/det/dom* ADJ-*e/a* N-DEF

that is, the standard form of such NPs in Swedish. (Comparatives and superlatives were excluded from this count.) This is equivalent to about once in ten minutes of conversation, or once in five printed pages. In addition, it turns out that a few adjectival lexemes had a rather dominant place among those examples: about 40 per cent consisted of tokens of the four adjectives *stor* 'big', *liten* 'small', *gammal* 'old', *ny* 'new'. It is probably no accident that these items are among the cross-linguistically prototypical adjectives in the sense that they show up in practically every language that has a separate class of adjectives.[1] In written dialect texts, which are either direct renderings of spoken language or else tend to be close to spoken language in form, the corresponding patterns also show up very sparingly.

4.2 Definite marking in attributive constructions: The typological perspective

As it turns out, it is quite common cross-linguistically for attributive constructions to show some peculiarities with respect to definiteness marking. Thus, we find languages in which definiteness is only marked when a noun phrase contains a modifier, as in Latvian which has suffixed definite articles on adjectives, although it does not otherwise use definite marking, as illustrated by the following examples.

(2) Latvian

    a. *liel-a*   *māja*
       big-F.NOM.SG house
       'a big house'

    b. *liel-ā*   *māja*
       big-F.NOM.SG.DEF house
       'the big house'

In another pattern, an article that usually sits on the noun shows up on the adjective in an attributive construction, as exemplified by Amharic:

(3) Amharic

    a. *bet-u*
       house-DEF
       'the house'

    b. *təlləq* *bet*
       big-DEF house
       'the big house'

---

[1] According to Dixon (1977), the adjectives that occur most frequently across languages are 'large', 'small', 'long', 'short', 'new', 'old', 'good', 'bad', 'black', 'white'.

Finally, the phenomenon of double articles is by no means restricted to Scandinavian. Consider, for example, Standard Arabic, in which the noun and the adjective each take the identical article *al*:

(4) Standard Arabic

  a. *al-bayt*
    DEF-house
    'the house'

  b. *al-bayt   al-kabir*
    DEF-house DEF-big
    'the big house'

From Germanic languages, we can mention Yiddish, where double articles are optional and more likely to appear when the adjective is postposed (Plank 2003: 342-347)

(5) Yiddish

  a. *di grine   oygn*
    DEF green.PL eye.PL
    'the green eyes'

  b. *di oygn di grine*
    DEF eye.PL DEF green.PL
    'the green eyes'

Even closer to home, in Old Icelandic, we find cases where two preposed definite articles are combined with a suffixed definite article on the noun. This triple marking is certainly a challenge for any theory that supposes that each morpheme fills a separate slot in the underlying structure. The following example is from the saga of Gísli Súrsson. The protagonist is having recurrent dreams where two dream-women, one good and one bad, appear:

(6) Old Icelandic
    *Hann segir, att nú kom   at honum **draumkona-n**   **sú hin***
    he   say.PRS that now come.PRS to he.DAT **dreamwoman-DEF DEF DEF**
    verri...
    worse
    '[Reporting Gísli's answer to a question about his dreams:] He says that now came to him the evil dream-woman...' (Gísla saga Súrssonar 33)

See Dahl (2003) for further examples and discussion.

4.3 Survey of attributive definite NP constructions

4.3.1 The deprecated standard: The Scandinavian preposed article

Like the suffixed article, the preposed definite article in Scandinavian goes back to medieval times, and the earliest attestations are from texts from Iceland and Norway where the pronouns *hinn* and *enn* were used early on in this function. In Early Written Medieval Swedish, as described by Larm (1936), there was competition between several different ways of expressing definite NPs with preposed attributes. Most often, only one article was used, but it could be either a preposed or a suffixed one, thus either *þæn gamli man* or *gamli mannin*. The preposed article – in the beginning sometimes *hinn* but more frequently *þæn*, another originally demonstrative pronoun – was more common in poetic language and the suffixed one most frequent in prose, although even there the preposed alternative was preferred – the overall ratio between the two articles was 10:1. The alternative with double articles seems to have become a serious contestant only later The distribution of the two articles over genres suggests that the preponderance of the preposed article in poetry "essentially depends on foreign influence" (Larm 1936: 68).[2] According to Larm, there is a difference in deictic force between the two alternatives as used in prose, in that *þæn* tends to be used in contexts that are more similar to those of "normal" demonstratives. Larm thus concludes that contrary to what earlier researchers such as Falk-Torp and Nygaard had proposed, the preposed article *þæn* cannot be older than the suffixed one[3] (Larm 1936: 64).

It is consonant with this view to assume that the preposed article arrived later in the Swedish dialect area than the suffixed article. In fact, as we shall now see, the use of the preposed article is still more restricted in Standard Swedish than in Standard Danish.

In Dahl (2003), I discuss in some detail two classes of cases where the preposed article does not show up, viz. what I call SELECTORS and NAME-LIKE USES. I use "selectors" as a cover term for three categories that are usually treated separately in Swedish grammars (all examples are Swedish):

1. a subset of what Teleman, Hellberg & Andersson (1999: 435) call "relational pronouns": "ordinative pronouns", e.g. *först(a)* 'first', *sist(a)* 'last', *nästa* 'next', *förra* 'previous', "perspectival pronouns", e.g. *höger/högra* 'right (hand)', *vänster/vänstra* 'left (hand)', *norra* 'north' etc., *övre* 'upper' etc., and *ena* 'one (of)'

---

[2] "...att den rika frekvensen av typen *þæn gamli man* i poesien till väsentlig grad beror på främmande inverkan."

[3] "*Þæn* såsom artikel kan ej vara äldre än suff. artikel."

2. ordinal numerals

3. superlatives

All these categories share a common semantics – they are all "inherently definite" in that the noun phrases they are used in normally have definite reference by virtue of their meaning. The term "selector" is motivated by the fact that they pick out a member or a subset of a specific superset by the help of some relation between that member or subset and the set as a whole. In other words, if I say e.g. *yngste sonen* 'the youngest son', I pick out one of the sons by relating him in age to the others: he may not at all be young if considered in isolation.

All three types of selectors show up with nouns in the definite form without a preposed article, e.g. *norra delen* 'the northern part', *första gången* 'the first time', *äldsta dottern* 'the eldest daughter'. In addition, the first type ("relational pronouns") also occurs without any definite marking at all, in spite of the noun phrases in question having definite reference: *nästa sommar* 'next summer', *höger hand* 'the right hand'. It appears that the interpretation of the unmarked cases tends to involve the deictic center. Often, the corresponding phrases in English are also articleless, and the pattern also shows up in the other Central Scandinavian languages. Selectors with a suffixed but no prefixed article are only found in Swedish and to some extent in Norwegian Bokmål but not at all in Danish. As I showed in Dahl (2003), they also appear to be considerably less popular in the vernaculars from the Southern and Göta dialect areas within the Swedish dialect area, judging from the Cat Corpus material. Compare the following sentence in Swedish and the text from Träslövsläge in Halland (similar examples are also found in texts from Skåne, Bohuslän, and Västergötland):

(7) a. Swedish
Äldsta pojken hade rest till Amerika.
old.SUPERL.WK boy.DEF have.PST go.SUP to America

b. Träslövsläge (Halland)
Den gamlaste päjken hade fåt te Amerka.
DEF old.SUPERL.WK boy.DEF have.PST travel.SUP to America

'The eldest boy (i.e. Granny's son) had gone to America.' (Cat Corpus)

A similar situation shows up with "name-like uses" of definite articles. This includes, on one hand, lexicalizations of noun phrases containing an adjectival modifier and a head noun as in *Vita huset* 'the White House', and on the other, expressions that have not yet reached the status of lexical items but which are used to refer to well-known objects, typically chosen out of a small set. For instance, if you own two houses next to each other but of different size, it is very natural to call them *stora huset* 'the big house' and *lilla huset* 'the little house', even before these denominations have become so "entrenched" that capital letters would be used in writing. We can see that such cases are fairly similar to the cases with selectors discussed above. Name-like uses are treated quite differently in the Central Scandinavian languages. In Danish, we find either (i) the usual pattern with a preposed article and no definite marking on the noun (*Det Hvide Hus* 'the White House'), (ii) no definite marking whatsoever (*Nordisk Råd* 'the Nordic Council') or (iii) definite marking only on the adjective, i.e. by choosing the weak form (*Store Bælt* 'the Big Belt, i.e. the sound between the islands of Sjælland and Fyn'). In no case do we find a definite form of the noun, however. All three Danish patterns are also found in Swedish, more or less marginally. The first pattern is found in archaic expressions such as (i) *den helige Ande* 'the Holy Ghost' and the second occasionally in names such as *Svensk Uppslagsbok* 'The Swedish Encyclopedia'. The third pattern is represented in toponyms such as Store Mosse 'Large Peatbog' over most of the South Swedish and Göta dialect areas. As for Norwegian, Bokmål, which in other cases has double articles, goes with Danish here, but Nynorsk stands out by using double articles even in these contexts (e.g. *Det Kvite Huset* 'the White House').

Generalizing from these patterns, it can be said that all Central Scandinavian languages (in which I do not count Nynorsk) show tendencies to have less definiteness marking with selectors and name-like uses than in other cases of definite noun phrases with preposed modifiers. In general, there tends to be less marking of noun phrases whose definiteness is in one way or the other "inherent"; in diachronic developments, they tend to be the last ones to receive marking. With respect to the preposed article, it appears fairly clear that it is generally stronger in Denmark than in the other Scandinavian countries, especially Sweden. If we consider also the non-standard varieties, we can see that there is in fact a cline going from south-west to north-east, with the preposed article becoming gradually weaker as we move along it. In south-western Jutland, the preposed article is used universally and the suffixed article does not exist. Southern Swedish vernaculars are less restrictive than Standard Swedish in the use of the preposed article, that is, they are more like Standard Danish. On the other hand, in the Peripheral Swedish area, in particular the more conservative parts, preposed definite articles of the Central Scandinavian type are quite restricted and are possibly largely ascribable to influence from Swedish.

4.3.2 The celebrated competitor: Adjective incorporation

Adjective incorporation is one of the more well-known peculiarities of the vernaculars of the Peripheral Swedish area, although the term itself has come into use only fairly recently (probably first in Sandström & Holmberg 2003); traditionally, the phenomenon has been seen as "compounding". Now, compounds consisting of an adjective and a noun are quite common in all varieties of Scandinavian, as in other Germanic languages. It is often noted in the literature that adjective-noun compounds are found more often in Northern Swedish vernaculars than in Central Scandinavian, but it is important to see that there is also a semantic difference, and that adjective-noun combinations found in Northern Scandinavia tend to be used in ways that are not normally possible with adjective-noun compounds. Consider, for example, the following Elfdalian sentence:

(8) Elfdalian (Ovansiljan)
Inǫ guävę   add   an laggt   ien   filt   briewið
on floor.DEF.DAT have.PST he lay.SUP INDF blanket next_to
wåtjakku.
wet_jacket.DEF.ACC
'On the floor, he had put a blanket next to the wet jacket.' [S9]

In Swedish or English, a compound like *våtjacka* or *wet-jacket* could only be used for a special kind of jacket that is permanently wet, or perhaps more plausibly, for a jacket intended for use in wet conditions. Similarly, *wetland* or the synonymous Swedish *våtmark* denote an area characterized by being permanently water-soaked. By contrast, the Elfdalian expression refers to a jacket that is in a temporary state of wetness. In other words, it functions just like the English phrase *the wet jacket*. One way of thinking of the distinction is in terms of the number of concepts involved. In the case of ordinary compounds, such as *wetland*, we are dealing with a unitary concept, more or less permanently established. In the case of the phrase 'the wet jacket', we have a more or less accidental combination of the two concepts 'wet' and 'jacket'. It is the possibility of using the Elfdalian expression in such an "occasional" way that motivates using the term "incorporation" rather than "compounding".

In some cases, we get quite distinct readings of one and the same adjective-noun combination. Thus, the phrase *the new car* might mean either 'the car I just bought (in contrast to the one I had before)' or 'the recently fabricated car'. In Swedish, there is a compound *nybil* which has only the second reading in the standard language. In the vernaculars where adjective incorporation is possible, this tends to be true of the indefinite form, but the definite form *nybiln* will also have the reading of referring to a new car that is contrasted to a car I had before (Sandström & Holmberg 2003: 91). In fact, the presence of such readings of combinations with an adjective like 'new' is a relatively certain indicator that we are dealing with something more than "ordinary compounding".

In generative theory, where a sharp distinction between "lexicon" and "syntax" is normally postulated, it is natural to assume, as Sandström & Holmberg (2003) do, that compounding belongs in the lexicon and incorporation in the syntax. However, the distinction between incorporation and compounding is a tricky one and should probably rather be seen as a continuum, as I argue in Dahl (2004 Ch.10) where I discuss incorporating patterns in general. In fact, this distinction between incorporation and compounding often becomes blurred. In a relatively large number of cases, it is not possible to determine whether we are dealing with a unitary concept or not. Many of the examples in the literature which are quoted as examples of the tendency to use adjective-noun compounds instead of ordinary attributive constructions are indeterminate in this way, making it hard to pinpoint the geographical distribution of the phenomenon. I think it is fairly clear that in addition to the use of clear cases of adjective incorporation in the Peripheral Swedish area, there is also a general predilection for adjective-noun compounding which raises the general frequency of such compounds relative to other Germanic languages. This means that one-word adjective-noun combinations are more common not only in definite but also in indefinite NPs. I shall return to the issue of indefinite NPs after an excursion into language typology.

Typological considerations. In the general linguistic literature, adjective incorporation is a somewhat neglected phenomenon, at least in comparison to noun incorporation, that is, the process by which a noun stem is incorporated into the verb of a sentence. Still, in some languages, adjective incorporation is the normal way of adding an attributive adjective to a noun, either generally, as in Lakota, a Siouan language (Boas & Deloria 1941), or under certain conditions, as in Chukchi (Muravyova 1998: 526), a Chukchi-Kamchatkan language in which attributive adjectives are obligatorily incorporated when the head noun is in a non-absolutive case.

There are also many examples of attributive constructions which cannot be regarded as full-fledged incorporation but which are still "tighter" than normal adjective-noun constructions. As a general tendency, these tighter constructions seem to be favoured by a low prominence of the adjective and are often restricted to a few adjectives, usually "prototypical" ones, such as 'big', 'small', 'old', 'new', 'good', 'bad', i.e. the ones that show up in languages in which adjectives are a closed class with a small number of members (see fn. (1)). It has been observed (Croft & Deligianni 2001) that preposed modifiers are more tightly integrated into a noun phrase than postposed ones, for instance by lacking normal grammatical markings. This can be illustrated by pairs such as Spanish *el gran libro* 'the great book' – *el libro grande* 'the big book'. Italian, the Celtic languages, Persian, Komi and Southern Ute also exhibit this kind of phenomenon.

For a more detailed survey of adjective incorporation from a typological point of view, see Dahl (2004: 225-236).

Indefinite adjective-noun combinations. I claimed above that there is a general predilection in Peripheral Swedish vernaculars for one-word adjective-noun combinations, not only in definite NPs (see also Delsing 2003b: 44, Fn 19). Many references in the literature to the phenomenon do not distinguish indefinite and definite noun phrases and the examples given are often indefinite ones (for a case in point, consider the examples from Hedblom 1978 quoted below in §4.4).

The question, then, is what is the status of these indefinite adjective-noun combinations. Acknowledging that "Northern Swedish", i.e. primarily Westrobothnian, has a "relatively productive formation of adjective-noun compounds", Sandström & Holmberg (2003: 91) claim that there are two major differences between (i) compounds as used in indefinite noun phrases and (ii) what they see as true cases of adjective incorporation in definite noun phrases.

According to Sandström & Holmberg, the first difference is that indefinite adjective-noun compounds are restricted to monosyllabic adjective stems. Thus, they say, examples such as **en vackerkweinn* 'a beautiful woman' and **en duktipajk* 'an able boy' are impossible. However, Bergholm, Linder & Yttergren (1999: 47) provide counterexamples from Burträsk (Northern Westrobothnian) and Sorsele (Southern Westrobothnian) such as *magersteint* 'lean girl' and *vackerkwinn* 'beautiful woman'. In the Cat Corpus, we find *magerstackar* 'lean poor thing' in the text from from Sävar (Southern Westrobothnian) and the following example with the bisyllabic stem *gåmmel-* 'old' from Northern Westrobothnian:

(9) Skelletmål (Northern Westrobothnian)
     ...hä ha   vorte   möittje bättär seda I bört   å
     it   have.PRSS become.SUP much   better since I begin.PST INFM
     *håå   ä   **gåmmel-kattskinn** där   om netträn.*
     have.INF INDF **old-catskin**   there at night.DEF.PL

     '...it [my back] has become much better since I began to put an old cat skin there at night.' (Cat Corpus)

From the Ovansiljan area we can cite Levander (1909: 52) examples *klakkug-dsieter* 'horn-less goats' and *digger-frunt* 'fat woman' (both Elfdalian), and from the Cat Corpus, *nog blickna-blad* (Älvdalen) 'some withered leaves' and *no blitse-blar* (Mora, same meaning). A more extreme example is *nykuäkaðpärur* 'newly boiled potatoes' (Elfdalian, Åkerberg 2012: 201). (Cf. also the examples from Nederkalix quoted below.) Thus, it is possible that the restriction holds for some variety, but definitely not generally for the Peripheral Swedish area and not even for Westrobothnian.

The other difference between definite and indefinite adjective-noun combinations cited by Holmberg & Sandström is semantic and thus potentially of a more fundamental nature. According to them, indefinite adjective-noun compounds do not have all the readings of the definite incorporated ones; thus, (10) can only mean that the person in question has bought a newly made car, not one that is "new for him":

(10) Westrobothnian
    Han ha   tjöfft   sä   n   nybil.
    he   have.PRS buy.SUP REFL INDF new.car
    'He's bought himself a new car.'

Yet, it does appear that indefinite adjective-noun combinations in Peripheral Swedish have uses that would not be expected of "normal" compounds, in particular in cases where the adjective signals an accidental or "occasional" property of the referent rather than forms a designation of a "unitary concept" together with the noun. Consider the following example from Elfdalian (Levander 1909: 142):

(11) Elfdalian (Ovansiljan)
    Gok   etter ien   sturwiðåbörd!
    go.IMP after one.F.DAT big.firewood.load
    'Go and get a big load of firewood!'

Rutberg (1924: 141) gives a number of examples from Nederkalix (Kalixmål), some of which have a definite "occasional" ring: *in litn artibåt* 'a nice little boat', *i vokkert röbat* 'a beautiful red band', *småswartskou* 'small black boots', *i vokke-liλ-bån* 'a beautiful little child', *in lil-fåti-ståkkar* 'a poor little thing', *i sta-skallat-kou* 'a big hornless cow'.

In fact, Levander (1909: 51) says explicitly that Swedish indefinite adjective-noun combinations "usually" correspond to compounds in Elfdalian, and in his general treatment of Dalecarlian (Levander 1928: 142), he echoes this statement by saying that "at least in Älvdalen" compounding is "incomparably much more frequent" than the syntactic construction.[4] It is possible, as Delsing (2003b: 44, Fn 19) suggests, that the tendency is stronger in Dalecarlian than in Upper Norrland, or in parts of it, if we consider the examples from Nederkalix above. Dahlstedt (1962: 98) says about Vilhelmina (Southern Westrobothnian) that "it does not seem to offend linguistic intuitions to use relatively occasional word combinations as compounds ... but this type of formation is not the usual one." His examples are *n gammbjärkbränne* 'an old forest clearing, overgrown by birch' and *n tôkken gammstyggôbb* 'such an ugly old man' (at least the first one seems like a possible lexicalization to me, though).

I think these circumstances give support to the idea that there is no clear borderline between compounding and incorporation and also that indefinite one-word adjective-noun combinations can have incorporation-like properties in Peripheral Swedish vernaculars. In any case, it seems unlikely that the one-word combinations we find in indefinite and definite NPs are diachronically wholly separate from each other.

Combinations with other determiners. In the simplest possible case of adjectival modifiers, there are no other elements in the NP than the adjective and the head noun. A definite noun phrase may also contain other elements, however, notably demonstratives (which, as we shall see in §4.3.3.2, are often used much like preposed definite articles). There is considerable variation as to the extent to which adjectives are incorporated in such contexts, which partly seems to be dependent on word order. In many Norrlandic varieties, the typical demonstrative pronoun is postposed and indeclinable, and there incorporation tends to take place in the same way as in simple noun phrases, thus:

(12) Skelletmål (Northern Westrobothnian)
      Kattkalln låg oppa bolä å beunnrä **konsti-burken**
      tomcat.DEF lie.PST on table.DEF and admire.PST **strange-can.DEF**
      dänna...
      that
      'Cat on the table admiring that strange can...'

When the demonstrative precedes, incorporation may or may not take place. The most common case appears to be that it does not. Rather, the adjective appears

---

[4] "Dylik sammansättning av adj. och subst. är åtminstone i Älvd. ojämförligt mycket vanligare än de båda ordens uppträdande bredvid varandra som skilda ord."

with or without an ending (but sometimes with a change in pitch accent, see below), as in the examples quoted in §4.3.3.2. But incorporation is not always excluded. Thus, Vangsnes (2003: 159), quoting personal communication from Ann-Marie Ivars, mentions examples such as *honde gamälbókjen* 'that/the old book' from Närpes (Southern Ostrobothnian); and in questionnaire material from Österbotten, also provided by Ann-Marie Ivars, there are similar examples from Munsala (Northern Ostrobothnian) and Västanfjärd (Åbolandic). Reinhammar (2005: 38) quotes cases from Hammerdal (Jamtska) such as *'n dân li'hllpöytjen* 'that small boy' (see further §4.3.3.2).

Origins of adjective incorporation. In Swedish, adjectives in definite noun phrases take what is traditionally called a "weak" ending (possibly a development of an erstwhile definite article on adjectives), normally *-a*. Plural adjectives always take the ending *-a*, regardless of where they occur. Over a large area in Scandinavia, final vowels have historically been deleted in the process referred to as apocope (illustrations are easily found in the example sentences in this book e.g. the infinitive forms *berätt* 'tell' in Arvidsjaur (Northern Settler dialect area) and *skaff* 'get' in Kall (Jamtska) – cf. Standard Swedish *berätta* and *skaffa*.) Since the adjective incorporation area is by and large included in the apocope area, it would not be implausible to connect the genesis of adjective incorporation with such a process. Dahlstedt (1962: 102), however, wants to explain it through a slightly different process by which the connecting vowel between the element of compounds is deleted. He does not really give any clear examples, but the precondition, he says, is that the adjective-noun combination is kept together in one "beat".[5] The problem, however, is how the adjective-noun combination came to have the same prosody as ordinary compounds. Vangsnes (2003: 159) (citing personal communication from Görel Sandström) suggests that it was rather the other way around: the final vowels were apocopated, and this created the conditions for incorporation: there was nothing – "except perhaps prosody" – that distinguished the combination of an ending-less adjective and a noun from a compound. This again seems to play down the importance of prosody.

Apocope was probably originally a wholly phonologically conditioned process applying to word-final but not utterance-final unstressed vowels after a stressed long syllable (a syllable which contained at least one long segment).

In modern vernaculars, apocope is contingent on a combination of phonological, morphological and lexical factors. Thus, in modern Elfdalian, many words

---

[5] "Vokalbortfallet (synkopen) ... är i princip samma slag som hos övriga sammansättningar med tvåstavig förled...Förutsättningen för vokalbortfallet torde från början ha varit att adjektiv och substantiv sammanhölls till en språktakt..."

still alternate between apocopated and non-apocopated forms depending on the position in the sentence. The process is no longer purely phonological, though, since many words (especially new additions to the lexicon) do not participate in it. In many vernaculars, apocope leaves a trace behind in that the distinction between the two Scandinavian tonal word accents is preserved even though the resulting word might consist of a single syllable: the tone contour "spills over" on the first syllable of the next word, as it were. Apocope did not apply to words whose stressed syllable is short (i.e. both the vowel and the following consonant are short).

The prosodic pattern in a phrase consisting of an apocopated adjective and a noun is relatively similar to that of compound nouns, at least in the dialects where apocope leaves a trace in the form of a grave accent. It is not identical, however. If we see the syntactic construction as the direct historical source for the incorporated adjective-noun construction, we have to assume that the prosodic patterns were similar enough for the identification to be possible. However, the situation is complicated by the existence on one hand of incorporations that cannot be blamed on apocope, and on the other, by cases where apocopated adjectives have not been incorporated. Thus, at least in the Ovansiljan varieties, not only apocopated adjectives but also those with short stem syllables – where the ending is not apocopated – take part in the incorporation pattern. We thus get forms such as (13), where the weak ending, which due to vowel balance (see §6.1) comes out as -*o* in these words, is preserved in the incorporated adjective:

(13) Elfdalian (Ovansiljan)
      ber-o-kwi-n
      naked-wk-belly-DEF
      'the naked belly' [S9]

It thus seems necessary to complement the hypothesis by assuming that the incorporating pattern has been extended to cases other than the original apocopated ones.

Another problematic type of cases are one-word adjective-noun combinations in indefinite NPs. In the case of definite NPs, the assumption is that incorporated forms arose from the endingless adjectives that were the result of apocope, and that this process was helped by the similarity of the prosodic patterns involved. Endingless forms are also common in the indefinite ("strong") adjectival paradigm, but in a vernacular such as Elfdalian there is a prosodic distinction between forms which historically involve apocope and those that do not, in that only the former induce a grave accent and can be seen as possible sources of univerbation:

(14) Elfdalian (Ovansiljan)
     *Ien **stúr**   kall* ↔ *flier   **stùr**   kaller*
     one big.NOM.M.SG man   several big.NOM.PL man.PL
     'one big man: several big men' (Åkerberg 2012, 188)

In addition, the pattern illustrated in (13) shows up also with indefinite nouns, such as *twerobåkk* 'steep slope' (Levander 1909: 52). Again, it seems that the one-word pattern must have undergone generalization from the cases where it was essentially conditioned by phonological developments. Dahlstedt (1962: 103) also assumes an expansion of the pattern from "one-beat" cases to more complex ones.[6] At this point, however, it may not be possible to empirically distinguish between a straightforward extension of the compounding pattern and an assimilation of endingless attributive adjectives to that pattern.

4.3.3 The obscurer alternatives

In addition to the standard double-marked construction and adjective incorporation, there are also a couple of other possibilities for expressing definite NPs with attributes found in the Peripheral Swedish area. These are not always given proper attention in the literature.

4.3.3.1 Non-incorporated modifiers without preposed articles but with definite head nouns

We saw above that in Swedish there are frequent cases where a NP contains a preposed modifier but no preposed article. In Written Medieval Swedish, such cases were more common and apparently not restricted to the contexts where they are normal in Modern Swedish. Compare

(15) Written Medieval Swedish
     *Migdonia gik   tel **mørko**   huset.*
     Migdonia go.PST to dark.WK house.DEF
     'Migdonia went to the dark house.' [S8]

The distribution of this construction in Written Medieval Swedish as described by Larm (1936) and the virtual absence of standard preposed articles in conservative Peripheral Swedish vernaculars suggests that this was the normal way of expressing definite attributive NPs in large parts of medieval Sweden, and the

---

[6] The example he provides is perhaps not wholly obvious, though: *stor övervalls dalasäkken* '?'

more general use of the pattern without a preposed article has in fact survived in some vernaculars in the Peripheral Swedish area. Compare:

(16) Leksand (Nedansiljan)
    *Sô jä får   ingôn trevnâ   ti **fin rommä**...*
    so I get.PRS no   nice_feeling in **fine room**.DEF
    'So I don't like it in the fancy room.' [S48]

As we see in this example, the construction in the vernaculars has typically undergone apocope of the weak adjective ending, which means that the adjective seems to be undeclined. The ending has not disappeared but undergone what is sometimes called "Cheshirization": it leaves a prosodic trace in the form of a "grave" pitch accent. Consider the following examples from Levander (1928: 148) with marking of the pitch accent:

(17) Ore (Ovansiljan)
    nȳ'   ruttjin
    new.WK coat.DEF
    'the new coat'

(18) Leksand (Nedansiljan)
    lìssl   påjtjôn
    little.WK boy.DEF
    'the little boy'

(19) Nås (Västerdalarna)
    gvìt   sôkkor
    white.WK sock.PL.DEF
    'the white socks'

Similar examples can be found in texts from Estonia, although without the pitch accent:

(20) Nuckö (Estonian Swedish vernaculars)
    stor re staina   opat krusat sånd butne
    big red stone.DEF.PL on   rippled sand bottom.DEF
    'the big red stones on the rippled sand bottom' [S39]

Sandström & Holmberg (2003: 110) argue that definite attributive NPs without incorporation and without a preposed article violate the "argument rule" proposed by Delsing (1993) which prohibits leaving the D (determiner) position empty in argument NPs. This would seem to exclude examples like those above. Admittedly, the rule is not supposed to apply to languages with morphological case (such as Icelandic), which might explain away at least the vernaculars which have retained some of the old case system. On the other hand, among the examples given, Nås and Estonia are clearly outside the area which preserves cases so that would be a counterexample to their claims.

4.3.3.2 Non-standard preposed articles

We saw in §4.3.1 that the Central Scandinavian preposed article is on the whole absent from the Peripheral Swedish area, at least as far as headed noun phrases in the more conservative vernaculars of the Peripheral Swedish area go. However this statement has to be qualified: preposed articles can be found, but they do not look quite the same as in the standard languages. Thus, in Elfdalian, in addition to the incorporation construction, as exemplified in (21a), we may have (21b), where the demonstrative *an dar* 'that' can be used without its original deictic force.

(21)   Elfdalian (Ovansiljan)

    a.   *swart-rattj-in*
        black-dog-DEF.NOM.SG
        'the black dog'

    b.   *an   dar   swart rattj-in*
        that there black dog-DEF.NOM.SG
        'the black dog'

What we see here is apparently yet another and at least partly independent instance of the common grammaticalization process by which a definite article develops out of a distal demonstrative pronoun, in this case *an dar* 'that', that is, a combination of the pronoun *an* 'he' and the adverb *dar* 'there'.[7]

    This phenomenon turns out to be quite wide-spread in the Peripheral Swedish area. In fact, several descriptions indicate constructions involving demonstratives as the primary alternative for expressing attributive definite noun phrases, or at least, as an alternative on a par with adjective incorporation. Thus, Ivars (2005) says that the major alternative for definite NPs with preposed modifiers

---

[7] For convenience, I will gloss such pronouns as demonstratives, even if they are clearly used as definite articles.

in southern Ostrobothnian is the construction "demonstrative *hande* + agreeing adjective + noun with suffixed definite article". That is, rather than the incorporated *röhu:se* 'the red house', one finds *hede rött hu:se* and rather than *röstugon* 'the red hut' one finds *honde ryö: stugon.* (See Vangsnes (2003: 158) for further examples from southern Ostrobothnian).

As for Nyland, where the preposed article is possible in the vernacular, Lundström (1939: 21) says that the vernacular prefers to use a demonstrative pronoun when speaking of "already familiar or previously mentioned objects".[8] It thus appears that the demonstrative is encroaching on the territory of the preposed article, but has not yet taken it over totally.

A further variation on the theme is found in Jämtland. Reinhammar (2005: 38) says about the vernacular of Hammerdal that the demonstrative *'n dânn* is used in a way that comes close to a preposed definite article. Primarily, however, this occurs with headless adjectives and adjective-noun compounds (incorporated adjectives) combinations, as in *'n dân li'hllpöytjen* 'that small boy'.

In his section on definite forms of adjectives in Dalecarlian, Levander (1928: 147) translates, without comment, Ore (Ovansiljan) *an-da gammblȧsta* as 'the oldest one', and he also has a suspiciously high number of examples with demonstratives from different parishes where he nevertheless keeps the demonstratives in the translation.

Regrettably, it is not possible to establish the exact geographical distribution of the construction discussed here, since it is usually hard to prove that examples in text cannot be understood as normal demonstratives. Except for statements like the above in published descriptions, where one has to rely on the author's judgement, systematic occurrences in translations provide the best evidence for the claim that a demonstrative in a vernacular has been grammaticalized as a definite article. I shall return to the geographical distribution in the following section, but it should be noted here that there are no attestations of extended uses of demonstratives in the Norrbothnian, Westrobothnian and Angermannian dialectal areas. This may possibly have something to do with the fact that, in many of those vernaculars, the most frequent way of forming a demonstrative NP tends to be by adding an adverb such as *daNNa* 'there' after the noun, e.g. *hässtn daNNa* 'that horse' (Skelletmål, Marklund 1976: 41).

---

[8] "förut bekanta eller tidigare omtalade föremål"

4.4 Distribution of attributive definite NP constructions

In the preceding section, we saw that there are at least four possible ways of handling definiteness marking in noun phrases with preposed modifiers in the Peripheral Swedish area: (i) standard preposed articles; (ii) adjectives incorporated in nouns with suffixed articles; (iii) non-incorporated modifiers without preposed articles but with definite head nouns; and (iv) preposed articles derived from complex demonstratives. We shall now look more closely at their distribution in the individual vernaculars.

Delsing (2003b: 49) identifies two areas in northern Scandinavia in which definite NPs with preposed modifiers behave differently from Central Scandinavian. The first and larger one is shown in his Figure 3.2 as comprising the traditionally Swedish-speaking parts of the following provinces: Norrbotten, Västerbotten, Lappland, Jämtland, Ångermanland, Medelpad, and Härjedalen, as well as the Dalecarlian area. Here, Delsing says, adjective incorporation is the normal way of forming a definite noun phrase with an adjectival attribute. There are two types of exceptions to this generalization. The first type concerns so-called "absolute positives", which I shall return to in §4.8. The second type is referred to by Delsing as "emphasis, in particular with superlatives and other expressions where the preposed article tends to be omitted in Standard Swedish"[9] – here the pattern used is an adjective with a weak ending without a preposed article. In the three provinces of Norrbotten, Västerbotten, and Ångermanland, preposed articles are not attested at all. In addition to the core area of adjective incorporation, there are also, says Delsing, "smaller areas", viz. Hälsingland, Gästrikland, Österbotten och Trøndelag, where "the same pattern is used", but "double definiteness shows up in the emphasis case".[10]

The claim that preposed articles are totally absent from the three northernmost coastal provinces is a bit too categorical. Thus, Rutberg (1924: 141) gives a number of examples from Nederkalix (Kalixmål) such as *dän stora gårn* 'the big farm', *dom höa höusa* 'the high houses', *de öyntjelia liλbåne* 'the poor little kids'. Her generalisation is that "adjectives show up as independent words when the adjective has stronger stress and especially when it is preceded by a demonstrative pronoun ...". Wikberg (2004: 114) notes several types of cases where preposed definite articles are used in Rånemål, including dates, NPs modified by *äänn* 'other', and before numerals, e.g.

---

[9] "dels vid emfas, särskilt vid superlativer och andra uttryck som gärna utelämnar den framförställda artikeln i rikssvenska"

[10] "I mindre områden (Hälsingland, Gästrikland, Österbotten och Trøndelag) används samma mönster men dubbel definithet uppträder i emfas-typen."

(22)   Rånemål (Lulemål)
       Di truy päjkan   *sparke   ball*
       DEF three boy.DEF.PL kick.PST ball
       'The three boys were playing ball.'

The Cat Corpus material also confirms that in the northernmost provinces definite NPs containing 'other' tend to contain a preposed article of the standard
kind, e.g.

(23)   a. Nederkalix (Kalixmål)
          Den *aann kårvit'n*   *har   'a   meste tåppe   ein ini*
          DEF other sausage_end.DEF have.PST she almost stuff.SUP in   into
          öre.
          ear.DEF
       b. Skelletmål (Northern Westrobothnian)
          Dän ann eenn   *hadd   hon ståppä   ein inni airä.*
          DEF other end.DEF have.PST she stuff.SUP in   into ear.DEF
       c. Sävar (Southern Westrobothnian)
          *...å   **den aann körv-enn**   sättä   'na mot öre.*
          ...and DEF other sausage_end.DEF put.PST she to   ear.DEF
          'The other (sausage) end she had almost stuffed into her ear.' (Cat
          Corpus)

Similarly, in the text [S16] from Älvdalen, where there are otherwise few if any
preposed articles, *oðer* 'other' is fairly consistently preceded by what looks like
a preposed article:

(24)   Elfdalian (Ovansiljan)
       Diär odrä   **gesslkallär**   *ad   ve   tungnäd kåit   upi*
       DEF other.PL herder boy.PL have.PST be.SUP forced.PP run.INF in
       budär   etter fuätsą...
       shielings after people.DAT
       'The other herder boys had been forced to run to the shielings for
       people...' [S16]

There are also other patterns, however, as in:

(25) Junsele (Angermannian)
Anner korvään *stôppe na nästan in i öre.*
other sausage_end.DEF stuff.PST she almost in into ear.DEF
'The other sausage end she had almost stuffed into her ear.' (Cat Corpus)

With regard to the use of adjective incorporation in general, it is not quite easy to verify the southern border of the area where incorporation is the preferred or even only possible, construction, but it does appear that it is fuzzier and more complex than Delsing makes it. Thus, for Njurunda in Medelpad, which would belong to the larger core area according to Delsing, Stenbom (1916: 59) gives examples such as *n dänn stygge pôjken* 'the nasty boy < that there nasty boy' as one of two possible constructions, the other being adjective incorporation. In other words, there is competition here between incorporation and a non-standard preposed article construction. In the case of the province of Hälsingland, we find that Delsing's own account is slightly contradictory. On the one hand, he says that it belongs to the peripheral incorporation area, on the other, in his discussion of the use of the preposed article, he says that it is used about as much as in the standard language, basing himself on what he has found in written texts. In several descriptions of Hälsingland vernaculars, incorporation is described in a way that suggests that it is the primary alternative. Hjelmström (1896: 82) says that "like other Norrlandic vernaculars" the Delsbo vernacular uses compounds such as *storboļe* 'the big table' and *gammeļjænta* 'the old girl' instead of Swedish *det stora bordet* and *den gamla flickan*. According to, According to Franck (1995: 31), incorporation is frequent in Forsa (his examples are *fịnhátten* 'the fancy hat', *stọrträ* 'the big tree', *svả\fthästen* 'the black horse'). Hedblom (1978: 62), in his discussion of the speech of some descendants of emigrants from Hanebo (Helsingian) in Bishop Hill, Illinois, says that they prefer compounds instead of adjectival attributes. His examples are *hå'ļvatt'n* 'hard water', *skar'pbrö'* 'crisp bread (knäckebröd)', *på gammeḷda'ganô* 'in the old days'. However, most of these could also be interpreted as lexical compounds and are difficult to evaluate out of context. On the other hand, as Delsing says, the written material from Hälsingland contains a considerable number of preposed articles, although partly differing in form from Standard Swedish. In the following example we find two instances of the demonstrative *-en* used as a preposed article. (It looks confusingly like an indefinite article, but the weak forms of the following adjectives and the definite form of the noun tell us that it has to be the demonstrative.)

(26) Delsbo (Helsingian)

[Marget o jɵ jɷle, sum mɷra sa]

o	*fleg*	*å*	*upp jenne dä*	*bratte*	*trampan*	*evver*	**en**
and	fly.PST	on	up that there	steep.WK	staircase.DEF	across	DEF

mɵrska bɵtten	*o*	*in i*	**en**	**liλla, jusa**	**kammarn.**
dark attic	and	in to	DEF	little well-lit.WK	chamber.DEF

'[Marget and I did as the old woman said] and flew up that steep staircase across the dark attic and into the small, well-lit room.' [S18]

Likewise, in the Cat Corpus we find that incorporation is used in the following sentence in two of three Hälsingland texts:

(27) a. Färila (Helsingian)

*...**vitgardinân***	*fḷaddrâ.*
...white_curtain.DEF.PL	flutter.PST

'...the white curtains fluttered.' (Cat Corpus)

b. Forsa (Helsingian)

*...**vitgardinene***	*jussom*	*vinka*	*at-en.*
...white_curtain.DEF.PL	like	wave.INF	at_one

'...the white curtains waved at you as it were.' (Cat Corpus)

Moving south along the Swedish east coast, Gästrikland appears to be fairly similar to Hälsingland, to judge from the description in Lindkvist (1942: 79). Having given some examples with preposed articles, Lindkvist says that they are not so frequent "since the vernaculars have other, more convenient means of expression",[11] quoting examples such as: *gammɵlprost'n* 'the old dean', *gammɵlgubbɵn* 'the old man', *unghäst'n* 'the young horse', *ungfôltji* 'the young people', *ludimyssâ* 'the hairy cap', *lillmiss'n* 'the little cat', *liss-stintâ* 'the little girl'. These examples do look like fairly typical incorporation cases. In Uppland, which is not included in Delsing's list, the standard preposed article appears to be the most common case but there are a couple of indications that incorporation also occurs, or used to occur.

Hesselman (1908: 523) quotes examples from the 17th century author Schroderus such as

---

[11] "ty målen ha andra, bekvämare uttrycksmedel"

(28) Upplandic (17th century)

    a. *Finsk   kyrkian*
       Finnish church.DEF

       'the Finnish Church' (apparently used as a proper name)

    b. *först resan*
       first time.DEF

       'the first time'

    c. *anner-sidon*
       other-side.DEF

       'the other side'

and claims, with no indication of sources, that "Modern Upplandic" ("nyuppländska") has expressions such as

(29) Upplandic

    a. *rö(d)-boken*
       red-book.DEF

       'the red book'

    b. *på ander-sidan*
       on other-side.DEF

       'on the other side'

In fact, the spelling of some of the 17th century examples suggest that they may rather be of the type discussed in §4.3.3.1, that is, non-incorporated modifiers without preposed articles but with definite head nouns. A further example is found in the transcribed text from Alunda in Västerlund (1988: 56), *red på ên vi't-kamp* 'rode on a white horse', but although Västerlund refers to it as "a compound with an adjective as first member according to the Norrlandic pattern", it is at least not a prototypical case of incorporation, since it occurs in an indefinite noun phrase.

    In Finland, on the other hand, incorporation is rather weaker than what is suggested by Delsing. For southern Ostrobothnian, Ivars (2005) says that adjective incorporation is not obligatory, but does occur. Her quest for examples, however, gave "meagre results", and she thinks the usage is receding. She found that adjective incorporation in southern Ostrobothnian is productive for "common adjectives such as *gammal* 'old', *ny* 'new', *lång* 'long', *stor* 'big', and colour adjectives. She says that her intuitive feeling is that incorporation is on the retreat, yielding to the construction with a preposed demonstrative (see §4.3.3.2). Likewise, Eriksson & Rendahl (1999) found only two indisputable examples of adjective incorporation in their relatively extensive questionnaire material from Ostrobothnian. About the use of the demonstrative construction, Ivars says that it often retains the function of demonstrative pronouns to "indicate, contrast and actualize" referents. This, I assume, is natural as long as no new dedicated distal demonstrative has developed and the old one still has to serve both as a demonstrative and as a definite article.

Delsing's smaller area also includes Trøndelag in Norway. It is rather hard to get clear documentation of the use of adjective incorporation in Trøndelag beyond the fact that it exists. For instance, Vangsnes (2003: 161) mentions it in passing, without giving examples. Faarlund, Lie & Vannebo (1997: 161) say that in Trøndelag Norwegian compounds with an adjectival first member are used more frequently than in Norwegian otherwise and give two examples, of which at least the first one cannot be seen as a straighforward lexical compound:

(30) Norwegian
Han er   spent på   dette, har   hørt   mye snakk om
he   be.PRS thrilled about this   have.PRS hear.PP much talk   about
nypresten.
new_clergyman.DEF
'He is thrilled about this, he has heard much talk about the new clergyman.'

(31) Norwegian
Stakkars Jon og Lise som må   gå   på skolen i **gammelklær.**
poor   Jon and Lise who must.PRS go.INF on school in **old_clothes.PL**
'Poor Jon and Lise, who have to go to school in old clothes.'

An Internet search yields a fair number of examples from Norway with incorporated *ny-* 'new'. The following, which is from a transcript of a story told by a woman born in Ålesund in 1901, suggests that the area where the usage is found extends at least into the province of Møre og Romsdal:

(32) Ålesund (Norway)
Og vi va   flytta   inni **nyhuset,**   *vi.*
and we be.PST move.PP into **new_house.DEF** we
'And we had moved into the new house.' (Internet)

It is harder to document clear cases of incorporation with other adjectives than *ny-* 'new', though, and my general impression is that the construction is rather restricted.

Delsing does not mention Estonia among the areas where incorporation is found. However, Tiberg (1962: 98) mentions examples such as *rödköttet* 'the red meat', *hvitöken* 'a white horse', which again, admittedly, could be taken to be ordinary compounds.

In the Dalecarlian area, the incorporation construction is undoubtedly strong Levander (1928: 148) claims that "the usual counterpart of standard language expressions such as 'the black horse', 'the old tables' etc. is the compounding of the adjective and the noun into one word".[12] He gives examples from Ovansiljan and Nedansiljan:

(33) Elfdalian (Ovansiljan)

    a. *swarrt-esstŋ*
       black-horse.DEF
       'the black horse'

    b. *gąmm-būärðe*
       old-table.DEF
       'the old tables'

(34) Sollerön (Ovansiljan)
    nȳ-ruttjen
    new-coat.DEF
    'the new coat'

(35) Rättvik (Nedansiljan)
    nīr-tjŏλlŋ
    new-skirt.DEF
    'the new skirt'

At the same time, however, it is clear that the strength of the construction varies, and that it may also have changed over time. We may consider some questionnaire responses to the sentence 'Put the red lid on the big can' (given in the context 'You have got two lids and two cans.') from two locations in the Ovansiljan

---

[12] "Dalmålets vanliga motsvarighet till riksspråkssuttryck som 'den svarta hästen', 'de gamla borden' o.d. är emellertid sammansättning av adjektivet och substantivet till ett ord".

area, Sollerön and Orsa. From Sollerön, only one informant used the incorporation construction. The two other informants used a preposed demonstrative, or what looks like a endingless non-incorporated adjective:

(36) Sollerön (Ovansiljan)

    a. *Sätt **rod-lutjä** upå **stur-buttn**.*
       put red-lid.DEF on big-can.DEF

    b. *Sätt **eta** rod lutjä upå **stur burtjän**.*
       put that.N.SG red lid.DEF on big can.DEF

    c. *Sätt **eta** rod lutjä upå **donda stur buttu**.*
       put that.N.SG red lid.DEF on that.F.SG big can.DEF
       'Put the red lid on the big can.'

The three informants from Orsa uniformly used a preposed demonstrative, varying only in the presence of the weak ending of the adjective:

(37) Orsa (Ovansiljan)
    *Setj **deda** röd luk uppo **denda** stur(a) butt'n!*
    put that.N.SG red lid.DEF on that.F.SG big.(WK) can.DEF
    'Put the red lid on the big can!' (questionnaire)

However, this does not mean that adjective incorporation does not occur in Orsa. The following sentence was translated with an incorporated adjective by several informants (the questionnaires from Sollerön show the same pattern as for the other sentence):,

(38) Orsa (Ovansiljan)
    *Wi trajvdöst bättör börti **gambölstugun**.*
    we like_it.PST better in old.house.DEF
    'We liked it better in the old house.' (questionnaire)

Some, however, prefer the preposed demonstrative here too:

(39) Orsa (Ovansiljan)
    *Wi trajvdös bättör börti **doda** gamla stugo.*
    we like_it.PST better in that.F.SG old.WK house.DEF
    'We liked it better in the old house.' (questionnaire)

The questionnaire material shows that there is competition between two or even more ways of handling adjectival modifiers of definite NPs in the Ovansiljan area. It also suggests that the variation between the constructions is not arbitrary, but the data are not rich enough to give clear indications of the tendencies.

Turning now to the most conservative vernacular of the Ovansiljan area, Elfdalian, we find that Levander (1909: 53) again expresses himself quite categorically, in that he states under the section on definite attributive adjectives: "This form is obtained by compounding the adjective and the noun." He gives a number of examples:

(40)　Elfdalian (Ovansiljan)

　　a.　*gambelwaisur*
　　　　old.song.PL.DEF
　　　　'the old songs'

　　b.　*frekolislkulla　　　mai*
　　　　kind.little.girl.DEF my.F.SG
　　　　'my kind little girl'

　　c.　*sturkasungen*
　　　　big.fur-coat.DEF
　　　　'the great fur-coat'

　　d.　*småkrippär*
　　　　small.children.DEF.PL
　　　　'the small children'

In spite of this, however, it is clear that modern Elfdalian also allows for the use of distal demonstratives in the function of preposed definite articles. Compare the following questionnaire sentence:

(41)　Elfdalian (Ovansiljan)
　　　An dar lissl wait mass kåjt　in i　e　dar stur roð
　　　that there little white cat　　run.PST in　in that there big　red
　　　ausað.
　　　house.DEF
　　　'The little white cat ran into the big red house.' (questionnaire)

It appears that speakers feel reluctant to incorporate more than one adjective at a time. This is in contrast to vernaculars from Upper Norrland, where informants are quite happy to do that:

(42) Arjeplog (Northern Settler dialect area)
      Lill-vit-katt-n   *sprang in i* **sto-rö-hus-e.**
      little-white-cat-DEF run.PST in in big-red-house-DEF
      'The little white cat ran into the big red house.' (questionnaire)

It is also in contrast to Levander's example (40b) above, where the two adjectives *frek* 'kind' and *lisl* 'little' have been incorporated together.

Thus, we have seen that the Ovansiljan area is generally characterized by the competition between adjective incorporation and preposed demonstratives in the function of definite articles, although it is not easy to see the principles for the choice.

From the Nedansiljan and Västerdalarna areas, there are some examples of incorporation, e.g. (35) above, but more commonly we seem to get other patterns. The Cat Corpus contains examples of both the standard preposed definite article construction and of what looks like the use of demonstratives as articles (although there is some uncertainty due to possible influence from the source text). What is peculiar to these areas, however, is the tendency to use unincorporated adjectives without any preposed article, as in the examples (16)-(19) above. This construction is also found in Åland (Eva Sundberg, personal communication), as in the following questionnaire sentence:

(43) Brändö (Ålandic)
      Sätt   **röd locket** *på* **stor burken!**
      put.IMP red lid.DEF on big can.DEF
      'Put the red lid on the big can!' (questionnaire)

However, in Åland, like in Southern Finland and Estonia, preposed articles are also regularly used, although their form often differs from that found in Swedish. This suggests that there have been at least partly independent paths from demonstratives to definite articles, as in the following examples, where the articles have the form *hon* and *he tän*, respectively:

(44) Brändö (Ålandic)
      Hon   **lill** **vit** **kattan** *sprang in i* **he**   **tän stor röd**
      that.F.SG little white cat   run.PST in in that.N.SG that big red
      huset
      house
      'The little white cat ran into the big red house.' (questionnaire)

4.5 Definiteness marking in special contexts

Let us now consider Delsing's claim that the larger northern area uses a weak adjective without a preposed article in the 'emphasis type'. His examples (given without a location) are *siste gånga* '(the) last time' and *störste husa* 'the biggest houses' – in other words what I have above (§4.3.1) referred to as "selectors" although it is not obvious that they are necessarily emphatic. To judge from the Cat Corpus material, there is considerable variation in the vernaculars in the area delineated by Delsing. Consider the first sentence of the Cat story in some Peripheral Swedish varieties, listed from north to south:

(45)   a. Nederkalix (Kalixmål)
        [Män voj voj, tuken ståckar,]
        *saar   mårmora når 'a så   'en   Murre **fårstgjaka**.*
        say.PST Granny when she see.PST PDA.M Cat   **first_time**.DEF

       b. Skelletmål (Northern Westrobothnian)
        *sa   Mormora **förstgånga**   hon feck   sei   kattkalln*
        say.PST Granny **first_time**.DEF she get.PST see.INF tomcat.DEF

       c. Sävar (Southern Westrobothnian)
        *sa   Mormora **först-gånga**   hon vart   vis   Kattgöbben.*
        say.PST Granny **first_time**.DEF she become.PST aware tomcat.DEF

       d. Junsele (Angermannian)
        *sa   Momma **först ganga**   hun såg   Katta.*
        say.PST Granny **first** time.DEF she see.PST cat.DEF

       e. Lit (Jamtska)
        *...sa   a Momma **förste** **gången** hu såg   Fresn*
        say.PST Granny   **first**.WK time.DEF she see.PST cat.DEF

       f. Elfdalian (Ovansiljan)
        *sagd   Mumun, **fuäst gandsin** o såg   Masse.*
        say.PST Granny **first** time.DEF she see.PST Cat

       ['But my, what a poor thing',] said Granny the first time she saw Cat.'

Thus, we see that the Norrbothnian and Westrobothnian vernaculars (a-c) actually use incorporation here. Among the three southern vernaculars, it is only Lit that uses a form like the one cited by Delsing – in the other two (Junsele and Älvdalen), the weak ending of the ordinal has been apocopated. We thus have at least three possibilities rather than one here: (i) incorporation; (ii) no preposed article and an unreduced weak form of the modifier; (iii) no preposed article and an apocopated form of the modifier. If we check some other sources, this variation is confirmed:

In Nordström (1925: 61) we find *först-bilje'ttn* 'the first label' from Lulemål. Likewise, in another description of a Lulemål variety, Wikberg (2004), which treats the vernacular of Böle (Råneå), there is a translation of the first chapters of Genesis, referred to as *Först-Mosebaoka*, and the seven days of the creation are consistently referred to by incorporated forms: *förstdän* 'the first day', *änndän* 'the second day', *trididän* 'the third day', etc.

In two questionnaires from the northern Westrobothnian area (Norsjö and Glommersträsk, Arvidsjaur), the informants give forms such as *elschtsöstra hennasch Anna* 'Anna's eldest sister'.

In [S5] from Edsele (Angermannian), I have on the one hand found forms such as *föşţvägga* 'the first wall' and *fjâlvägga* 'the fourth wall', on the other hand (on the same page) *annër vägga* 'the second wall' and *trejjë vägga* 'the fourth wall'.

In addition to the example above from the Lit Cat Corpus text, we also find apocopated examples such as *gamlest pöjkn* 'the eldest son', and there are many similar examples in written texts. For instance, in a published translation of the parable of the Prodigal Son, in three instances we find the phrase *feitest kæhlfven* 'the fattest calf'. The variation in apocopation is probably not free, but contingent on the number of syllables in the word, trisyllabic words being more prone to having their final vowel apocopated than bisyllabic ones.

The Elfdalian example is in accordance with the terse statement in Levander (1909: 57): "Compounding of comparatives and superlatives with nouns does not occur"[13] and his example:

(46)   Elfdalian (Ovansiljan)
       *I kam   **nylest lovdan.***
       I come.PST last   Saturday
       'I came last Saturday.'

For the "smaller area" consisting of Hälsingland, Gästrikland, Österbotten and Trøndelag, Delsing claims that "double definiteness shows up in the emphasis case".[14] Again, it is not clear what Delsing has in mind when he speaks of "emphasis", and he gives no examples, but it is possible to read this as saying that preposed articles are more common here than in Standard Swedish. If we look

---

[13] "Sammansättning av komp. l. superl. med subst. brukas ej."
[14] "dubbel definithet uppträder i emfas-typen"

at the usage with selectors, it appears that, at least for Hälsingland, which is the only province represented in the Cat Corpus, this is not the case. Franck (1995: 31) gives examples from Forsa (Helsingian) such as *(dän) sìsste dan* 'the last day' and *hèle hösten* 'the whole autumn'. Here, the preposed article is like that used in Swedish, only as an alternative. The Cat Corpus material suggests a consistent pattern without a preposed article at least for the expression 'the first time':

(47) a. Forsa (Helsingian)
    *...sa   Momma når   ho   såg   Fräsen **fårsta   varve**.*
    say.PST Granny when she see.PST cat.DEF **first.WK time.DEF**

  b. Färila (Helsingian)
    *...sa   Momma **förstâ   gönnjen** ho såg   Fresn.*
    say.PST Granny **first.WK time.DEF** she see.PST cat.DEF

  c. Järvsö (Helsingian)
    *...sa   Momma **fôrsta   gånjen** ho feck si   Fräsen.*
    say.PST Granny **first.WK time.DEF** she get.PST see.INF cat.DEF

  ['But my, what a poor thing',] said Granny the first time she saw Cat.'

4.6 Competition between constructions: A case study

In order to see more clearly how the competition between the two constructions works, I looked at the translation into Elfdalian of a Swedish novel from 1986, *Hunden* 'The dog' by Kerstin Ekman [S9].[15] The novel was translated in 2000 by Bengt Åkerberg, with consultations with a number of other native speakers.

Elfdalian is primarily a spoken language, and Bengt Åkerberg's translation is one of the longest written texts ever published in it. As I mentioned above, definite NPs with adjectival modifiers are rather infrequent in spoken language – something like one occurrence in 2000 words, corresponding to once in five written pages. By contrast, in Kerstin Ekman's novel, the frequency of this construction was 279 in about one hundred pages, that is, on average three per printed page, or approximately ten times as many as in the spoken corpus. In addition, the distribution of different adjectival lexemes is very different. The four "top" adjectives *stor* 'big', *liten* 'small', *gammal* 'old', and *ny* 'new', which make up about 40 per cent of all adjectives in definite NPs in spoken Swedish (see §4.1), account for only 26 tokens or less than 10 per cent of the total in *Hunden*.

---

[15] The investigation was also reported in Dahl (2004).

It is fairly clear that definite NPs with adjective modifiers have a rather different role in the genre represented by this novel than in spoken language. Instead of simply helping to identify the referent of the NP, adding a modifying adjective to a definite NP in such texts is often a device to add subtle details – consider examples such as *det starka ljuset från himlen* 'the strong light from the sky' or *den mörkgröna bladfällen* 'the dark-green pelt of leaves'. Someone who wants to translate such a text into a language with a very restricted written tradition faces a peculiar situation: it is necessary to decide how to say things that have never or very seldom been said before in that language. In this sense, the translated text is not a natural sample of the language, and this might call the results into doubt. On the other hand, the translation may also be seen as a (partly unintentional) grammatical experiment – what happens if a native speaker is forced to express all these definite NPs with the adjectival modifiers retained? And the patterns in the results turn out to be quite significant.

Among the adjectives that are incorporated, we can first note that there are 16 occurrences of the three "prototypical" adjectives, *stur* 'big', *lissl* 'small' and *gambel/gamt* 'old' (the fourth adjective from the top group – *ny* 'new' – occurs only once in the original and the translation is not incorporated). In particular, the adjective *stur* 'big' is incorporated 10 out of 12 times. In other words, these prototypical adjectives have an incorporation propensity that is about three times higher than that of adjectives in general in this text. Among other adjectives that are incorporated more than once, we find *gryön* 'green', *guäl* 'yellow', *langg* 'long', *swart* 'black', and *wåt* 'wet'. Except for the last one, all of these belong to semantic groups that are likely to show up as adjectives.

There were also clear correlations between propensity for incorporation and parameters such as frequency and length. Out of 29 examples of (single) adjectives with more than one syllable, only four were incorporated. Only once were two Swedish adjectives translated as a double incorporation (*lausug-wait-kwi'n* 'the lice-ridden white belly').

Generalizing about the competition between the two constructions in Elfdalian, it appears that the incorporating construction survives better with "core" or "prototypical" adjectives, and that it has particular difficulties in the case of multiple modifiers.[16] This is also congruent with what we have seen in other vernaculars

---

[16] One would also expect such difficulties to occur when the adjective is modified by an adverb. However, it turns out that there are no such cases in the material! The conclusion is that even in a literary text such as Kerstin Ekman's novel with a comparatively high frequency of definite NPs with adjectival modifiers, the adjectives are themselves seldom modified. An Internet search reveals that such cases do occur, although much more infrequently than with indefinites (this goes for both Swedish and English). Thus, the string *a very big* is about twenty

outside the northern core area – such examples of incorporation that are found tend to involve the four most frequent adjectives ('big', 'small', 'old', 'new'). With those adjectives, it is not impossible to find examples that look like incorporation even outside the Peripheral Swedish area, even sometimes in Standard Swedish. Consider the following example from the (unpublished) Swedish version of the Cat text:

(48)   Swedish
[Det första han såg när han kom ut på gården var]
en   ekorre som satt   i **stortallen**   bortom brunnen och skalade
INDF squirrel REL sit.PST in **big.pine.DEF** beyond well.DEF and peel.PST
kottar.
cone.PL

'[The first thing he saw when he went out into the yard was] a squirrel that sat in the big pine behind the well, peeling cones.' (Cat Corpus)

In this sentence, most of the translations of the Cat story use a compound *stortallen* 'the big pine'. By itself, this could of course be explained by influence from the Standard Swedish text that was the original for most of the translations. What is noteworthy, though, is that several translations from southern Sweden – Västergötland, Bohuslän, and Skåne are exceptions: they prefer the standard preposed article construction, suggesting that compounds with adjectives may be less natural in those vernaculars.

It is tempting to suggest that adjectival incorporation has been more general in older times and has been pushed back. What speaks in favour of this is that – like several other phenomena discussed in this book – it seems to be strongest in the most conservative parts of the Peripheral Swedish area.

4.7 Definite suffixes on adjectives

In many Peripheral Swedish area dialects, adjectives may take definite suffixes, identical to those of nouns, if they are used in definite noun phrases without a lexical head noun, i.e. as translations of English examples such as *the small one*. Compare the following example from Elfdalian:

---

times as frequent as the string *the very big*.

(49)   Elfdalian (Ovansiljan)
  *Ir eð i **lisslun**   eld **sturun?***
  be.PRS it in little.DEF.SG.DAT.F or big.DEF.SG.DAT.F
  'Is there [coffee] in the little one or the big one?' (Levander 1909: 53)

The definite suffixes are in general identical to the ones used with nouns. It should be noted, however, that adjectives with definite suffixes generally have a grave accent, e.g. *lìsslun* and *stùrun* in (49) (for Upper Norrland, see Holmberg & Sandström 2003). Definite suffixes on nouns do not in general induce a grave pitch accent if the noun does not have it by itself. Compare Elfdalian *stùrn* 'the big one' from *stur* 'big' with *kálln* 'the man' from *kall* 'man'. (The -n suffix is here syllabic, which means that the definite forms are bisyllabic and can carry grave accent.) This suggests that the definite suffix was originally added to an adjective with a weak ending: *sture-n*. (Holmberg & Sandström, who assume that these forms arise by the movement of the adjective to the D position, assume that the grave accent is a "phonological reflex of the empty pronoun into which the adjective is incorporated". They do not explain how an empty pronoun comes to induce a grave accent.)

 Delsing (2003b: 51) reports adjectives with definite suffixes from Norrbotten, Västerbotten, Ångermanland, Jämtland, Härjedalen, Medelpad, and Dalarna. He did not find them in Österbotten or Värmland, but notes that they are attested in Norway (Trøndelag and Nordmøre). The use in the Cat Corpus is basically in accordance with this.

 In Standard Swedish, *Lillen* and *Lillan*, masculine and feminine weak forms of *liten* 'little', are used as hypocoristics for small children. Like the Peripheral Swedish forms, they have a grave accent. By contrast, a form like *försten* 'the first one', which is also sometimes used, is often pronounced with an acute accent.

4.8 "Absolute positives"

A rather curious construction is found in a relatively large number of Scandinavian varieties, including Standard Swedish. It involves an adjective with a weak ending followed by a definite noun:

(50)   Swedish
  *Han är ju redan **stora karn.***
  he be.PRS PRAG already big man.DEF
  '(lit.) He is already the big man.'

The Swedish Academy Grammar (Teleman, Hellberg & Andersson 1999: 3:20) mentions such cases, almost in passing, as examples of lexicalized phrases parallel to other cases of omitted preposed articles. However, we are rather dealing with a productive construction with quite specific properties. (Delsing refers to it as "absolute positives" without indicating any source for this term.) Typical uses are in predicative position, where there is no apparent motivation for the use of a definite form of the noun, but the construction is also found in prepositional phrases. The expressions give an emphatic impression and there seems to be a common element of "completeness" or "maximalness" to many uses of the construction, but there are also examples of combinations with negation where this element is not present. Thus, consider the following examples from southern Westrobothnian and Bokmål Norwegian, respectively:

(51) Hössjö (Southern Westrobothnian)
Det är **köLsvarte** **mörkre** *ne* *ända* *till Mosjö.*
it be.PRS pitch-black.WK darkness.DEF down all_DEF_way to Mosjö
'It is pitch dark [lit. the pitch-black darkness] down to Mosjö.' [S44]

(52) Bokmål Norwegian
Jeg veide *bare 1440 gram og* *var ikke* **store** **gutten.**
I weigh.PRET only gram and be.PST NEG big.WK boy.DEF
'I weighed only 1440 grams and wasn't a [lit. the] big boy.' (About the narrator's premature birth) (Internet)

For the Peripheral Swedish vernaculars, there is an additional feature that makes this construction stand out: the adjectives used are not incorporated and the weak ending may not undergo apocope. The pattern has been noted in the literature, e.g. for Skelletmål by Marklund (1976: 34), who notes that in Skelletmål, it is found "in certain expressions that indicate a rather high degree, a 'rather' or 'only', which either restricts or emphasizes the property",[17] as in (53).

(53) Skelletmål (Northern Westrobothnian)
gode bitn	'a good (i.e. substantial) bit'
store kæN	'a big man'
tonge læsse	'a heavy load'
blåe mjôLLka	'pure skim milk'
raNe vættne	'pure (mere) water'
rette såTTn	'the right sort'

---

[17] "i vissa uttryck som innebär en rätt hög grad, ett 'ganska' eller 'bara', som antingen begränsar eller betonar egenskapen (adjektivet)"

Likewise, after saying that definite attributive adjective are formed by compounding in Elfdalian, Levander (1909: 53) adds that adjectives are "exceptionally" used as words of their own when heavily stressed:

(54)   Elfdalian (Ovansiljan)

   a. *bero   bokken*
      naked.WK ground
      '(the) naked ground'

   b. *Al   du renn   jär i twero   bjärre?*
      shall.PRS you run.INF here in steep.WK mountain
      'Are you going to ski here on the steep mountain?'

   c. *Og du ir   aut o   kåiter i mörk notn.*
      and you be.PRS out and run.PRS in dark night.DEF
      'And you are out running around in the dark night.'

However, Elfdalian differs from Skelletmål in that these examples follow the normal rules for apocope. Thus, in (54c) the weak ending is apocopated, but not in (54a)–(54b) because the stems are short-syllabic.

   In the Cat Corpus, the "absolute positive" pattern is mainly found in the translations of the following sentence, quoted here in the Standard Swedish version, and in a version from Våmhus (Ovansiljan):

(55)   Swedish
       Det är   ju   inte långa   biten   ner   till oss.
       it   be.PRSis PRAG NEG long.WK piece.DEF down to us
       'It is not far (to go) down to us.' (Cat Corpus)

(56)   Våmhus (Ovansiljan)
       Ä i   ju   int launga bi:tn   nið a wuoss.
       it be.PRS PRAG NEG long.WK piece.DEF down to us

Most of the examples in the Cat Corpus are from Dalarna but there are also examples from Hälsingland and Bohuslän, e.g.:

(57)   Sotenäs (Bohuslän)
       D'ä   jo   'nte lánge bedden   ner   te ûss
       it be.PRS PRAG NEG long piece.DEF down to us

The apocopated pattern is found in the Ovansiljan area (but cf. example from Våmhus, without apocope) and also in a couple of other places in Dalarna, e.g.

(58) Aspeboda (Dalabergslagsmål)
      *Hä ä   ju   nt   **lång bitn**   ne   tä ôss*
      it   be.PRS PRAG NEG **long piece**.DEF down to us

The distribution in the Cat Corpus texts from Dalarna and Hälsingland is shown in Figure 4.1.

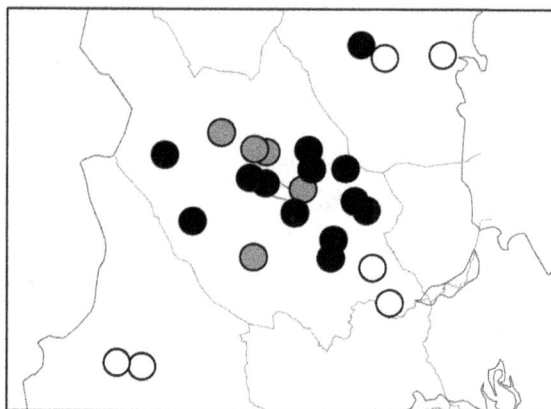

Figure 4.1: Occurrences of absolute positives in the Cat Corpus. Black circles: absolute positives with apocope; grey circles: absolute positives without apocope; white circles: no absolute positives attested.

5 Possessive constructions

5.1 General background

The topic of this chapter is possessive noun phrases, that is, noun phrases that involve a possessive modifier, the latter being roughly everything that is functionally equivalent to genitives. Following what is now established terminology, I shall speak of "possessor" and "possessee" for the two entities involved in the possessive relation. It should be noted from the start that possessive constructions may express a diversity of relations that sometimes have very little to do with "ownership", which has traditionally been seen as their basic meaning.

When it comes to the expression of possessive relations in noun phrases, Scandinavian languages display a bewildering array of constructions. Quite often, we find a number of competing possibilities within one and the same variety. In this chapter, my main concern will be with lexical possessive NPs – constructions where the possessor is a full NP rather than a pronoun. This includes possessor NPs with different kinds of heads – most notably, the head may be either (i) a proper name or an articleless kin term such as 'father', or (ii) a common noun, usually in the definite form. Delsing (2003b) treats these two types under separate headings, which is motivated by the fact that some constructions show up with the first type only. However, as he himself notes, there are no constructions which categorically exclude this type.

A caveat here about the available material: noun phrases with full NP possessors are less frequent in spoken and informal written language than one would like as a linguist studying this construction, making it difficult to collect enough data to formulate safe generalizations about usage.

5.2 *S-genitive*: Old and new

The traditional device for marking possessive constructions in Indo-European is the genitive case. In older Germanic, like in its sister branches, the genitive also had various other functions – thus, both verbs and prepositions could govern the genitive. This situation is still preserved in some of the modern Germanic languages, such as (Standard) German and Icelandic. In most Germanic varieties, however, the genitive case has either been transformed or has disappeared altogether. Thus, in languages such as Dutch and West Frisian, like in many spoken Scandinavian varieties, we obtain what Koptjevskaja-Tamm (2003) calls "deformed genitives". In these, what is kept from the traditional genitive case is primarily the suffixal marking, usually a generalized suffix such as *-s*. Other common characteristics of deformed genitives are that the possessor phrase is preposed relative to the head noun and that there are restrictions on what kinds of NPs can occur as possessors – in the strictest cases, only proper names and name-like kinship terms. Syntactically, deformed genitives tend to behave more like "determiners" than like "modifiers", which, among other things, means that they do not co-occur with definite articles. Even in Standard German, where the old genitive is in principle fairly well preserved, there is arguably an alternative "deformed" construction of this kind (e.g. *Peters Buch* 'Peter's book'). If we look at Central Scandinavian, we find a possessive construction which resembles the "deformed genitives" in several ways, but which also differs significantly from it. What is rather curious is that a construction with almost exactly the same properties is found in English – the so-called *s*-genitive. The English and Scandinavian constructions share with each other and with the garden-variety deformed genitive at least three properties: (i) the preposed position in the noun phrase; (ii) the generalized *s*-suffix; (iii) the lack of definite marking on the possessee NP or its head noun. They differ from other deformed genitives in not being restricted to proper names and kinship terms and in being possible with basically any noun phrase, regardless of syntactic complexity. The marker *-s* is always on the last element of the noun phrase, which may entail "group genitives" such as Swedish *far mins bok* 'my father's book' or English *Katz and Fodor's theory*, where the *-s* is not suffixed to the head noun but rather to a postposed modifier or to the last element of a conjoined NP.

S-genitives, so characterized, are not found generally in Scandinavian, but are in fact essentially restricted to "Central Scandinavian", that is, standard Danish and Swedish, with a somewhat reluctant extension to some forms of standard Norwegian and the spoken varieties of southern Scandinavia (south of the *limes norrlandicus*). Even in parts of southern Sweden, however, deviant systems are found. Thus, in central parts of the province of Västergötland, according to the description in Landtmanson (1952), the ending *-a* is commonly found with proper names and kinship terms. This is also in accordance with the usage in the single Cat Corpus text from that province, the title of which is *Mormora Misse* 'Granny's cat' (likewise, in the same text: *Allfrea käring* 'Alfred's wife'). The ending *-s* is found with a few types of proper names and also with common nouns, "to the extent they can be used in the genitive at all" (Landtmanson 1952: 68). Genitive forms in *-a* are also found in some Upplandic dialects. In Written Medieval Swedish, Wessén (1968: I:142) notes that the original *-ar* ending of *i-* and *u-*stems, often reduced to *-a*, survived for quite a long time with proper names, "especially in foreign ones". "In Västergötland and Småland it even still survives: *Davida* 'David's' etc." The *-ar* ending, in non-reduced form, is also found in Orsa (Ovan-siljan): *Alfredar keling* 'Alfred's wife' (but *Momos Måssä* 'Granny's cat', with an *s*-ending).

More elaborate genitive forms are sometimes found. Thus, in the Cat Corpus text from Träslövsläge (Helsingian) we find the ending *-sa*, as in *Mormosa katt* 'Granny's cat' and *Alfredsa käring* 'Alfred's wife'. The ending *-sa* is apparently a combination of the two endings *-s* and *-a*. It is also found in Faroese possessives, and in the Alunda vernacular (Uppland) as described in Bergman (1893). In the text from Sotenäs in Bohuslän the ending is *-ses*, apparently a doubling of *-s*: *Mormorses pissekatt* 'Granny's pussy cat' and *Alfreses kjäreng* 'Alfred's wife' (see Janzén (1936) for a discussion of *-ses* forms in Bohuslän vernaculars). Compare also similar examples from Hälsingland with definite forms of the possessee under §5.3.

In the vernaculars of the Peripheral Swedish area, like in most of Norway, the *s*-genitive, at least in its canonical form as described above, is generally absent or weakly represented in a way that suggests late influence from acrolectal varieties. Delsing (2003b: 41) says that the *s*-genitive is totally absent in the "old dative vernaculars" of Norrbotten and coastal northern Västerbotten, as well as in Jämtland and Härjedalen as well as in the Dalecarlian area. In the rest of northern and middle Norrland there are only few attestations, he says, and they seem to be a "young phenomenon". On the whole, the weak support for the *s*-genitive in the vernaculars of peninsular Scandinavia, with the exception of the Southern Swedish/East Danish dialect area, is striking. In fact, it appears to me that the development of the *s*-genitive, as described e.g. by Norde (1997),[1] may be essentially restricted to Danish, Scanian and prestige or standard varieties of Swedish, and possibly some parts of Götaland.

---

[1] Norde describes the development of the *s*-genitive as an essentially internal phenomenon in Swedish and does not treat deviant developments in vernaculars or draw parallels to Danish.

5.3 Definite in *s*-genitives

A construction which is fairly analogous to the standard *s*-genitive – differing from it primarily in that the head noun takes the definite form – is found in a relatively large part of the Peripheral Swedish area on both sides of the Baltic (Delsing 2003b: 27).

In Mainland Sweden, the strongest area seems to be Hälsingland. In the Cat Corpus, it is found in all three texts from this province, although alternating with the regular *s*-genitive construction. Thus, for 'Alfred's wife' we find *Alfreds käringa* from Järvsö (Helsingian) and *Alfreses tjeringa* from Färila (Helsingian) with a doubled ending *-ses*, and *frua Alfreds*, with the order possessee-possessor from Forsa (Helsingian). Further north, it is less common, but does occur. Bergholm et al. found cases such as *Pers bole* 'Per.GEN table.DEF' and *mine brorn* 'my brother.DEF' in Burträsk (Northern Westrobothnian). Delsing (2003b: 27) enumerates quite a few examples from the literature and from written texts, covering all the coastal provinces in Norrland except Norrbotten, and also the Laplandic parts of the Westrobothnian area.

The construction is also found in Gotland, as in the Cat Corpus examples *Mormors sänge* 'Granny's bed' from Fårö (Gotland) and *Mårmårs sänggi* 'Granny's bed' from Lau (Gotland). In Gotland, definite forms can also be used with pronominal possessors, as in (1).

(1) Lau (Gotland)
    De jär   min kattn.
    it be.PRS my cat.DEF
    'It is my cat.' (Cat Corpus)

The construction seems to be general in the whole Trans-Baltic area. In most cases, the possessor takes the affix *-s*, but in Ostrobothnian *-as* is also quite common – I shall return to this in §5.4.2. In Ostrobothnian, Eriksson & Rendahl (1999) also found considerable variation between definite and indefinite possessees – roughly 50 per cent of each.

From older times, Hesselman (1908: 523) quotes examples from the 17th century lexicographer Ericus Schroderus such as

(2) Upplandic (17th century)
    Lijffzens   Träet
    life.GEN.DEF tree.DEF
    'the tree of life'

and from Bureus, another 17th century writer:

(3) Upplandic (17th century)
     hos Anders Burmans   i Rödbäck systren
     at   Anders Burman.GEN in Rödbäck sister.DEF
     'at the sister of Anders Burman in Rödbäck'

and says "in the same way as modern Upplandic: *Geijers dalen* [Geijer's Valley],
bokhandlarens pojken 'the bookseller's boy' etc." This is the only place in the
literature known to me where definites with *s*-genitives are said to be found in
Upplandic. (The first example is clearly a compound in the modern language,
spelled *Geijersdalen.*)

As for the alternative construction with the possessee-possessor word order,
found in the example from Forsa (Helsingian) above, Delsing quotes a number
of examples, some of them, as he says, "from unexpected places" such as Värmland and Västergötland. The word order possessee-possessor was normal in Old
Nordic and is still used in Icelandic (although without definite marking on the
possessee). It is thus possible that it is an archaism at least in some places –
although hardly for the Laplandic vernaculars mentioned by Delsing.

5.4 Constructions with the dative

5.4.1 The plain dative possessive

In many Peripheral Swedish vernaculars, a common possessive construction involves a dative-marked possessor. In most cases, the word order is possessed-
possessor, but preposed possessors also occur. The possessee NP is normally
morphologically definite only when it precedes the possessor. I shall call this
construction THE PLAIN DATIVE POSSESSIVE. The following two phrases exemplify
the postposed and preposed variants of this construction:

(4) Skelletmål (Northern Westrobothnian)
     POSSESSEE   POSSESSOR
     skoN   *paitjåm*
     shoe.SG.DEF boy.DAT.SG.DEF
     'the boy's shoe' (Marklund 1976: 22)

(5) Nederkalix (Kalixmål)
     POSSESSOR   **POSSESSEE**
     Mårmorn   *kjaatt*
     Granny.DEF.DAT cat
     'Granny's cat' (Cat Corpus, title of translation)

Even in those vernaculars where the dative is preserved, cases of zero-marking are common. Thus, many examples of this construction look like plain juxtaposition of two NPs:

(6) Elfdalian (Ovansiljan)
     POSSESSEE **POSSESSOR**
     kalln   *Smis-Margit*
     man.DEF.SG Smis-Margit
     'Smis-Margit's husband' (Levander 1909: 97)

In examples such as (6), the possessor NPs can be regarded as being in the dative – the lack of overt marking is in accordance with the grammar of the vernacular. However, there are also examples where an expected overt marking is lacking. For instance, in the Cat Corpus, we find in addition to the dative-marked (5) an example such as (7), with the nominative *mårmora* 'Granny':

(7) Nederkalix (Kalixmål)
     *Hån   Murre sprant   åopp å   laar 'se opa **måan**   **mårmora**.*
     PDA.M Murre jump.PST up   and lay REFL on **belly.DEF Granny.DEF**
     'Murre jumped up and lay down on Granny's belly.' (Cat Corpus)

Källskog (1992: 161–163) treats the possessive dative in the Överkalix vernacular (Kalixmål) in some detail and says that it is "perhaps the most common way of expressing the genitive concept".[2] She enumerates five possibilities (Table 5.1). The first, third and fourth possibilities clearly represent the postposed variant of the plain dative possessive, and the second possibility the preposed variant. In the fifth case, the dative has been replaced by the nominative.

Rutberg (1924), in her description of Nederkalixmål, presents paradigms where the genitive and the dative are identical throughout. Both Källskog (1992: 161) and Delsing (2003b: 42) take this as an indication that dative-marked possessors are

---

[2] "Det kanske vanligaste sättet att uttrycka genitivbegreppet i överkalixmålet är att använda en omskrivning med dativ." It is not clear why Källskog uses the term *omskrivning* 'periphrasis' here – it would seem that the dative construction is not more periphrastic than the *s*-genitive.

Table 5.1: Possesion in Överkalix (Kalixmål)

1 Definite possessee + definite possessor in the dative

POSSESSEE	POSSESSOR		POSSESSEE	POSSESSOR	
stjella	*faːren*	*iert*	*möylhn*	*stäjntn*	*hina*
bell	sheep.DAT	your.N	ball.DEF	girl.DAT	this.F
'the bell of your sheep'			'this girl's ball'		

2 Definite possessor in the dative + indefinite possessee

POSSESSOR	POSSESSEE	POSSESSOR	POSSESSEE
färssfeːro	*djeyλ*	*kwäjen*	*kaλv*
paternal_grandfather.DAT	field	heifer.DAT	calf
'Grandfather's field'		'the heifer's calf'	

3 Indefinite possessee + indefinite possessor in the dative

POSSESSEE		POSSESSOR	
in	*hesst*	*ino*	*åokonna kär*
INDF	horse	INDF.DAT.M	unknown man
'an unknown man's horse'			

4 Indefinite possessee + definite possessor in the dative

POSSESSEE		POSSESSOR
in	*såːn*	*sistern*
INDF	son	sister.DEF.DAT
'a son of my sister'		

5 Possessor without case-marking + indefinite possessor

POSSESSOR	POSSESSEE	
mäjn	*baːn*	*laigseker*
my	child.PL	toy.PL
'my children's toys'		

possible. Indeed, the Cat Corpus text from Nederkalix contains at least three clear examples – (5) above and also the following:

(8)   Nederkalix (Kalixmål)
Utimila   var   'e för varmt baki   röyggen mårmorn.
sometimes be.PST it too hot   behind **back.DEF Granny.DEF.DAT**
'[The cat thought:] Sometimes it was too hot behind Granny's back.' (Cat Corpus)

(9)   Nederkalix (Kalixmål)
mårmorn   vé
Granny.DEF.DAT firewood
'Granny's firewood' (Cat Corpus)

For *Lulemål*, Nordström (1925) says that the genitive, like the dative, takes the ending *-o*. He gives the example *färo mööss* 'father's cap'. In the Cat Corpus, there are examples from Lulemål such as *Mormoro lillveg* 'Granny's little road'. Källskog (1992: 163) quotes two proverbs from transcriptions done by E. Brännström, interpreting the *o*-ending as a dative marker:

(10)   Nederluleå (Lulemål)

a. *Fisk o   bröd jer   bånndo   fööd.*
fish and bread be.PRS **farmer.DEF.DAT food**
'Fish and bread are the farmer's food.'

b. *He jer   ållt   bånndo   arrbäjt.*
it be.PRS clearly **farmer.DEF.DAT work**
'It is clearly the farmer's work.'

She also mentions an expression *måora pappen* 'father's mother', said to be obsolete, by a speaker born in 1898.

From Böle in Råneå parish (Lulemål), Wikberg (2004: 113) quotes examples such as *gråsshändlaro daoter* 'the wholesale trader's daughter' and *maoro klening* 'Mother's dress' together with juxtapositional cases such as *pappen råck* 'Father's coat' and *mammen tjaol* 'Mother's skirt'.

For Pitemål, Brännström (1993: 11) mentions the postposed construction as "obsolete" (ålderdomligt) and gives the example *påtjen fàrom* 'Father's boy'.

Moving south to northern Westrobothnian, we have already seen one case of the possessive dative from Skelletmål as described by Marklund (1976: 22), who also gives the following examples: *löNa pi'gen* 'the maid's pay', *rissla græ'nnåm* 'the neighbour's sleigh', *kæppa n'Greta* 'Greta's coat', *löngNeN n'Lova* 'Lova's lies', *hästn åm Jâni* 'Johan's horse'.

In his discussion of the Lövånger (Northern Westrobothnian) vernacular, Holm (1942: 208) says that "there are a great number of other possibilities" than the *s*-genitive of the standard language (which he says is not possible in the vernacular), and gives as an example juxtaposition with the order possessee–possessor, as in *rävapälsen pastor Holm* 'the Reverend Holm's fox fur coat'.

Larsson (1929: 125) reports postposed possessives both with and without dative marking from Westrobothnian, without indicating any specific geographical locations. About the juxtapositional construction, he says that it is "very common" and gives examples such as the following:

(11) Westrobothnian

skon pötjen	'the boy's shoes'
nesdutjen stinta	'the girl's handkerchief'
lönja piga	'the maid's pay'
tjettn fara	'the sheep's pen'
legden Jonson	'Jonsson's former fields'
bökjsen n Nikkje	'Nicke's trousers'
strompen a Greta	'Greta's stockings'

For the last two examples, he gives the alternatives *bökjsen hanjs Nikkje* and *strompen hanasj Greta*, both of which should more properly be treated as *h*-genitives (see §5.5).

For the dative-marked construction, he gives the following examples: *boka prestum* 'the clergyman's book', *lönja pigen* 'the maid's pay', *löngnen n kesa* 'Kajsa's lies'.

With the reservation that Larsson does not specify the location of his examples, it appears that no attestations of the dative construction are found in southern Westrobothnian, which is perhaps not so astonishing, given that the dative has more or less disappeared there. In order to find further examples of the plain dative construction, we have to move about 700 kilometers south to the Ovansiljan area, where Levander (1909: 97) gives this construction as the normal way of expressing nominal possession in Elfdalian:[3]

(12) Elfdalian (Ovansiljan)

fjosbuðę   sturmasum

stable-shed.DEF Stormas.DEF-PL

'the shed of the Stormas people'

---

[3] "Genitivbegreppet uttrycks vanligen genom postponerad dativ"

As a modern example, we may cite the following:

(13) Elfdalian (Ovansiljan)
*Ulov add   taið   **pennskrineð kullun.***
Ulov have.PRET take.SUP pen_box.DEF girl:DAT.SG.DEF
'Ulov had taken the girl's pen case.' (Åkerberg 2012: 120)

According to Levander (1928: 112), the plain dative possessive construction is (or was) found in many places in the Dalecarlian area. Outside Älvdalen, he quotes the following examples:

(14) Boda (Nedansiljan)
skųônną Ierrka
shoe.PL Erik.DAT
'Erik's shoes'

(15) Sollerön (Ovansiljan)
gǡrdi   Sǡrim
work.PL Zorn
'[the painter Anders] Zorn's works'

(16) Transtrand (Västerdalarna)
hätta   dränndjan
cap.DEF farm-hand.DAT
'the farm-hand's cap'

For Sollerön, Andersson & Danielsson (1999: 357) mention the plain dative possessive as "a nice old locution",[4] with examples such as the following:

(17) Sollerön (Ovansiljan)
katto   Margit
cat.DEF Margit
'Margit's cat'

(18) Sollerön (Ovansiljan)
biln   prässtim
car.DEF priest.DEF.DAT
"the priest's car"

---

[4] "en gammal och fin ordvändning"

In the Cat Corpus, we find the following examples without overt case-marking:

(19)   a. Mora (Ovansiljan)
          sendjen Mårmår
          bed.DEF Granny

          'Granny's bed'

       b. Mora (Ovansiljan)
          kelindje Alfred
          wife.DEF Alfred

          'Alfred's wife'

       c. Sollerön (Ovansiljan)
          kelindji Alfred
          wife.DEF Alfred

          'Alfred's wife'

From these data, it appears that the plain dative construction is or has been possible over the whole dative-marking part of the Dalecarlian area.

Summing up the geographical distribution, we find two areas where dative marking of possessors is employed: Norrbotten and northern Västerbotten, and the Dalecarlian area. A possible difference is that the examples from the northern area tend to involve common nouns whereas proper names also show up fairly frequently in the Dalecarlian examples.

It may seem a little unexpected to find the dative as a marker of adnominal possession, but there is a relatively plausible diachronic source for it, namely what has been called "external possession" or "possessor raising constructions". This is a very widespread but by no means universal type of construction in which the possessor of a referent of a noun phrase in a sentence is expressed by a separate noun phrase, marked by an oblique case or a preposition. (English is an example of a language that has no external possessor construction, where adnominal possessors have to be used instead.) The prototypical cases of external possessor constructions involve relational nouns, above all body-part nouns (which are sometimes incorporated into the verb).

In many Indo-European languages, the possessor NP is dative-marked, as in (20a), which is more or less synonymous to (20b), where the possessor is expressed by an adnominal genitive:

(20)   German

       a. *Peter wusch   seinem   Sohn die   Füße.*
          Paul wash.PST his.DAT.M.SG son   DEF.NOM.PL foot.NOM.PL

  b. *Peter wusch*   ***die***   ***Füße***   *seines*   *Sohns.*
  Paul wash.PST DEF.NOM.PL foot.NOM.PL his.DAT.M.SG son
  'Paul washed his son's feet.'

In the older stages of Scandinavian, dative-marked external possessors were also possible. The following example is quoted from the Västgöta provincial law (Wessén 1956: 15), Norde (1997: 212):

(21) Early Written Medieval Swedish
     Skiær tungu   *ör*   ***höfþi***   ***manni...***
     cut.PRS tongue.ACC out_of **head**.DAT **man**.DAT
     'If one cuts the tongue out of a man's head...' [S2]

In many Scandinavian varieties, the dative-marked external possessor construction disappeared together with the dative case in general. As a replacement, a periphrastic construction, where the external possessor phrase is marked by the preposition *på* 'on', is used in Central Scandinavian including many vernaculars, as in the following example from the Cat Corpus:

(22) Grytnäs (Dalabergslagsmål)
     Sen huppa   *han åpp i* ***knäna***   *på na.*
     then jump.PST he   up in **knee**.DEF.PL on she.OBL
     'Then he jumped onto her lap.' (Cat Corpus)

As we shall see later, however, in the Peripheral Swedish area, it is more common for another preposition – a cognate of Swedish *åt* and English *at* – to be used in this way.

   There are a few examples from early Scandinavian which seem more like adnominal possessors. Thus:

(23) (Wessén 1956: 15, Norde 1997: 211)
   a. Runic Swedish
      stuþ   *trikila i* ***stafn***   *skibi*
      stand.PST manly in **stem**.DAT ship.DAT
      'He stood manly at the stem of the ship.' [S35]
   b. Early Written Medieval Swedish

> *Dræpær maþer   man,   varþær   han siþen dræpin a*
> kill.PRS man.NOM man.ACC become.PRS he   then kill.PP at
> ***fotum   hanum***
> foot.DAT.PL he.DAT
> 'If a man kills a man, and is then killed at his [that man's] feet.' [S2]

Norde (1997: 212) cites *hanum* in (23b) as a clear example of an adnominal posses-sor. Her criterion is the role of the referent of the dative phrase: "the dead man at whose feet the man who murdered him is killed himself, can hardly be seen as beneficiary of this killing; in this example the dative *hanum* strictly belongs to *fotum*, not to the whole clause". I do not find this argument wholly convincing, but given their borderline character, examples like (b) could act as a basis for the reinterpretation of external possessor NPs as adnominal possessors. There is little evidence that the process really got off the ground in Written Medieval Swedish.

For Medieval Norwegian, Larsen (1895) claims that the dative tended to be con-fused with the genitive (which was at the time disappearing) and quotes exam-ples such as *Kiæxstadom vældi* 'the property of the Kekstad manor'. It is difficult to say how common this phenomenon was, and standard histories of Norwegian such as Saltveit & Seip (1971) do not mention it. To me, it looks more like occa-sional confusion than a systematic usage – the examples cited by Larsen often seem to have occurred in contexts which would tend to induce the dative (such as following a preposition governing the dative). In any case, there seem to be no traces of the plain possessive dative in Modern Norwegian varieties. On the other hand, it is far from excluded that confusion of this kind may have contributed to the rise of the dative possessive constructions also in Swedish vernaculars. (Some of Larsen's examples look more like the complex dative possessive, see below.)

5.4.2 The complex dative possessive

The dative-marking constructions that we have spoken of up to this point in-volve a straightforward combination of a possessee noun with a dative-marked possessor. Another possibility, which I shall refer to as THE COMPLEX DATIVE POSSESSIVE, is productive only in Dalecarlian, notably in Elfdalian. The construc-tion I am referring to is superficially quite similar to the Swedish *s*-genitive, and is also treated as a kind of genitive construction by Levander (1909). Let us thus look at his treatment of the genitive in Elfdalian.

According to Levander, all the traditional four cases of Germanic — nomina-tive, genitive, dative, and accusative are found in Elfdalian. However, Levander

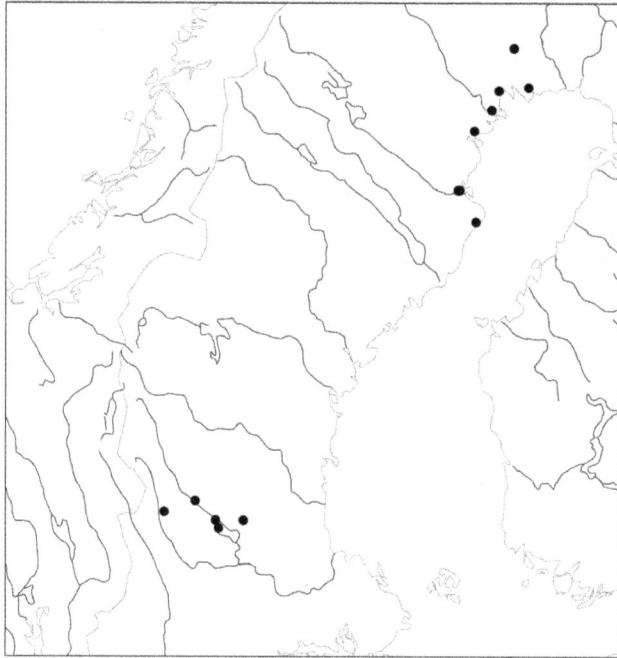

Figure 5.1: Attestations of the plain dative possessive construction.

himself notes that the genitive is fairly rare, especially in the indefinite, where it is basically restricted to two kinds of lexicalized expressions, viz.

- after the preposition *et* 'to', in expressions such as *et bys* 'to the village', *et messer* 'to the mass', *et buðer* 'to the shielings'

- after the preposition *i* 'in', in expressions of time such as *i wittres* 'last winter', *i kwelds* 'yesterday evening'

In these uses, the genitive preserves the original endings (*-s* in masculine and neuter singular; *-er* in feminine singular and generally in the plural). This is not the case for the definite forms. Consider the following example (Levander 1909: 96):

(24) Elfdalian (Ovansiljan)
      *Ita jar ir   **kullum-es**   **saing.***
      this here be.PRS girl.DEF.PL.DAT-POSS bed
      'This is the girls' bed.'

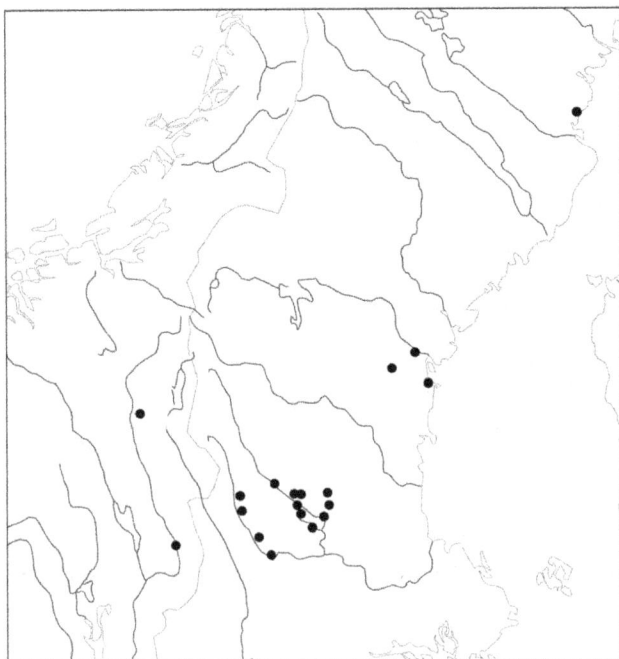

Figure 5.2: Attestations of the complex dative possessive construction.

We would expect to find here something like *kuller* but instead we have something that looks like the dative plural form *kullum* followed by an ending *-es*. This kind of formation is in fact perfectly general. Thus, we get examples such as *smiðimes* 'the black-smith's', where *-es* is added to the dative singular definite form *smiðim* of *smið* 'black-smith'. Further examples:

(25)   Elfdalian (Ovansiljan)

    a.   *An-dar skuägen   ir   **bym-es.***
        that   forest.DEF be.PRS village.DEF.DAT-POSS
        'This forest belongs to the village.'

    b.   *Isn-jär byggnan   ir   **sån-es.***
        this   building.DEF be.PRS saw-mill.DEF.DAT-POSS
        'This building belongs to the saw-mill.'

Moreover, as Levander notes, the *-es* ending may be added to the last word in a complex noun phrase, in which case the possessor noun will still be in the dative:

(26)   Elfdalian (Ovansiljan)

a. *Ann*[5]   *upp i budum-es*   *etta*
Anna.DAT up in shieling.DAT.PL-POSS hood
'Anna-at-the-shieling's hood'

b. *An bar*   **pridikantem**   **jär upp-es** *an.*
he carry.PRET **preacher.DEF.DAT.SG here up-POSS** he
'He carried the stuff of the preacher's [stuff] up here, he did.'

(In (b), the possessive noun phrase is headless, i.e. the possessee is implicit.)

Indeed, if the possessor is expressed by a noun phrase determined by a possessive pronoun, *-es* is added directly to that noun phrase, with the possessive pronoun in the dative case:

(27)   Elfdalian (Ovansiljan)

a. *Isу*   *jär lodǫ*   *ar*   *stendeð ǫ*
this.F.SG.NOM here barn.DEF.NOM.SG have.PRS.SG stand.SUP on
mainum   **faðer-es**   **garde.**
my.M.SG.DAT father-POSS farm.DAT.SG
'This barn has stood on my father's farm.'

b. *Eð war*   **uorum**   **fafar-es**   **fafar**
it be.PRET.SG **our.M.DAT.SG. father's_father-POSS father's_father**
so   *byggd*   *dǫ*   *dar tjyälbuðę.*[6]
who build.PRET that.F.SG.ACC there shelter.DEF.ACC.SG
'It was our great-great-great-grandfather who built that shelter.'

c. *Eð war*   **dainum**   **kall-es**   **mumun.**
it be.PRET.SG **your.M.DAT.SG. husband-POSS mother's_mother**
'It was your husband's maternal grandmother.'

The marker *-es* can also be added to headless adjectives with a definite suffix (see §4.7) and some pronouns:

(28)   Elfdalian (Ovansiljan)

---

[5] The dative form of *Anna* is given by Levander as *Anno* but the final vowel is elided here due to the morphophonological process known as apocope (see further in the main text).

[6] This word, which translates into regional Swedish as *(myr)slogbod*, denotes a structure somewhat similar to a bus stop shelter used during activities in remote places such as hunting, fishing and hay-harvesting.

a. *Oðrą   ir   ljuätam-es.*
   other.DEF.F.SG be.PRS evil.DEF.M.DAT-POSS

   'The other one belongs to the Evil One.'

b. *Ermkläd ir   dumbun-es.*
   scarf.DEF be.PRS dumb.DEF.F.DAT-POSS

   'The scarf belongs to the deaf-and-dumb woman.'[7]

c. *Eð ir   ingumdier-es   stjäl min.*
   it be.PRS neither.DAT.M.SG-POSS reason with

   'There is no reason for either one.'

It seems that there is a recent increase in the frequency of the *-es* construction in modern Elfdalian, which is most probably due to it being seen as the closest equivalent of the Swedish *s*-genitive. An interesting phenomenon in this connection is the tendency for native speakers to make *es* a separate word in written Elfdalian (or sometimes hyphenated, as in *bil-es stor* 'uncle's walking-stick'). Perhaps most strikingly, *es* is even used after a preceding vowel, although, due to extensive apocope, hiatus is not a common phenomenon in Elfdalian. Consider a proper name such as *Anna*, for which Levander gives the dative form *Anno* and the "genitive" *Annes*, the latter being the logical outcome of apocopating the dative form before *-es*. In modern Elfdalian, however, proper names in *-a* are normally treated as undeclinable and are shielded against apocope. Thus 'Anna's book' comes out as *Anna es buäk*.

The tendencies mentioned in the previous paragraph come out very clearly in one of the few longer texts written in Elfdalian, [S21], where the complex dative construction is the most frequent way of expressing nominal possession, and *es* is fairly consistently written separately. There are several examples where the preceding noun ends in a vowel such as *Kung Gösta es dågå* 'King Gösta's days' and *Sparre es klauter* 'Sparre's clothes'. Whereas proper names are generally not case-marked, most definite possessor nouns are in the dative, but there are also examples of nominative possessor preceding *es*. ([S21] is on the whole heavily influenced by Swedish – there are also a fair number of literal transfers of *s*-genitives, such as *Luthers katitsies* 'Luther's catechesis'.) Compare (29), where the nominative form *prestsaida* 'the clergy side' is used rather than the dative *prestsaidun*:

---

[7] The feminine ending of the adjective indicates that the referent is a woman.

(29) Elfdalian (Ovansiljan)

Nu war ed prestsaida es tur at tytts at
now be.PST it **clergy-side**.DEF POSS **turn** INFM think.INF that
muotstonderer språked um nǫd eller eld ed dier
adversary.DEF.PL speak.PST about something other than it they
uld tag stellning ad ǫ stemmun.
shall.PST take.INF position to on meeting.DEF.DAT

'Now it was the turn of the clergy side to think that the adversaries were talking about something other than what should be decided at the meeting.'

The construction *eð ir NP es tur at V-inf* 'it is NP's turn to V' is calqued quite directly on the corresponding Swedish construction *det är NPs tur att V-inf*, but seems to have been firmly entrenched in Elfdalian for quite some time. Compare the following example from a speaker born in the 1850's:

(30) Elfdalian (Ovansiljan)

...å se vart ed bumuǎr es tur tä tag riäd
and then become.PST it **shieling hostess** POSS **turn** to take.INF care
o mjotsin da gesslkallär ad fer ad
about milk.DEF.DAT when herder_boy.PL have.PST go.SUP to
raisǫ.
forest.DEF.DAT

'...and then it was the shieling hostess's turn to take care of the milk when the herder boys had gone to the woods.' [S16]

Here, however, the noun form *bumuǎr* 'shieling hostess' is ambiguous between nominative and dative. Notice also that whereas the infinitive marker in (29) is the Swedish-inspired *at*, (30) has the more genuine Elfdalian *tä* (see §6.5.2).

Much of what has been said about the Elfdalian construction carries over to other Ovansiljan varieties. According to Levander (1928: 170), "definite genitive forms" formed by adding a suffix to the definite dative singular are found in most Dalecarlian varieties where the dative is preserved. In Ovansiljan (except Orsa) and Nedansiljan, the suffix is *-s* preceded by some vowel whose quality varies between *e, å, ä, a,* and *ô*. In Västerdalarna and Orsa, the suffix is simply *-s*, except in Äppelbo, where it is *-säs*. Examples can also be found in modern texts. Consider the following example from Mora:

(31) Östnor-seljamål (Ovansiljan)

*Welsignarn e   an så   kum   i **Ärram-ås**   **nammen!***
blessed   be.PRS he who come.PRS in Lord.DEF.DAT-POSS name

'Blessed is he who comes in the name of the Lord!' (Matthew 21:9) [S20]

In *Ärram-ås*, the suffix -*ås* has been added to the definite dative form *Ärram*. In texts from other villages, however, -*ås* is also sometimes added to the nominative:

(32) Utmeland, Mora (Ovansiljan)

*Då   stod   **Ärran-ås**   **angel** framåmin   dem...*
then stand.PST Lord.DEF-POSS angel in_front_of they.OBL

'And then the angel of the Lord stood before them...' (Luke 2:9) [S20]

In the following example, the suffix is added to a postposed possessive pronoun:

(33) Önamål (Ovansiljan)

*Wennfe si   du twårpär i **bror**   **denås**   **öga...***
why   see.PRS you speck.PL in **brother** your-POSS eye

'And why do you see specks in your brother's eye...' (Matt. 7:3) [S20]

In other village varieties in Mora, the possessive pronoun is preposed and we get *den brorås*.

In Sollerön, according to Andersson & Danielsson (1999: 357), the suffix -*as* is added to the dative, or in modern varieties of the vernacular, to the nominative: *donda kallimas kelingg* or *donda kallnas kelingg* 'that man's wife'. Proper names in -*a* such as *Anna* have genitive forms such as *Annonas* (but in a questionnaire from Sollerön *Annaas* is given as an alternative).

There is also some sporadic evidence of similar constructions outside of Dalecarlian. Thus, Larsson (1929: 124) quotes an unpublished description of the vernacular of Byske (Northern Westrobothnian), Lundberg (n.y.), as mentioning "a genitive with an *s* added to the dative form, in the same way as in Dalecarlian", e.g. *pajkoms* 'the boy's, the boys'', *sanoms* 'the son's', *sönjoms* 'the sons'', *kooms* 'the cow's, the cows', but claims that no such form has been attested by later researchers (including himself). However, Larsson adds: when questioned directly, informants confirm that *s* can added to dative of masculines "in independent position", e.g. *he jer gobboms* 'it is the old man's'.

Hellbom (1961: 126) quotes Larsson and says that "similar constructions seem to have existed also in Medelpad, above all when a preposition precedes the genitive".[8] Medelpad is otherwise an area where the dative had already virtually disappeared at the end of the 19th century. Hellbom's first example is from Njurunda, his own native parish. The text, however, was already written down in 1874:

(34) Njurunda (Medelpadian)
 *Hæ var   en   tå **ryssôm-s**   **vaktknekter** sôm hadde*
 it be.PST one of Russian.PL.DAT-POSS sentinel.PL   who have.PST
 sômne   åv å låg å snarke.
 fall_asleep.SUP off and lie.PST and snore.PST

 'It was one of the Russians' sentinels who had fallen asleep and lay snoring.' [S38]

Here, there is indeed a dative-governing preposition before the possessive construction. If this were an isolated example, we would probably interpret the form *ryssôms* as resulting from a confusion of two syntactic structures. (Delsing (2003b: 38) mentions (34) as an example of a "group genitive", which, however, presupposes the less likely interpretation 'a sentinel of one of the Russians' rather than 'one of the Russians' sentinels'.)

 Hellbom (ibid.) quotes an unpublished note by Karl-Hampus Dahlstedt to the effect that some people in the parish of Indal in the province of Medelpad used the form *bånôms* in the genitive plural of *bån* 'child'. He also enumerates a few examples of forms where the genitive *-s* is added to what looks like an oblique form of a weak noun, which at older stages of the language was ambiguous between genitive, dative, and accusative: *fårsjinnpälsa gubbas* 'the old man's sheep fur coat'; *gu'bbass bökksan* 'the old man's trousers'; *ti gu'bbass kammarn* 'to the old man's chamber'. His final example, however, is somewhat more spectacular,[9] in that it appears to exemplify the addition of the genitive *-s* as a phrasal clitic to an NP in the dative.

(35) Stöde (Medelpadian)
 *in   par   jänter   ... som fôdde   mä   på **fara***
 INDF couple girl.PL.DAT   who follow.PST with on **father.DAT**
 senne-   -s joLsättning
 their.REFL.DAT POSS funeral

 '...a couple of girls ... who took part in their father's funeral.' [S15]

---

[8] "Likartade bildningar ser ut att ha förekommit även i Medelpad, främst då när en prep. föregått genitiven."
[9] "Slutligen ett mera tillspetsat belägg från Stöde 1877"

Genitive forms where the -*s* is added to an oblique form of a weak noun are quite common in Medieval Scandinavian. (Recall that weak masculine nouns had a single form for genitive, dative and accusative in the singular.) A form such as *bondans* 'the farmer's' is actually fairly straightforwardly derivable from something like *bonda hins*. In other forms, we have to assume an extension by analogy of this formation, as in *kirkionnes* 'of the church' instead of the older *kirkionnar* (Wessén (1968: I:143)). The Medelpadian *gubbas* could be interpreted in the same way, although it might perhaps also be derivable from an older *gubbans*. A genitive ending -*as* is in fact found in various vernaculars. In Vätö (Uppland), as described by Schagerström (1882), weak stem proper names take the endings -*as* (masc.) and -*ôs* (fem.). In Ostrobothnian, -*as* as a genitive ending can be added to the definite form of masculine common nouns, such as *rävinas* 'of the fox' and *varjinas* 'of the wolf'. This is a more radical extension than what we find in Vätö, since in these forms there is no historical motivation for the *a* vowel. In these cases, on the other hand, there is no connection to the dative case, which has been wholly lost in Ostrobothnian. However, there is an intriguing parallel to the Dalecarlian construction. Eriksson & Rendahl (1999: 43) found a variation among their Ostrobothnian informants between -*s* and -*as* as a genitive or possessive marker, with a possible concentration of -*as* in the southern part of the province. The general pattern was for the -*as* marker: possessor noun + -*as* + possessee + definite suffix. In two of the examples in the questionnaire, the possessor noun was the proper name *Anna*. Here, "the informants felt forced to mark an orthographic boundary", yielding spellings such as *Anna'as haanden* 'Anna's hand' and *Anna as gamlest systren* 'Anna's eldest sister', which closely parallel the Elfdalian forms quoted above (except for the definite form of the head noun).

In his discussion of the confusion between the dative and the genitive in Medieval Norwegian, Larsen (1895) mentions a few examples which look like complex dative possessives, for instance in this document from Rendalen in 1546:

(36) Rendalen (Hedmark, Norway, 16th century)
...med ...   *theyriss*   **bondomss** *Karls*   *Jonsszon*
...with their **husband.DAT.PL-POSS** Karl.GEN   Jonsszon
Engilbrictz   Asmarsszon oc Trondz   Eyriksszon oc theyriss
Engilbrict.GEN Asmarsszon and Trond.GEN Eyriksszon and their
barnomss   *godom*   *vilie...*
child.DAT.PL-POSS good.DAT.SG.M will..

'...with the good will of their husbands Karl Jonsson Engelbrikt Asmarsson and Trond Eyriksson and their children...'

In addition, he mentions that in the Norwegian Solør vernaculars where the dative is still preserved, the construction *for NP's skull* 'for NP's sake' commonly employs genitives formed from the dative, as in *for gutas (jintns, bånis, ongoms) skull* 'for the boy's (girl's, child's, kids') sake'.

Returning to the complex dative possessive in Elfdalian, we can see that it has a number of specific properties: (i) there is a general syllabic marker *(-)es*; (ii) the marker is combined with a dative form of the possessor; (iii) the marker has the character of a clitic added to a full noun phrase rather than an affix added to a noun. The last point is supported by the following facts: (a) modifiers of the possessor NP are in the dative (at least in more conservative forms of the language); (b) the vowel of the marker is not elided after nouns ending in vowels; (c) the marker is placed on the last word of an NP rather than on the head noun; and (d) native speakers tend to write the marker as a separate word. In the Peripheral Swedish area outside Dalecarlian, we find sporadic examples of possessive constructions that share some of these properties but hardly any that have all of them. In fact, with respect to (iii) there are also parallels with the *s*-genitive of Central Scandinavian and English.

What can we say about the possible evolution of the complex dative construction?

The geographically quite dispersed although sporadic and rather heterogeneous manifestations suggest that the construction was more widespread earlier. It is likely that the general demise of the dative has made it either disappear or be transformed. We may note that the examples from modern Elfdalian suggest that *(-)es* now tends to be added to a noun phrase that has no case-marking, and that is also the case for the Ostrobothnian examples. It is also possible that the tendency to treat *es* as a clitic with no influence on the form of the previous word is a relatively recent phenomenon in Elfdalian.

The most natural approach to the genesis of the complex dative construction would *prima facie* be to try and explain it as a result of a development similar to that described for the *s*-genitive by e.g. Norde (1997), that is, by a "degrammaticaliz⟨⟩ of the genitive *s*-ending of early Scandinavian. After the introduction of suffixed articles, the *s*-ending was found in indefinite masculine and neuter singular strong nouns and in all definite masculine and neuter singulars. Later on, it spread to other paradigms, and was then typically grafted on to the old genitive forms. If these were non-distinct or similar to the dative forms, it is possible that they were reanalyzed as such, which could have triggered a generalization of the pattern dative + *s*-ending. Such a hypothesis is not unproblematic, however. If we suppose that the source of the Elfdalian *uksa-m-es* 'of the ox' is a medieval

Scandinavian form such as *oksa-ns* 'ox.DEF.GEN.SG', we have to assume that the apparent dative form of the stem would trigger the choice of a dative definite suffix, and we also have to explain where the vowel in the suffix comes from.

One peculiar circumstance around the complex dative possessive is that its functional load was apparently rather small in the pre-modern vernaculars where it existed. We have seen that there are only very sporadic examples from the Norrlandic dialects, and even in Elfdalian around 1900 it was, according to Levander (1909: 98-99), "rare",[10] the simple dative possessive being the preferred alternative (On the other hand, this claim is in a way contradicted by the fact that Levander himself provides no fewer than 17 examples of the complex dative construction in his grammar.)

Why was it, then, kept in the language at all? One possible explanation is that the complex dative possessive had a specialized function. Something that speaks in favour of this is that a surprisingly large number of the examples quoted in the literature from older stages of the vernaculars displays the possessive NP in predicate position. This goes for the only example that Larsson quotes as still acceptable to his informants from Byske in Västerbotten, and out of Levander's 17 examples, 12 directly follow a copula. It is also striking that ten of these are headless – which parallels Larsson's claim that the complex dative construction is allowable "in independent position". We might thus hypothesize that the complex dative possessive developed as an alternative to the simple dative possessive primarily in predicate position and/or when used without a head noun.

If we look around in the Germanic world, the constructions discussed in this section are not without their parallels. Consider the following examples:

(37)   Middle English (13th century)
    *of Seth ðe   was **Adam is   sune***
    of Seth who be.PST **Adam POSS son**

    'of Seth, who was Adam's son' [S3]

(38)   Middle Dutch
    Grote   Kaerle   sijn soon
    Great.DAT Charles.DAT his son

    'great Charles' son'

---

[10] "Bestämd genitiv är likaledes sällsynt..."

(39)   Dutch
       Jan z'n   boek
       Jan POSS book
       'Jan's book'

(40)   Afrikaans
       Marie se   boek
       Mary POSS book
       'Marie's book' ((38)-(40) quoted from Norde 1997: 56)

Following Koptjevskaja-Tamm (2003), we can call these constructions LINKING PRONOUN POSSESSIVES. In the most elaborated type, exemplified here by Middle Dutch, they contain a possessive pronoun between the case-marked possessor noun phrase and the head noun. In the Middle Dutch example (38), the possessor noun is in the dative case,[11] as it is in the following Modern German title of a best-selling book on German grammar (Sick 2004):

(41)   German
       *Der   Dativ ist   **dem   Genitiv sein***
       DEF.M.SG.NOM dative be.PRS DEF.M.SG.DAT genitive POSS.M.SG.NOM
       Tod
       death
       'The dative is the death of the genitive.'

However, genitive possessor nouns are also attested in Middle Dutch/Low German:

(42)   Middle Dutch
       alle des   konincks sijn landen
       all DEF.M.GEN king.GEN his land.PL
       'all the king's lands' (Norde 1997: 58)

In Germanic varieties where the dative case is no longer alive, e.g. Middle English, Modern Dutch and Afrikaans, the possessor NP in linking pronoun possessives has no case marking (cf. (37)-(41)). In Afrikaans, we can also see that the linking morpheme *se* has been differentiated in form from the masculine possessive *sy* and has been generalized also to feminines (and plurals).

---

[11] This analysis is questioned in Allen (2008).

In Scandinavian languages, there are at least two types of linking pronoun constructions. One involves non-reflexive possessive pronouns and was apparently quite common in written Danish from the Late Middle Age on (Knudsen 1941: 61): *Graamand hans vrede* 'Gramand's wrath'; *en enkkæ hennes søn* 'a widow's son'. This construction is now only marginally possible in bureaucratic style (Modern Norwegian: *Oasen Grillbar Dets Konkursbo* 'the insolvent estate of the grill bar *Oasen*' (Internet)). The construction was often used in cases where a group genitive might be expected in the modern Central Scandinavian, such as *prestens i Midian hans queg* 'the priest in Midian's cattle' (16th century Bible translation). As the last example illustrates, the head noun could also be genitive-marked (according to Knudsen this was relatively uncommon, however). The construction still exists in Jutland, "in particular northern Jutish" (Knudsen 1941: 62: *æ skrædder hans hus* 'the tailor's house').

The second Scandinavian linking pronoun construction is found in Norwegian (at least originally predominantly in western and northern varieties) and involves reflexive linking pronouns:

(43) Norwegian
      mannen sin   hatt
      man.DEF POSS.REFL.3SG hat
      'the man's hat'

This construction is generally assumed to have arisen under German influence and is therefore traditionally called "garpegenitiv", *garp* being a derogatory term for 'German'.

Typological parallels to the Germanic linking pronoun possessives are found, for example, in Ossetian (Iranian; Koptjevskaja-Tamm 2003: 669). One could also see them as the analytic analogue to possessive constructions in which a possessive affix on the head noun agrees with the possessor noun phrase, as in Hungarian:

(44) Hungarian
      a   szomszéd kert-je
      DEF neighbour garden-3SG.POSS
      'the neighbour's garden' (Koptjevskaja-Tamm 2003: 648)

The Germanic linking pronoun possessive constructions are controversial, both with respect to their origin and their possible role in the history of the *s*-genitive. They could have originated, as claimed by some scholars, from a reanalysis of an indirect object construction (Behaghel 1923: 638), such as:

(45) German

> *Er hat*   ***meinem***   ***Vater*** *seinen*   *Hut genommen.*
> he have.PRS my.DAT.M.SG father *his.ACC.M.SG* hat take.PP
> 'He has taken from my father his hat.'?'he has taken my father's hat.'

Some Dutch scholars, quoted by Norde (1997: 58), have suggested that the linking pronoun is a "pleonastic addition", added for clarity. For Middle English, a common view is that the linking pronoun *(h)is* is actually a reanalysis of the old genitive ending.

Independently of what the origin of the linker is, it may or may not have played a role in the development of the English *s*-genitive (Janda 1980). The reanalysis of the *s*-ending as a pronoun could have facilitated the rise of group genitives, where the possessive marker was placed at the end of the noun phrase. Norde (1997: 91) comments on this hypothesis as follows: "Even though this may seem to be a plausible scenario for English, it should be borne in mind that the emergence of the Swedish *s*-genitive was not mediated by RPP's [linking pronoun constructions]." Her argument for this is that (i) there was no homonymy between -*s* and the possessive pronouns in Swedish, and (ii) "there are no indications that RPP-constructions were ever relevant in Swedish". Although the latter claim is true of Standard Swedish, it is, as we have seen, not true of Scandinavian as a whole. In particular, it is not true of Danish, which has probably provided the model for the Swedish *s*-genitive. Nor is it necessarily true of the Peripheral Swedish varieties, where homonymy between a possessive and a genitive ending is far from excluded. In Elfdalian, there are two forms of the 3rd person masculine singular possessive pronoun: *onumes* and *os*. The former is analogous to what we find with lexical possessors in the complex dative construction: it consists of the dative pronoun *onum* and the possessive marker -*es*. The latter – *os* – has developed out of the old genitive form *hans* 'his'. In other Ovansiljan varieties, the shorter forms of the possessive pronouns seem to have been replaced by the longer ones. However, as has already been mentioned, the quality of the vowel in the possessive marker is highly variable and at times must have been identical to what was found in the short possessive pronoun (when it still existed). This would give the Dalecarlian complex dative possessives the same make-up as the linking pronoun constructions in German and Middle Dutch.

As we have seen, the origin of the linking pronoun constructions in the West Germanic languages is disputed. Still, the documentation of the medieval stages of these languages is much better than that of the corresponding period of Dalecarlian and other Peripheral Swedish varieties. This fact makes it rather doubtful whether we shall ever be able to find out the details of the early history of the complex dative possessive in Scandinavian. It is not unlikely, however, that its origin involves more than one source – probably both re-interpreted oblique forms of nouns and linking pronoun constructions have played a role.

5.5 "H-genitive"

Following Delsing (2003a), I shall use the label 'h-genitive' for the pronominal periphrasis construction *huset hans Per* '(lit.) the-house his Per'. This construction is superficially somewhat similar to the linking pronoun constructions discussed in §5.4.2, and it may not be out of place to point to the major difference between them: although both involve pronouns in the middle, the order of the lexical parts is the opposite: the h-genitive has the structure possessee – pronoun – possessor, the linking pronoun constructions possessor – pronoun – possessee.

An account of the geographical distribution of the h-genitive in Norway, Sweden and Iceland is given in Delsing (2003b: 34). The Scandinavian h-genitive area can be conveniently divided into four zones, in which the construction has somewhat different properties:

1. Iceland

2. Norway (excluding a few areas in the south)

3. an inland zone in Sweden comprising parts of Jämtland and Medelpad, Härjedalen, Västerdalarna and probably also the previous Norwegian parishes Särna and Idre, and parts of Värmland

4. a coastal zone in Sweden comprising the provinces of Västerbotten and Norrbotten (but excluding Lapland).

It may be noted that the two Swedish zones are non-contiguous: there seem to be no examples of the construction in the intermediate area: eastern Jämtland, Ångermanland and southern Lapland.

The pronoun that precedes the possessor noun in h-genitive looks like a prepropial article, and the geographical distributions of these two phenomena are also very similar. However, as Delsing (2003a: 67) notes, there are discrepancies: prepropial articles are used in the area between the inland and the coastal h-genitive zones, and there are certain parts of Norway (the inner parts of Agder and Western Telemark) where h-genitives occur without there being any prepropial articles. Furthermore, in the Northern Västerbotten dialect area, the h-genitive is also possible with common nouns such as *saitjen hansj hannlaråm* 'the shop-owner's sack' (Skelletmål, Marklund 1976: 23). Here, the possessor noun is in the dative, a fact that I shall return to below. In addition, as noted in Holmberg & Sandström (2003), there are also attested examples from the same area where a possessive pronoun and a preproprial article are combined. Thus, in the Cat Corpus we find the following:

(46) Skelletmål (Northern Westrobothnian)
*Kattkalln   begrifft   att händäna var   **kelinga håns n***
tomcat.DEF understand.PRET that that   be.PST wife.DEF his   PDA.M
Alfre.
Alfred
'Cat understood that that was Alfred's wife.' (Cat Corpus)

Dahlstedt (1971: 51) quotes several examples from Sara Lidman's novel *Tjärdalen:*[12]

(47) a. *golvet hans n'   Jonas*
floor his   PDA.M Jesus
'Jonas' floor' [S23]

b. *bokhyllan   hans n'   Petrus*
bookshelf.DEF his   PDA.M Petrus
'Petrus' bookshelf' [S23]

c. *tjärdalen hans n'   Nisj*
tar_pile his   PDA.M Nisj
'Nils's tar pile' [S23]

Similar cases are also found in Norrbothnian and Southern Westrobothnian. Thus for Pitemål, Brännström (1993) gives examples like the following as the major way of expressing possessive constructions:

(48) Pitemål

a. *båoka   haNs en   Erik*
book.DEF his   PDA.M Erik
'Erik's book'

---

[12] In Dahlstedt's opinion, however, these examples represent "an unequivocal hyperdialectism without support in the spoken vernacular" ("en otvetydig dialektism utan stöd i det talade folkmålet"). This conclusion, which he bases on a term paper by a native speaker of Northern Westrobothnian, seems somewhat rash, given the quite numerous attestations of the construction in question. Also, "hyperdialectisms" do not seem to be characteristic of Sara Lidman's work.

b. *lärjunga   haNs en   Jesus*
disciple.DEF.PL his   PDA.M Jesus
'the disciples of Jesus'

The Cat Corpus provides us with an example also from Southern Westrobothnian:

(49) Sävar (Southern Westrobothnian)
Kattgöbben församst,   att   hanna va   källinga hansch 'n
tomcat.DEF understand.PST that DEM   be.PST wife.DEF his   PDA.M
Allfre.
Alfred.
'Cat understood that this was Alfred's wife.' (Cat Corpus)

Apparently, in these varieties, the possessive pronoun can be combined with a complete noun phrase rather than with a bare proper name. It may be concluded that the analysis of the *h*-genitive as consisting of a head noun followed by a proper name with a preproprial article is not correct for Västerbotten. Delsing draws the conclusion that the preproprial article analysis of the *h*-genitive is generally inadequate and proposes that it instead involves an "ordinary possessive pronoun", amenable to a unified analysis for all *h*-genitives within generative syntax. Koptjevskaja-Tamm (2003) also questions the applicability of the preproprial article analysis, at least for some Norwegian and Swedish dialects where the pronouns showing up in the *h*-genitives "have become analytic construction markers".

It seems relevant here that one of the competitors of the *h*-genitive in the coastal zone is the dative possessive construction (see §5.4). In many cases the two constructions will differ only in the form of the pronoun: cf. Skelletmål examples in Marklund (1976): *kæppa n'Greta* 'Greta's coat' (dative possessive) vs. *kLänninga hännasj Lina* 'Lina's dress' (*h*-genitive), or Överkalix *sjåongmaːLe henars/n/en Anna* 'Anna's voice' (Källskog 1992: 153). Also in this connection, notice examples like the following from Larsson (1929: 125), *bökjsen n Nikkje* 'Nicke's trousers' and *strompen a Greta* 'Greta's stockings', where the pronouns are in the nominative, and where Larsson also gives the alternatives *bökjsen hansj Nikkje* and *strompen hannasj Greta*.

It would not be too amazing if the two constructions tended to be confused, especially in a situation where the vernacular in general becomes unstable. Such a confusion is arguably found in the above quoted Skelletmål example *saitjen hansj hannlaråm* 'the shop-owner's sack', which differs from the "normal" *h*-genitive in at least two ways: the possessor is not a proper name but a common noun, and in addition this noun is in the dative case. Marklund (1976: 23) says that dative marking on the noun is "usually" present in this construction, other examples being

(50)   Skelletmål (Northern Westrobothnian)

    a. *vävsjea hännasj mo'rrmon*
       reed   her   granny.DAT
       'Granny's reed'

    b. *bökkreN   däres skolbâNåm*
       book.DEF.PL their school-child.DEF.PL.DAT
       'the books of the school-children'

Similar examples are *i galar* 'on Grandfather's farm', in a text from Burträsk quoted in Wessén (1966: 104), and *hemme hannasj mormorn* 'Granny's home', quoted as Westrobothnian without specification of the location by Larsson (1929: 131). We may see the rise of the mixed construction as a special case of the more general process (hinted at in the quotation from Koptjevskaja-Tamm 2003 by which the pronoun becomes gradually detached from the possessor NP and is reinterpreted as a marker of the possessive construction. The arguments for treating the pronoun in the *h*-genitive as a preproprial article seem to be strongest for Icelandic, where the pronoun and the following noun both take the genitive case: *húsið hans Péturs* 'Peter's house', and the possessor noun phrase can also be interpreted as an associative plural, if the pronoun is in the plural: *húsið þeirra Jóns* 'Jon and his family's house' (Delsing 2003a: 69). This (as Koptjevskaja-Tamm 2003: 632 suggests) can be seen as indicating that Icelandic represents an early stage in the development of the construction, and that the first step towards the dissociation of the pronoun from the possessor NP comes when the genitive marking is lost, as has happened in all mainland Scandinavian dialects. The coastal zone vernaculars would then represent a further developmental stage, which, however, seems rather unstable. Thus, the dative marking is disappearing with the general deterioration of that case. The following example from the Cat Corpus is from the same vernacular as (50a), and the grammatical construction is identical, except for the form of the possessor noun (here a definite unmarked for case):

(51) Skelletmål (Northern Westrobothnian)

leill-vegän   hännärs Mormora
little_road.DEF her   Granny.DEF

'Granny's little road'

The final stage in the transition from preproprial article to possessive construction marker is possibly seen in the following Cat Corpus example from the South Westrobothnian Sävar vernacular: *lill-vegen hansch Mormora* 'Granny's little road', where a masculine pronoun is combined with a female kin term. A parallel to this is found in Romanian (Koptjevskaja-Tamm 2003: 632), where the masculine pronoun *lui* is also used with feminine nouns, as in the example *casa lui Mary* 'Mary's house'.

What has been said so far applies to the coastal *h*-genitive zone (Westrobothnian and Norrbothnian). The inland vernaculars where the *h*-genitive is found, on the other hand, have chosen a rather different route. Here, we do not find double pronouns or an extension to common nouns. Instead, there has been a differentiation between the pronoun used in the *h*-genitive and 3rd person genitive pronouns used independently. In most Scandinavian vernaculars, the feminine possessive pronoun has taken on the -*s* ending originally characteristic only of the masculine *hans*. We thus find forms such as *hännärs* which was quoted above from Skelletmål. This has also happened in the inland vernaculars, but only when the pronoun is used by itself, not in the *h*-genitive construction. We thus get different forms in sentence pairs such as the following example from the Cat Corpus (Västhärjedalen):[13]

(52) Ljusnedal (Härjedalian)

a. ... *ô   kahtta   hadde   håhppâ ohppi **knea**   **hinnjis**.*
    and cat.DEF have.PST jump.SUP up   in   **knee.DEF her**

    '...and the cat had jumped up on her lap.' (Cat Corpus)

b. *Ho håhppâ   ohpp i **knea**   hinnji   mor.*
   she jump.PST up   in **knee.DEF PDA.F.GEN** mother

   'She [the cat] jumped up on Granny's lap.' (Cat Corpus)

For Malung (Västerdalarna), Levander (1925: 2:211) gives the form *hännäsäs* for 'her' – in the *h*-genitive construction, however, the form is *in*:

---

[13] The same for Tännäs (Härjedalian) (Olofsson 1999: 22).

(53)   Malung (Västerdalarna)

    *O   hôpp   ôpp ô   sätt   sä'   ti **knenon**   in   Mormor.*

    she jump.PST up and set.PST REFL in **knee.DEF.PL PDA.F.GEN mother**

    'She jumped up and sat on Granny's lap.' (Cat Corpus)

For Hammerdal (Jamtska), Reinhammar (2005) gives *en* as the form used in the *h*-genitive construction, and in Lit (Jamtska), we get *pyne sängâ n Momma* 'under Granny's bed' (Cat Corpus). This means that in the inland area, the pronoun used with feminine names in the *h*-genitive is identical to the preproprial dative pronoun, rather than to the independent genitive pronoun. (However, in the older text [S11] from Kall (Jamtska), we find the form *henn* in *rättuheita henn mor* 'Mother's rights' as opposed to both the independent possessive pronoun *hennes*, as in *bröran hennes* 'her brothers', and the preproprial dative *'n*, as in *i la ma 'n mor* 'together with mother'.) The masculine pronoun in the *h*-genitive construction, on the other hand, is unmistakably genitive, although it may also differ from the independent genitive. Thus, in Malung (Västerdalarna), we get *as* in the *h*-genitive – a straightforward development of the original *hans* – whereas the independent pronoun is *honômäs* – an expansion of the original dative form. In other places, the forms are identical (e.g. *hans* in Lit (Jamtska), *hâns* in Hammerdal (Jamtska)).

We thus find that the arguments for rejecting the preproprial article analysis of the *h*-genitive do not work very well for the inland zone. It may still be the case that a unified analysis of the *h*-genitive is possible, as Delsing proposes. On the other hand, there is much to suggest that preproprial articles are the diachronic source of the *h*-genitive, and it is not clear if the idea of a gradual movement away from that source is compatible with a unified synchronic analysis.

5.6   Prepositional constructions

Adnominal possession is frequently expressed by adpositional constructions – English *of* is a well-known example. Our interest here will be focused on those constructions which have grammaticalized far enough to be able to function more generally as possessives rather than being restricted to a certain class of head nouns. As noted by Delsing (2003b: 43), Standard Danish and Swedish lack prepositional constructions that can be used with non-relational nouns ("alienable possession") to say things like 'John's car' – here, the *s*-genitive is the only option. In many other Scandinavian varieties such prepositional constructions exist. In Standard Bokmål Norwegian, *til* is the most common preposition used:

boka til Per 'Per's book'. In Nynorsk Norwegian and various Norwegian dialects, an alternative is *åt* (Faarlund, Lie & Vannebo 1997: 263), Delsing (2003b: 43), which is a cognate of the English *at* – this preposition is also used in parts of the Peripheral Swedish area to form a periphrastic adnominal possessive construction, as in the title of the Cat story in the Lit (Jamtska) vernacular: *Fresn at a Momma* 'Granny's cat'. More generally in the Peripheral Swedish area, however, the same preposition is found in what is arguably an external possessor construction, plausibly representing an earlier stage in the evolution of the construction. I shall therefore discuss the external possessor construction first, but before doing so, I shall say a few words about the preposition *at* as such, since it has a rather interesting history of its own.

In Written Medieval Swedish, as well as in other earlier forms of Scandinavian, the preposition *at* could be used similarly to its English cognate, e.g. *aat kirkio* 'at church', but it also had several other uses (Söderwall 1884). Frequently, it indicated 'direction', as in

(54) Written Medieval Swedish
  *...for   han stragx   **ath danmark** j gen*
  ...go.PST he   at_once **to   Denmark** again
  '...he went at once to Denmark again.' [S13]

It could also signal 'beneficient' or 'path':

(55) Written Medieval Swedish

  a. *...göra   brullöp   **aat sinom**   son iohanni...*
    make.INF wedding **for** POSS.3SG.REFL.DAT.M.SG son Johan.DAT
    '...arrange a wedding for his son Johan.' [S13]

  b. *Þe   þär   fram foro   **at   väghenom.***
    they there forth go.PST.PL **along** road.DEF.DAT
    'They went along the road.' [S8]

In the modern Central Scandinavian languages, the prepositions descending from *at* in general have much narrower ranges of meaning. In Danish, *ad* mainly seems to be used in the 'path' meaning and as part of verb collocations such as *le ad* 'laugh at'. In Norwegian, *åt* is fairly marginal – some Bokmål dictionaries do not even list it. In Nynorsk, it appears to have more or less the same range as in Swedish, although it is rather infrequent. In Swedish, both the locational and the directional uses have more or less disappeared; instead the beneficiary use has expanded and *åt* is now commonly used as the head of an analytic counterpart to indirect objects with verbs of giving. This goes also for most vernaculars, although the directional use is preserved in at least parts of Ovansiljan and in Nyland and Åboland.

The form of the descendants of Old Nordic *at* also shows variation, with a somewhat unexpected geographical pattern. The vowel was originally a short *a*, which should not have changed in the standard languages, under normal circumstances. However, already in the medieval period, a "secondary prolongation" (Hellquist 1922: 1204) took place in Swedish and at least some forms of Norwegian. The long *a* then developed into *å*, in the Scandinavian Vowel Shift. What is peculiar here is that some Swedish varieties which otherwise took part in the *ā* > *å* shift seem to have missed out on the prolongation, and thus preserve the original short *a* in *at*. Such forms, to judge from the Cat Corpus, are predominant in the Dalecarlian area and in Jämtland and Hälsingland. (It may be noted that Jämtland does not follow the neighbouring Trøndelag here.) A hybrid form *ått* is found in Sävar (Southern Westrobothnian) and Åsele (Angermannian).

As a regular counterpart of Swedish *s*-genitive, the *at* construction is found most systematically in three of the Cat Corpus texts, viz. Åsele (Angermannian), Lit (Jamtska), and Junsele (Angermannian). The Lit text is the only one where the *at* construction shows up in the title of the Cat story, although *Fresn at a Momma* 'Granny's cat', quoted above, does not display the traditional dative form *n* of the preproprial article exemplified in the following example from the same text:

(56) Lit (Jamtska)
*...han skull   sväng   ta på lillvein   **at   n   Momma.***
...he   shall.PST turn.INF off on little_road.DEF POSS PDA.F.DAT Granny
'...he was going to turn into Granny's little road.'

In this corpus sentence, all three vernaculars mentioned use the *at* construction, as they also do in the following sentence:

(57) Junsele (Angermannian)
*Katta   begrep   att ä dänne va   **käringa åt'n***
Cat.DEF understand.PST that it there be.PST wife.DEF POSS-PDA.M
Alfred.
Alfred
'Cat understood that this was Alfred's wife.'

Here, the construction is also found in the text from Luleå:

(58) Lulemål

    *Kätta   förstöo   att hein vär   freo   **att n'   Alfri.***

    Cat.DEF understand.PST that this be.PST wife.DEF POSS PDA.M Alfred

    'Cat understood that this was Alfred's wife.'

In transcribed texts from Hössjö village in Umeå parish, we find several examples, thus:

(59) Hössjö (Southern Westrobothnian)

  a. *Hä va   n'   syster **åt   mamma min** som var   här i*
     it be.PST PDA.F sister POSS **mother   my**   who be.PST here in

     *Hössjö å   **en** syster åt   n'Ol   Orssa å   n'Anners   Orssa.*
     Hössjö and INDF sister POSS PDA.Ol Orssa and PDA.Anners Orssa

     'It was the sister of my mother who was here in Hössjö and a sister of Ol Orssa and Anners Orssa.' [S44]

  b. *Hä va   ju   **n'   doter   åt   mormora.***
     it be.PST PRAG PDA.F **daughter POSS Granny.DEF**

     'It was Granny's daughter.' [S44]

We thus have examples from Jämtland, Norrbothnian, the Angermannian dialect area, and Southern Westrobothnian. Delsing (2003b: 44) quotes examples from earlier descriptions of vernaculars from Västerbotten, Jämtland, Medelpad, and Värmland and text examples from Västerbotten, Medelpad, Jämtland, Hälsingland, and Värmland, but refers to the text examples as "sporadic".[14] This probably gives too bleak a picture of the strength of the construction. Hedblom (1978: 61)[15] says about Hälsingland that "the genitive is often expressed by a preposition in the older dialect", and gives the examples *mo´r at Gus´tav* 'Gustav's mother' and *bins´lene at ju´rene* 'the fastenings of the animals'. Källskog (1992: 157) says that in Överkalix *at* is common as a "paraphrase of the genitive concept, in particular with expressions denoting kinship".

Most of the ones quoted here seem to involve kin terms as head nouns. Bergholm, Linder & Yttergren (1999) are skeptical towards the possibility of using prepositional constructions with non-relational head nouns, noting that their informants in Västerbotten reject examples such as *hattn åt (n) Johan* 'Johan's hat' and *glassn åt (a) Lisa* 'Lisa's ice cream'. The examples from Lit (Jamtska) and Hälsingland above seem to show that this restriction is not general, and some

---

[14] "I dialekttexterna har jag funnit enstaka belägg från norra Sverige."
[15] "Genitiven uttryckes i äldre dial. ofta med preposition..."

of Delsing's examples from the southern part of the area also seem to be quite clearly non-relational. Källskog (1992: 157) quotes a number of non-relational examples from Överkalix, but they may be interpreted as meaning '(intended) for' (e.g. *kräfftfåore at kollo* 'the special fodder for the cows'), where also Swedish could have the preposition *åt* (perhaps somewhat marginally).

There are quite a few other texts in the Cat Corpus than the ones mentioned above where the *at* construction is used, but in a more restricted fashion. What I want to claim is that in those vernaculars, *at* is not a general possessive marker but rather signals an external possessor construction. This possibility has to my knowledge not attracted any serious attention – maybe because the notion of "external possession" has not been salient for most people who have worked in the area. Another reason is that the construction is rather infrequent in most texts. In the Cat Corpus, however, it happens to be very well represented, mainly thanks to the protagonist's jumping habits. The text with the largest number of examples is from Mora, where there are eight fairly clear examples, typical ones being:

(60)   Mora (Ovansiljan)

    a. *An upped   upp i knim   a Mårmår.*
       he jump.PST up in lap.DEF.DAT to Granny
       'He jumped up onto Granny's lap.' (Cat Corpus)

    b. *Men då   byrd   ä å   swäir i ogum   a Missan...*
       but then begin.PST it INFM smart in eye.DEF.PL to Cat...
       'But then Cat's eyes started smarting...' (Cat Corpus)

In the Mora Cat text, the preposition *a* is also used in the original, directional, sense, as in (61a), and in its modern Swedish beneficiary/recipient sense, as in (61b):

(61)   Mora (Ovansiljan)

    a. *Gamblest påjtsen add   fe   a Merikun...*
       old.SUPERL boy.DEF have.PST go.SUP to America.DEF
       'The eldest boy had gone to America...' (Cat Corpus)

    b. *A   du skreva   dånda lappen a me?*
       have.PRS you write.SUP that   slip.DEF to me.OBL
       'Have you written that note to me?' (Cat Corpus)

However, in this text, it is not used in examples of possession which cannot naturally be understood as external possession, such as (49). This might of course be an accident, but as it turns out, the same is true of more than ten other texts in which *at* is found in examples such as (60a-b). Figure 5.3 shows the distribution of external possessor *at* in the Cat Corpus. The vernaculars where *at* is used as an adnominal possessive marker are encircled. As we can see, the external possessor construction has a much larger geographical distribution, covering large parts of the Peripheral Swedish area.

My interpretation of the situation depicted in the map is that the adnominal uses of *at* are a more recent development, and that they have originated as a reanalysis of the external possessor construction. There are indications that an adnominal use is also developing in places where it has not yet become properly established. Thus, in Elfdalian, informants tend to find adnominal uses rather questionable, but it is possible to find examples, such as the following relatively old recording, which do not quite fit the criteria for external possession:

(62)   Elfdalian (Ovansiljan)
       Og ǫ   add   gaið fromǫ   gamman að nogum
       and she have.PST go.SUP in_front_of **front_roof** to **some.DEF.PL**
       momstaskallum.
       Månsta_people
       'and she had passed by the front roof of some Månsta people.' [S34]

If the hypothesis that the *at* construction has developed from external possession to an adnominal possession is correct, it may be the second time this has happened in the area: above, we saw that dative-marked adnominal possessors may have the same kind of origin.

5.7 Possessor incorporation

A further type of possessive construction found in some Peripheral Swedish vernaculars is possessor incorporation – alternatively described as a construction involving a compound noun whose first element is a noun referring to the possessor. Typologically, this is a relatively uncommon type which I discuss in Dahl (2004). The clearest examples outside Scandinavian are found in the Egyptian branch of the Afro-Asiatic languages. In the following two examples from Old Egyptian (Kammerzell 2000) as spoken around 2500 B.C.E., the possessor and the possessee are expressed in one word unit, and the possessee takes the special "construct state" form typical of possessive constructions in many Afro-Asiatic languages:[16]

(63)   Old Egyptian

   a. inalienable
      ħal-ʃan
      face.cs-brother
      'the brother's face'

   b. alienable
      t'apat-ʃan
      boat.cs-brother
      'the brother's boat'

Possessive constructions with incorporated possessors are remarkable in involving the incorporation of highly referential noun phrases (see Dahl (2004) for further discussion). This holds also for the Norrlandic examples. The examples in the literature tend to be of the type personal name + kin term (including "improper" kin terms in the sense of Dahl & Koptjevskaja-Tamm (2001), e.g. *Svän-Jons-pojken* 'Svän-Jon's boy' (quoted by Delsing 2003b: 38 from Delsbo). The last element can also be a noun denoting an animal:

(64)   Överkalix (Kalixmål)
   Per-Ajsja-mä:ra   *å*
   <firstname>-<patronymic>-mare.DEF and
   Läs-Ändersa-hesstn   *gär*   *din*   *opa*
   <firstname>-<patronymic>-horse.DEF walk.PRS there on
   aindjen.
   meadow.DEF.DAT
   'Per Eriksson's mare and Lars Andersson's horse are in the meadow.'
   (Källskog 1992: 164)

Inanimate possessees do also occur, although they are mentioned less frequently: *pappaskjorta* 'father's shirt' (Lövånger (Southern Westrobothnian), Holm 1942), *Ilmesnäsduken* 'Hilma's scarf' (Fasterna (Uppland), Tiselius 1902: 134), *Halvarluva* 'Halvar's cap' (Oscarsson 2007). (For some reason, all these examples involve items of clothing.)

---

[16] I am using Kammerzell's phonological representation rather than the traditional Egyptologist transcription that leaves out the vowels.

As for the distribution within the Peripheral Swedish area, Delsing gives attestations from Västerbotten (more specifically, Northern Westrobothnian) and Hälsingland; as the examples above reveal, the phenomenon is also found in Norrbotten and Jämtland. In addition, it is attested as far south as Värmland and Uppland.[17]

5.8 Pronominal possession

In the realm of possessive constructions with pronominal possessors, including both 1st and 2nd person possessive pronouns and what is traditionally called genitive forms of 3rd person pronouns, there has been less turbulence in the Peripheral Swedish than is the case for nominal possessors. In fact, the Peripheral Swedish vernaculars are on the whole rather conservative here, in that they have not in general followed the general trend towards preposed rather than postposed pronominal possessors.

In Runic Swedish, possessive pronouns were generally postposed, except when strongly stressed, and this is consistent with the oldest attested stages of Germanic varieties (Wessén 1956: 107ff.). The same holds for the Swedish provincial laws. However, the situation seems to have changed quickly and drastically: in the rest of Written Medieval Swedish post-position is a "rare exception" (Wessén 1956: 110ff.). Wessén comments that this change can hardly have taken place without external influence – he assumes that it spread from the West Germanic languages via Germany to Denmark and Sweden. In Central Scandinavian, preposed pronominal possessors are now the normal case, except for Norwegian where both orders are possible, although post-position seems to be preferred in spoken language and in Nynorsk. In written Standard Swedish, postposed possessors live on as a not too frequent alternative for kin terms in expressions such as *far min* 'my father'. In corpora of belletristic prose, such expressions make up 1-2 per cent of the combinations that contain the nouns in question. This situation appears to be relatively stable. The postposed variants have a clear colloquial or even "rustic" character.

Delsing (2003b: 32) has mapped the distribution of pronominal possession constructions in Swedish written dialect materials in detail. (Regrettably, for some

---

[17] Possessor incorporation may well turn out to be more common typologically than I have suggested here; it may just be something that has not been paid attention to. From his children's colloquial German, Wolfgang Schulze (pers. comm.) mentions examples such as *das ist der Lenny-Platz* 'that is Lenny's place [at the table]'.

areas, the number of attested examples in his statistics is really too low to allow
for any reliable judgments.) In Delsing's material, the Swedish dialect area di-
vides fairly nicely into three zones (see Figure 5.4): a southern one, coinciding
with the Southern Swedish area of traditional dialectology, with exclusively preposed pronominal possessors pronouns, a north-eastern one, roughly coinciding
with what I call the Peripheral Swedish area (but excluding Gotland and Estonia)
where postposed possessive pronouns predominate, and one intermediate area –
the rest, where preposed possessives are the norm but post-position is possible
with kin terms.

It appears that the postposed alternative is losing ground in present-day vernaculars. In the Cat Corpus, there are relatively few examples of possessive pronouns, and some of them are in focused position where the preposed alternative
is fairly general, but even in the others it can be seen that pre-position is used
in most of Dalarna, including the usually conservative Ovansiljan area. Levander (1909: 111) states that pre-position is possible only when the pronoun bears
strong stress (in the third person singular masculine, the preposed form is apparently a "reinforced" one, formed on the pattern of the complex dative possessive
discussed in §5.4.2):

(65) Elfdalian (Ovansiljan)

    a. preposed (strong stress)
       Eð ir   **onumes gard.**
       it be.PRS **his**   **farm**

       'It is his farm.'

    b. postposed (weak stress):
       Gardn -os ar   *buolageð*   *tjyöpt.*
       farm his have.PRS company.DEF buy.SUP

       'His farm has been bought by the company.'

In the intermediate area, pre- and post-position are equally probable with kin
terms in Delsing's material – 45 per cent of the occurrences are postposed. There
is considerable variation within the area, though. The following provinces have a
clear majority for the preposed alternative: Östergötland, north Småland, Bohuslän, (Halland), Närke, Dalsland. The following prefer the postposed construction:
Södermanland, (Västmanland), south Värmland, Västergötland. (Provinces with
total numbers that are too low are in parentheses.)

It thus appears that much of Sweden – not only the Peripheral Swedish area –
has for a long time withstood wholly or partly the trend towards preposed pro-

nominal possessors. What is somewhat remarkable in this context is that Written Medieval Swedish, except for the provincial laws, went further in this trend than virtually any of the vernaculars spoken within the borders of medieval Sweden, in that preposed possessive pronouns are the norm even with kin terms. Thus, in the Källtext corpus, I found only one instance of the phrase *fadher min* 'my father' as compared to about 30 instances with the preposed pronoun. Among the vernaculars, it is only the old Danish provinces and the adjacent southern Småland where the frequency of postposed pronouns in Delsing's material is as low or lower than in Källtext. The contrast with the Peripheral Swedish area is of course even more striking. It seems fairly clear that with regard to the placement of possessive pronouns, the usage in Written Medieval Swedish has little support in the surviving vernaculars. We may speculate that it was based on a prestige dialect heavily influenced by foreign models, probably primarily Danish ones.

5.9 Concluding discussion: The evolution of possessive constructions in the Peripheral Swedish area

It is not so easy to sort out the geographical patterns in the diversity of possessive constructions in the Peripheral Swedish area, especially in view of their frequent overlapping. Still, a possible scenario can be sketched.

Two constructions that do not overlap to any great extent but rather are in complementary distribution are the plain dative construction and the prepositional construction with *at*. As we can see from Figure 5.1, the plain dative construction has a discontinuous distribution, the two parts of which are the two parts of which are on opposite sides of the distribution of the *at* construction. Furthermore, the two constructions appear to have similar origins – from external possessor constructions. A dative external possessor construction is attested from Written Medieval Swedish, whereas an external possessor construction with *at* is found in a large part of the Peripheral Swedish area, notably in the areas where the plain dative construction is still alive. It is thus highly probable that the plain dative construction is the older one and that the *at* construction may have replaced it in Middle Norrland.

Even if there are some discrepancies (see §5.5), the distributions of the *h*-genitive and preproprial articles are similar enough for it to be likely that the former originates in the latter, and Norway is a likely candidate as the origin. Like the plain dative construction, the *h*-genitive has a discontinuous distribution; in fact, the "hole" in the middle is partly the same for the two constructions, and in both cases largely overlaps with the distribution of the *at* construction. Using the same logic

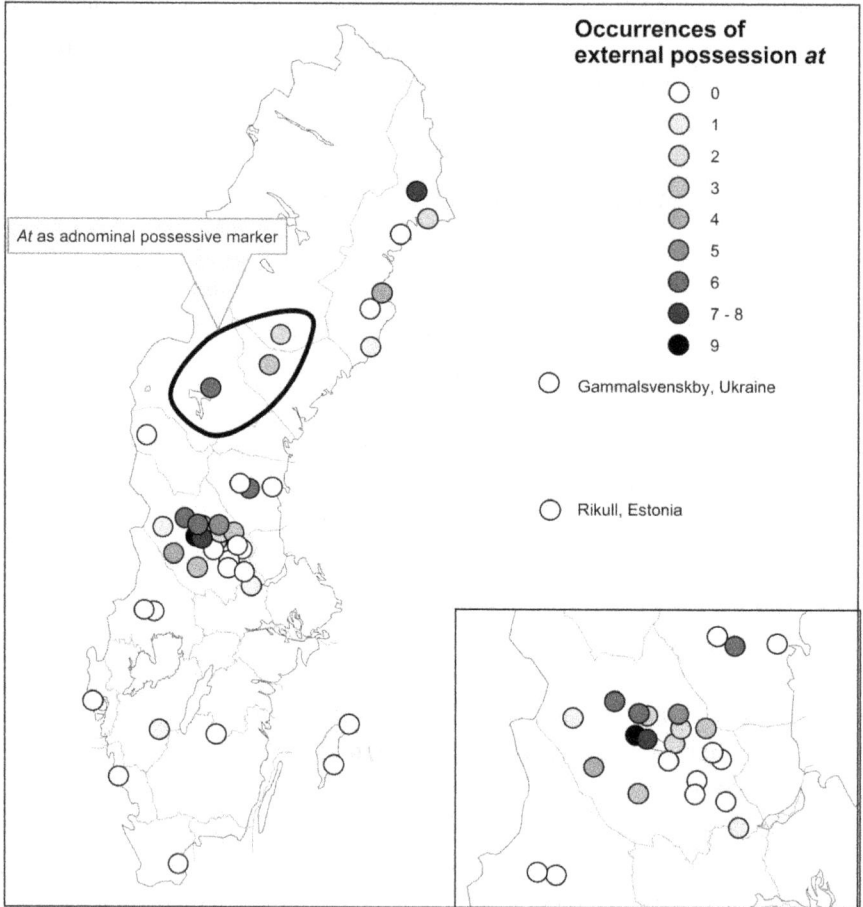

Figure 5.3: External possession in the Cat Corpus

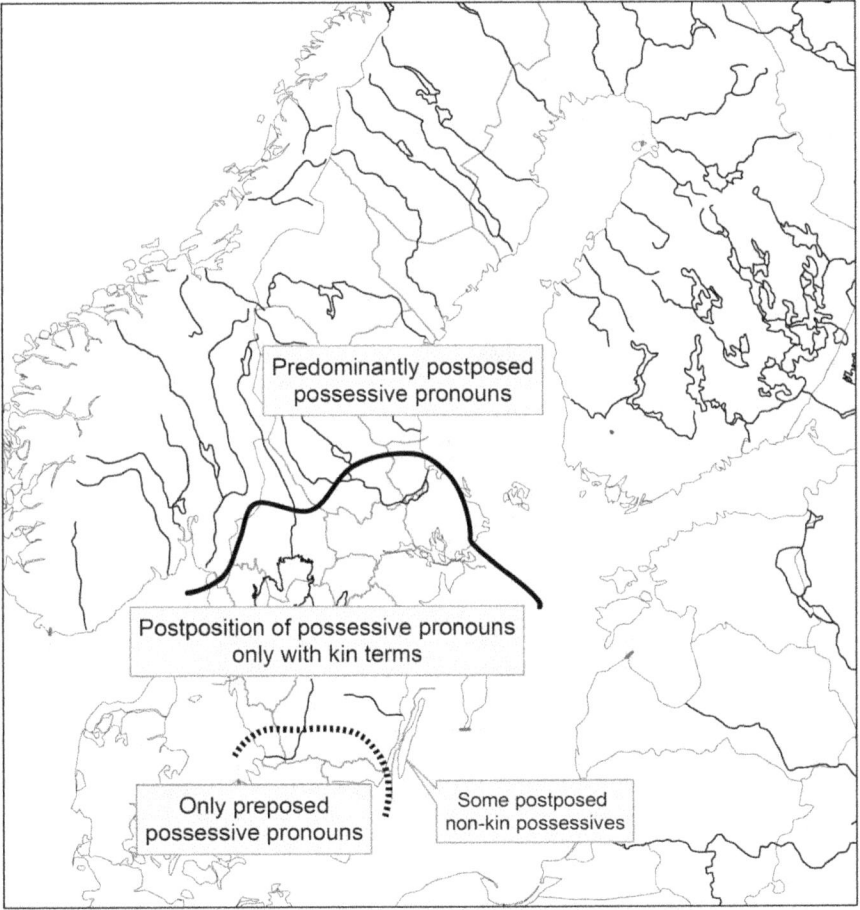

Figure 5.4: Placement of possessive pronouns (adapted from Delsing 2003b)

as before, we may assume as a possibility that the *at* construction has pushed out not only the dative construction but also the *h*-genitive in parts of Middle Nor rland. (Alternatively, the dative was first pushed out by the *h*-genitive, then the *at* construction took over.) Admittedly, we cannot exclude that the coastal *h* genitive is an independent development. However, one may wonder, if given all the possessive constructions they already had, these vernaculars would have developed another possessive construction if there were no pressure from the outside.

The geographical distribution of the *s*-genitive with a definite head suggests that it has expanded from the south along both sides of the Baltic.

6 The rise of Peripheral Swedish: Reconstructing a plausible scenario

6.1 General

In what precedes, we have been looking at a number of innovative linguistic phenomena that are spread over large, partly non-contiguous, geographic areas. If a particular linguistic phenomenon is found in two or different members of the same language family but did not exist at earlier historical stages of that family, there are a number of logical possibilities for how such a situation could arise:

1. There is no causal connection between the different manifestations of the phenomenon; it has developed quite independently in the various locations where it is found.

2. The developments are in principle independent of each other, but are triggered by the same internal factors which are due to shared properties inherited from their common ancestor.

3. The phenomenon is due to a common development. This is compatible with a variety of scenarios: the spread may have taken place through migration of speakers, or through influence from a cultural and economical centre, or through a vaguer process of dissipation, without any well-defined centre of origin.

Obviously, possibilities 2 and 3 shade into each other: if people in two close-by communities suddenly seem to get the same idea, it is not always possible to tell if they have influenced each other or if they are inspired by the same situation.

To see how one could argue for or against the different possibilities, let us look at one of the central processes discussed above, the extension of the use of definite forms to contexts which are not usually seen as definite. Is it, to begin with, possible that this development could have taken place independently, say, in Dalarna, Upper Norrland, and Finland?

One issue that has bearing on this question is the general typological probability of the development in question. Definiteness marking is found in many languages all over the world; we also know that it is not uncommon for definiteness markers to generalize in such a way that they no longer deserve that name. However, it does appear that developments that parallel the Scandinavian ones more closely are not so common – otherwise they ought to have attracted the attention of typologists to a greater extent. In §3.4.4, we saw a fairly close parallel in Moroccan Arabic and certain less clear tendencies among the Romance languages. Among the Germanic languages, nothing similar has been attested so far. These facts certainly speak against the assumption that the parallels between Dalarna, Upper Norrland and Finland are coincidental. But could there be factors that would favour a parallel development without there being a direct spread of innovations? One point of some importance here is that Scandinavian definiteness marking has reached a relatively "advanced" stage of grammaticalization in that it involves affixation and sometimes fusion between stem and affix, rather than the article being a free morpheme, which is the case in most European languages that have a definite article. It is likely that the further expansion of the definite article to, for instance non-delimited uses, is easier if the article is bound than if it is free. (The Arabic definite article is written orthographically as a separate word but in the spoken dialects, such as Moroccan Arabic, it is actually more like an affix.)

Could the innovations in Peripheral Swedish noun phrase syntax be due to a common spread from a centre? The obvious problem is to identify this centre, given that the phenomena that we are examining in several cases are found in discontiguous areas and that there is no common economic and cultural centre within their present-day territory. We do not have go very far to find such a centre outside the Peripheral Swedish area, however, as is suggested in the following quotation:

> "The Norrlandic and East Swedish [i.e. Trans-Baltic] dialects are in general ramifications of the Upper Swedish area. They hardly have any centre of their own, but point to Central Sweden, especially Uppland, as their original middle point. However, in these more peripheral dialect groups, several traits have been retained that have been pushed out from central Sweden by innovations from the south or by influence from the standard language." (Wessén 1966: 51, my translation)

Wessén seems here to be speaking of the retainment of conservative traits in the Peripheral Swedish area. It is natural to think of those traits as being inherted from Old Nordic, and to assume that they were once found in the whole Scandinavian linguistic area. In actual fact, the feature Wessén uses as an illustration in the same chapter – "vowel balance" – is not of this kind. Like another feature he mentions earlier in the book – "medial affrication" – vowel balance is an innovation that was never characteristic of all Scandinavian varietes. However, these features still covered a larger area in earlier times than they do today – particularly in parts of the central provinces of Uppland and Södermanland." The innovations from the south" that have pushed them out are thus not really innovations but rather a return to an original state; that is, the varieties that win out are the more conservative ones – at least as far as these particular developments go. Let us look at the details.

"Medial affrication" (in Swedish literature often referred to as *norrländsk förmjukning* 'Norrlandic softening') is the process that gives rise to forms such as Elfdalian *mjotję* 'the milk', where the stem-final *k* in *mjok* 'milk' has become a [tʃ] before the front vowel in the definite ending. This is different from the palatalization of *k* and *g* before stressed vowels that is found in most spoken varieties of Peninsular Scandinavian, including Standard Swedish and Norwegian. Medial affrication is usually described as applying generally in Swedish vernaculars north of a line more or less coinciding with *limes norrlandicus,* including parts of Swedish-speaking Finland (but not Estonia). In addition, it is also found in most of western and northern Norway. Figure 6.1 shows the borderlines of the medial affrication area according to Haugen (1970), which, like most other treatments, shows the border through Uppland as described in Kruuse (1908); this mapping may be assumed to represent the second half of the 19th century. In Källskog et al. (1993), the phenomenon is said to be "extremely rare" in Uppland except in the very north and is judged by the editors of the volume to be disappearing in this province – the only attestation in the texts in the book is from the parish of Hållnäs.

Wessén (1966: 43) says that there is evidence that medial affrication earlier covered a larger area, extending also to parts of Södermanland and the archipelago along the coast of Östergötland. (The footnote in Hesselman (1905: 36) which Wessén refers to says "all of eastern Västmanland, parts of Södermanland".) Geijer & Holmkvist (1930) demonstrated that sporadic occurrences of medial affrication were found in a large area in Västmanland south of the present borderline, again suggesting a wider distribution in the past. In other words, there appears to be a continuous receding movement northwards. Reinhammar (2005: 80) says that forms such as *bättjen* and *väddjen*, which are known from northern Uppland and northwards, may have spread from Uppland and may also have existed fur-

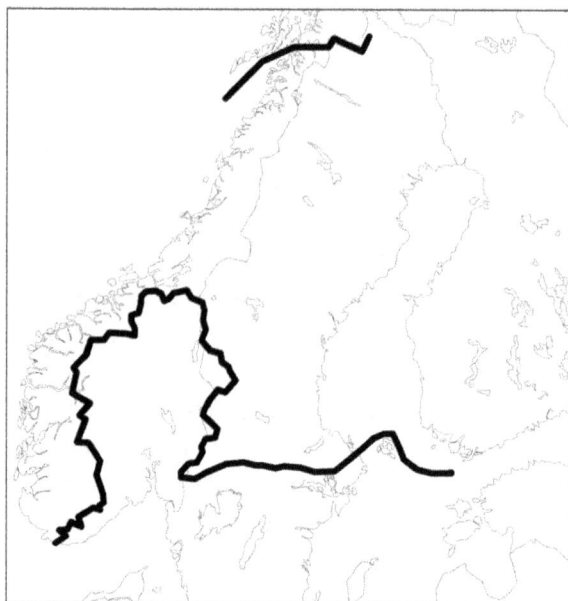

Figure 6.1: The borderlines of medial affrication according to Haugen (1970)

ther south, but were pushed out by the forms without affrication "which have as it were regained territory from the south".

The term "vowel balance" refers to the interdependence in length between a stressed syllable and a following unstressed one that characterizes many northern Scandinavian varieties, due to developments in the Middle Ages; this means in practice that unstressed vowels that followed a short stressed syllable were not subject to the reduction processes that hit other unstressed vowels, thus Written Medieval Swedish *faþir* 'father' (<Runic Swedish *faþer*) vs. *mōþer* 'mother'. In the varieties where vowel balance has been operative, it is hard to distinguish this as a phenomenon different from apocope, that is the deletion of unstressed final vowels, and "vowel leveling", that is the assimilation of the quality of the stem vowel to that of the non-deleted but raised final vowel. Thus, in Elfdalian, verbs with original long-syllabic stems show up with the infinitive ending *-a*, which is however apocopated in many positions, e.g. *jag(a)* 'hunt' (long stem vowel), whereas short-syllabic stems get the ending *-å* or *-o*, which is never apocopated and also colours the stem vowel, e.g. *båkå<baka* 'bake' (short stem vowel). The geographic distribution of these features is quite complex and I shall not try to disentangle it here. It should be noted, however, that similar processes seem

to have been common in large parts of the Germanic area, and it is not easy to reconstruct interrelationships between different varieties. Vowel balance is more directly preserved in Swedish varieties in Dalarna and southern Norrland (except Hälsingland and Gästrikland) but also in the neighbouring Norwegian varieties, covering most of Eastern Norway. In addition, it shows up in Finland and Estonia. Curiously enough, although medial affrication and vowel balance are strongly positively correlated in the Swedish dialect area, their distribution in Norway is almost perfectly complementary. Wessén (1966: 52) notes: "There are many traces of vowel balance also in Upper Swedish dialects, and it does appear that this regulation of final vowels earlier extended south to the border to the Göta area." Apocope was also apparently common in older forms of Upper Swedish (Wessén 1968).

What I want to show now is that there is in fact a fairly large number of other phenomena, both grammatical and lexical, that show similar patterns, that look like innovations that have been pushed back. I will also try to show that the geographical distribution of those innovations tends to resemble that of truly conservative features that have also been pushed back, which suggests a relatively early date for the innovations in question.

6.2 Pushed-back innovations in the pronoun system

Some of the most important innovative phenomena in the Peripheral Swedish area belong to the pronoun systems. Their distribution in time and space has been studied in detail by the late Swedish dialectologist Vidar Reinhammar (especially Reinhammar 1975).

6.2.1 *H-* and *d*-pronouns

The term "*h*-pronouns" is here used as a convenient label for demonstrative and 3rd person pronouns formed from stems beginning in *h*, as opposed to "*d*-pronouns" whose stems begin in a dental. This should not be taken as implying that *h*-pronouns all have a common origin. Nevertheless, this label nicely covers the innovative pronouns in the Peripheral Swedish area.

6.2.2 Adnominal *h*-pronouns

In Central Scandinavian, the pronouns *han* 'he' and *hon* 'she' are not used adnominally. By contrast, in many vernaculars throughout the Peripheral Swedish area, masculine *han* and feminine *hon* form a paradigm of adnominal demonstratives together with neutral *hä,* with the plural taken from the *d*-series, as in the neuter dative forms. In Elfdalian, we thus have the nominative forms *an kalln* 'that man', *o*[328?] *kulla* 'that woman', *eð auseð* 'that house', *dier kallär* 'those men', and the neuter dative form *dyö ausę* 'that house'. The geographical distribution is shown in Figure 6.2.

There are no attested examples of adnominal *h*-pronouns in Written Medieval Swedish (Reinhammar 1975: 114). The innovation must have taken place during the Middle Ages, but it is unclear if it had already happened during the "Early Old Swedish" period (ibid.).

Reinhammar reconstructs the following area for the maximal geographical distribution of adnominal *h*-pronouns: in addition to the present-day area, he assumes that *han* and *hon* were used more extensively in eastern Uppland, possibly also in eastern Södermanland (the Södertörn peninsula[1]). Similarly, adnominal *hä* was also used in SE Uppland and possibly in Södermanland, in addition in Öland and Gotland.

Reinhammar sees adnominal *han/hon* in Uppland, Estonia, Åland, Åboland, western Nyland, and northern and southern Österbotten as forming a unitary area, to which Öland would also belong. The innovation centre was probably Uppland and the innovation spread "along coasts and via water-ways" (Reinhammar 1975: 115).

"From the point of view of dialect geography" it can be assumed, says Reinhammar, that the Swedish east coast from Södertörn to Öland had adnominal *han/hon* during some period and that it was later pushed out by *d*-pronouns. Åland has "undoubtedly" had *han/hon,* although mainland Åland has shed it due to influence from the standard language. As for Österbotten, the adnominal *h*-pronouns can be assumed to have arrived via "the Swedish settlements in Satakunta" (the province south of Österbotten, presently only Finnish-speaking) rather than directly from Sweden, "since the Norrlandic dialects do not know the use in question and the distance to Uppland seems too large" (Reinhammar 1975: 116). The situation in Österbotten is complicated by the existence of an alternative pronoun paradigm *tan, ton* – I will not go into Reinhammar's discussion of these problems.

Concerning the use of adnominal *h*-pronouns in Dalarna, Reinhammar says that it is "less probable" that it has arisen as an internal development with no relation to the large area mentioned above. Although "it cannot be excluded" that the *h*-pronouns entered Dalarna through a colonization from Uppland, Reinham-

---

[1] Södertörn is the triangular peninsula directly south of Stockholm. It is best visible in Figure 6.19.

mar prefers to see the two areas as "remnants of an older unity". (Apparently
Reinhammar sees these alternatives as excluding each other.) He refrains from
taking a definite view on the extension of this unified area but conjectures that
it may have, in addition to the Dalecarlian area, also been comprised of parts
of Uppland, eastern Västmanland and southern Dalabergslagen, and perhaps a
part of Gästrikland. Now the problem arises as to how to explain the "inter-
mediary area" where adnominal *h*-pronouns are not found today. Reinhammar
speculates that the spread could have taken place through a "pincer operation"
but says that, in any case, we must assume that the *d*-pronouns have regained
part of the territory that they earlier lost to the *h*-pronouns. From Reinhammar's
rather lengthy discussion of this issue, I will just mention his claim that the competition between *d*- and *h*-pronouns in the Dalecarlian area may be explained by
the hypothesis that the innovation was never fully implemented there.

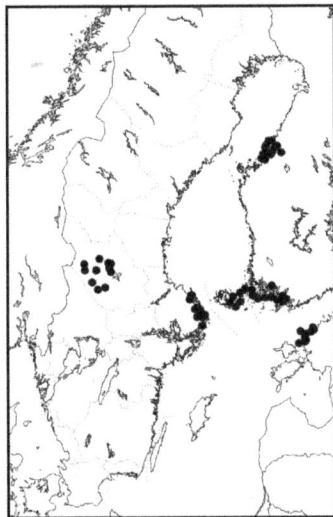

Figure 6.2: Distribution of adnominal masculine *h*-pronouns without adverbial
   expansions (Reinhammar's Figure 2.5).

Adnominal *hä* has a larger distribution than adnominal *han/hon*, and is in fact
combined with non-neuter *den* in one paradigm in an area comprising parts of
Uppland, Västmanland, Dalabergslagen and Gästrikland (Figure 6.2). "It does not
seem unlikely" that this area earlier had a full *h*-pronoun paradigm (Reinhammar
1975: 43). Combinations of *h*-pronouns with the deictic adverb *dar/där* also occur
in a wider area (Figure 6.3; in Standard Swedish, only *d*-pronouns are normally
possible.

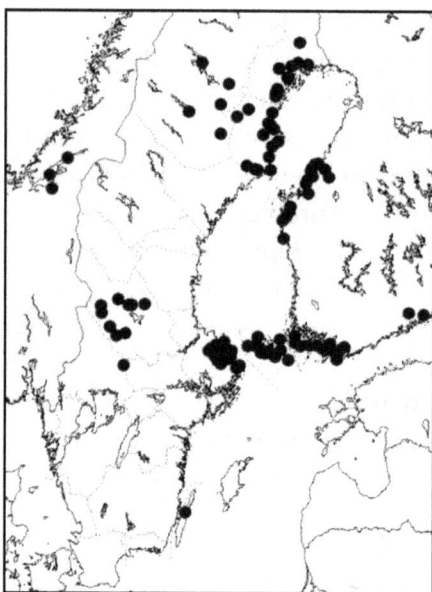

Figure 6.3: Distribution of adnominal masculine *h*-pronouns in combination with *dar* (Reinhammar's Figure 2.3).

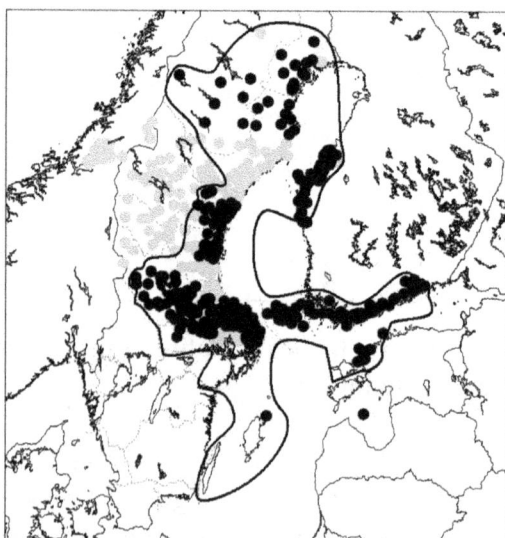

Figure 6.4: Modern distribution of stressed and enclitic independent *hä* (black and grey circles, respectively) and reconstructed maximal extent of stressed *hä* (enclosed area).

6.2.3 Independent *hä*

Forms such as *hä, ä, äd*, etc. are widely used as independent neuter pronouns in the Peripheral Swedish area. For simplicity, I shall refer to all these forms simply as *hä*. Figure 6.4 shows the present-day distribution of the stressed variants.

Reasoning out from dialect geography and older materials, Reinhammar deems it probable that *hä* was earlier used in a contiguous area comprising Norrbotten, Västerbotten and the present-day *hä*-areas in Lappland (to the extent that they were populated), eastern Ångermanland, Medelpad (except Haverö) and the easternmost corner of Jämtland, Hälsingland except the north-west, Dalarna except in north-west, Gästrikland, Uppland, Västmanland except possibly the south-western part, (at least) northern and eastern Södermanland, and possibly also Närke and the north-east corner of Östergötland. In addition *hä* existed in Öland, (the whole of) Gotland, and generally in Finland and Estonia. Reinhammar does not exclude the possibility that the use of *hä* was less general in some of the areas where it later receded, but says that the most probable assumption is that a relatively uniform system was prevalent as least as far as stressed and proclitic uses are concerned.

The Swedish mainland *hä*-area has been split up or "otherwise decreased in extent". The corresponding *d*-form, denoted as *dä* (corresponding to standard orthography *det*), has expanded "mainly from the south and partly from Stockholm" and replaced *hä* in Södermanland, SE Västmanland, S Uppland, "also infiltrating remaining *hä*-vernaculars in Uppland and NE Västmanland, as also partially in Dalabergslagen and Gästrikland" (Reinhammar 1975: 186). A similar process has taken place in Finland, affecting Åland (from the Swedish mainland) and Nyland (from Helsinki) (Reinhammar 1975: 187).

For Hälsingland, Reinhammar assumes a spread along the rivers Ljusnan and Voxnan and the coast in the south-west. Northwestern Hälsingland, on the other hand, belongs to an area with original *dä*, comprised of Härjedalen, Jämtland and W Medelpad (that is, areas under Norwegian influence – my remark) (Reinhammar 1975: 186). For Ångermanland, the picture seems to be somewhat confused – Reinhammar mentions several possibilites but does not want to choose between them. In Gotland, the reconstituted *dä* can be assumed to have spread from Visby (Reinhammar 1975: 188).

Finally, Reinhammar raises the questions of the age of *hä* and how its large distribution should be explained. He notes that early attestations of *hä* are found over a large area, such as Gotland from about 1550, Älvdalen from about 1600, and Uppland from 1620. This is an indication of an early spread. Reinhammar says that *hä* should be seen as having originated in the Old Swedish period (i.e. before

1520), "maybe already in the latter part of the Early Old Swedish period".[2] Since the period of Early Old Swedish is normally given as 1225-1375, this should be interpreted as meaning the three first quarters of the 14th century. On the other hand, he thinks that *hä* is not old enough to belong to the layer called "Birka Swedish" by Hesselman (see §6.2.6).[3]

Reinhammar proposes a somewhat complex mechanism: the unstressed variants, mainly *h*-less ones, have developed independently in the various dialects, but the extension to stressed variants has spread from an innovation centre – "for different reasons" – most probably in Uppland or at least in the Svea dialect area. What is most important for the theme of this book is the general picture of an early innovation which spread from the Mälar region basically over the whole Peripheral Swedish area but is later on "cancelled" by a new spread from more or less the same centre.

It may be noted that the border Reinhammar gives for *hä* in Uppland is not too different from that postulated for medial affrication by Kruuse (1908), although the *hä* line goes further south in the eastern parts of the province. Källskog et al. (1993) note that in their texts, *hä* (or *he*) is found only in Älvkarleby and Hållnäs in the very north – Hållnäs is also the only place where medial affrication is preserved in their material. In other words, we see a rather striking parallelism between the developments of these two quite disparate phenomena. (Regrettably, Kruuse did not describe the distribution of pronouns.)

6.2.4 Demonstratives of the *hissin* type

Demonstrative pronouns tend to exhibit a sometimes confusing diversity. One set of forms whose distribution is of interest here involves those forms which have a stem in *his-*, *tes-* or the like, such as the masculine singular forms Överkalix (Kalixmål) *hisin*, Elfdalian (Ovansiljan) *isin* or Kökar (Ålandic) *tesin*. Reinhammar (1988) describes the distribution as follows: Forms deriving from an original *his-* occur in Överkalix and Nederkalix, although they are obsolete in the latter. They may have been spread more generally in Norrbotten and Västerbotten in an earlier period. They furthermore occur in Ovansiljan, Nedansiljan and lower Västerdalarna, eastern Småland and Blekinge, Gotland, Österbotten, and Estonia. Forms in *t-* such as *tesin* occur mainly in southern Finland and Estonia. Rein-

---

[2] "Häd, äd bör därför antas ha sin upprinnelse i fsv. tid, kanske redan i senare delen av äldre fsv." (Reinhammar 1975: 189).

[3] "Med min här framlagda tolkning av hä, äd följer, att formerna inte har sådan ålder, att de kan hänföras till det gamla språkskikt, Hesselman trott sig kunna spåra i de ovan nämnda formerna." (Reinhammar 1975: 190).

nammar concludes that it is natural to assume that the present-day forms are relics from the periphery of an earlier contiguous area on the Swedish mainland connected to Gotland and the Trans-Baltic areas. Evidence from medieval runic inscriptions in Gotland suggest that the forms had spread no later than 1400.

5.2.5 Generic pronouns

Many Peripheral Swedish vernaculars use the third person pronoun *han* in a generic sense, corresponding to Swedish *man*, e.g.

(1) Hössjö (Southern Westrobothnian)
Sku **an** *bara hav* *se* *fölver* *ti* *tänk* *œpa, so*
shall.PST **one** only have.INF REFL self.M.SG INFm think.INF upon so
sku *e int va* *meir än* *halva* *komersen.*
shall.PST it NEG be.INF more than half.WK commerce.DEF
'If one only had oneself to think of, that wouldn't be more than half the commerce.'

According to Westerberg (2004: 84), this usage can be documented from the whole of Norrland and Dalarna, from the northern and eastern parts of Uppland, and from all Swedish vernaculars in Finland. In addition, according to Hellevik (1979: 48), the use of generic *han* is spread throughout most of Norway, although the most common generic pronoun in Norwegian is *e(i)n*. (Hellevik notes that this was already pointed out by the creator of Nynorsk, Ivar Aasen.)

In spite of its general spread, the use of generic *han* is not equally strong everywhere in the Peripheral Swedish area. I have not been able to find any examples from Norrbotten and, according to Westerberg (2004: 85), the usage is receding in the Norsjö vernacular (Northern Westrobothnian) that she describes, yielding to *man*. On the other hand, generic *han* is also found in some less conservative areas such as Hälsingland, Dalabergslagen and Uppland. The geographical distribution of *han* is thus not entirely in accordance with that of some of the other Peripheral Swedish phenomena. In Norrbotten and Västerbotten, the second person pronoun *du* has been extensively used in the role of a generic pronoun, and this may be one reason for *han* being weaker there than in other parts.

According to Wessén (1956: 73), the oldest forms of "our language" had no counterpart to the Modern Swedish generic pronoun *man*. Instead, he says, subjectless sentences were most often used:

(2)   Written Medieval Swedish

    a. *Värþär   dräpit hors eller nöt ... veit   eig hvar drap.*
       become.PRS kill.PP horse or   cow   know.PRS NEG who kill.PST
       'If a horse or a cow is killed, and one does not know who killed [it].'
       (Older Västgöta Law)

    b. *Fyrst skal   by   letä.*
       first shall.PRS village.ACC search.INF
       'First one shall search the village.' (Older Västgöta Law)

Man as a generic pronoun starts showing up in some later provincial laws. As Wessén (1956: 75) thinks, both internal "preconditions" and influence from German were operative in the rise of *man*. He sees *man* as "mainly a word belonging to written language" and says that "natural spoken language, especially dialects" have *en* instead, which is also used as the oblique form of *man* in the standard language. (Wessén's claim about the unnaturalness of *man* seems slightly exaggerated.) *En* as a generic pronoun is obviously derived from the numeral 'one' and is sometimes also claimed to be a result of German influence, like *man*. The fact that German uses forms such as *einem* and *einen* in oblique cases no doubt speaks in favour of a connection.

Given that older forms of Scandinavian had no overt generic pronouns, *han*, *man*, and *en* in their generic use all have to be seen as innovations; and the present-day geographical distribution of *han* suggests that it used to be general in the Svea area – although not exclusive to it, as its additional presence in Norway shows.

In the Cat Corpus data, a clear dominance for *en* is seen in Värmland, Halland, Västerdalarna, Västergötland, Skåne and Bohuslän – that is, mainly provinces in the south or west or along the Norwegian border. Some tokens are hard to interpret unambiguously, given that reduced forms such as *'n* may be derived from both *han* and *en*.

6.2.6 Hesselman's "Birka Swedish" theory

In 1936, the Swedish scholar Bengt Hesselman put forward a hypothesis about a specific language variety called "Birka Swedish" (*Birkasvenska*) which supposedly existed in the Viking period (Hesselman 1936). The "Birka Swedish" hypothesis seems to have received rather limited attention until it was taken up and further developed by Gun Widmark almost sixty years later (Widmark 1994, Widmark (2001), who prefers to speak of "Hedeby Nordic". (I discussed it in Dahl

2001 in connection with the question of the origin of the Scandinavian languages in general.) Birka (in Lake Mälaren) and Hedeby (Haithabu, close to the present-day city of Schleswig on the east coast of Jutland) were both parts of a network of trading centres around the Baltic and North Seas, and it is natural to assume that they played a central role in the spread of linguistic innovations in Scandinavia.

Figure 6.5: The distribution of forms such as *hjär* and *jär* for 'here' according to Hesselman (1936). Crosshatched areas represent modern vernaculars, dots earlier attestations.

Hesselman's main argument centres around a single phenomenon, the existence of alternate forms of the demonstrative adverb *här* 'here', such as *jär* (Figure 6.5). Such forms are or were found in Nordic dialects spoken in various parts of Scandinavia, including Upper Norrland and Dalarna in continental Sweden, Ostrobothnia in Finland, Gotland in the Baltic and the Swedish dialects in Estonia, but also in Danish dialects in an area of southern Jutland and Schleswig. Hesselman provides evidence that forms beginning with *j-* were earlier found over a larger area, in particular Uppland and other parts of the Mälar region, and draws the conclusion that there was a sound change *ē* > *ja* which spread from the Mälar region with Birka as the centre and was in fact one feature of "Birka Swedish", a language variety supposedly spoken "in a contiguous area around the Baltic Sea from Överkalix in the north to Slesvig (Hedeby) in the south" (Hesselman 1936: 158).[4] Widmark (1994) points to a number of other changes, such as the monophthongization of *au* to *o* and "breaking", illustrated by developments like **singwa* > *sjunga*, that could be connected with the Hedeby/Birka language which she characterizes as a "prestige language that spread over large areas" (1994: 199; my translation). Widmark also points to an important issue that Hesselman more or less manages to avoid: the later fate of "Hedeby Nordic". Since the traits in question are no longer characteristic of the language varieties spoken in the central regions of Denmark and Sweden, it seems to follow that "Hedeby Nordic" was later superseded by other prestige varieties, which may well have spread from other centres, although presumably still in southern Scandinavia.

As Widmark points out, the sound change *ē* > *ja* cannot have spread to the whole area at once, since there were no Swedish settlements in the northernmost part at that time, and the expansion of the Scandinavian-speaking population was not completed until several centuries later, in the the 13th or 14th centuries. The timetable is on the whole somewhat problematic. The spread of the Birka/Hedeby variety must have taken place quite early, in fact earlier than the spread of other changes that have been more general, such as the spread of definite marking. But what is notable in this context is the similarity between the distribution of the *jär* area and the other Peripheral Swedish phenomena discussed here, although *jär* is stronger in the south than many of the others.

6.3 Lexical innovations in the Peripheral Swedish area

Among the numerous lexical items specific to Peripheral Swedish vernaculars, the most interesting ones in this context are those which are represented in different parts of the Peripheral Swedish area and which lack cognates both in older forms of Scandinavian and in modern Standard Swedish – that is, items which can be taken to be shared innovations in the Peripheral Swedish area.

Given the old insight that each word has its own history, it is not easy to orient oneself in the geographical distribution of lexical items. What I shall point to here are a couple of high-frequency items that are fairly well represented in the Cat Corpus.

Words for 'run' appear to be relatively unstable in the sense that they are replaced frequently in languages. The most frequent word for 'run' in older forms

---

[4] As Widmark (1994) notes, this is clearly an exaggeration: the northern border of Scandinavian-speaking settlements most probably did not go as far north as Överkalix at this time.

of Scandinavian appears to have been *löpa* (or its cognates), but in modern Standard Swedish it has been replaced by *springa,* whose original meaning was 'jump'. This development appears to be peculiar to Swedish and is not found in the other Scandinavian languages, nor has it extended to all non-standard varieties, as we shall now see.

Words for 'run' occur on average about 10 times in the Cat stories, so there is relatively ample material for a comparison. There are two competitors to *springa,* which is the major alternative in about half the texts. One is *ränna,* which shows up in the two texts from Gotland (Fårömål also has *löpa* as a second choice).[5] The other one – *kuta* – is the most interesting from our point of view. The word exists also in Standard Swedish but the primary meaning indicated by older dictionaries is 'walk with a stoop'. In colloquial language, on the other hand, it does mean 'run'. Hellquist (1922: 371) thinks that the two readings are derived by parallel but historically separate processes from the obsolete word *kut* 'hump'. The reading 'run' is attested from the 16th century, and in this sense the word is probably identical to the one found in the vernaculars. The distribution in the Cat Corpus (see Figure 6.6) suggests that, as the major word for 'run', *kuta* is restricted to the Peripheral Swedish area, including Värmland. *Kute* 'run' exists in Norwegian dialects, but I have not been able to establish its distribution.

Another interesting item is the cognate set represented in Swedish by *häva* and found also in many other Germanic languages (e.g. English *heave*) with the original meaning 'lift, move upwards'. In Swedish vernaculars, it has expanded its meaning quite considerably. Thus, as far south as Småland, examples such as *häva dom i grytan* 'put them (the potatoes) in the pot' are common according to the materials collected for the Swedish Dialect Dictionary. In the Peripheral Swedish area, cognates of *häva* have developed into a general transitive verb of movement corresponding to English 'put', as exemplified by the following examples (they also show up in many lexicalized phrases):

(3) Skelletmål (Northern Westrobothnian)
  *han **ho**   päninge   ni plånboka*
  he   put.PST money.PL.DEF in wallet.DEF
  'He put the money in the wallet'

---

[5] As can be seen from (), the verb *renna* exists in Elfdalian, but may be used predominantly in the sense 'to ski'.

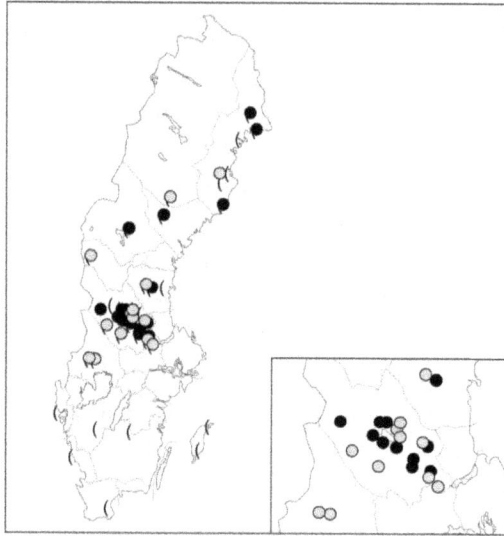

Figure 6.6: Distribution of *kuta* 'run' in the Cat Corpus.

(4)   Norsjö (Northern Westrobothnian)
      *ha   du **het** på de   vanta?*
      have.PRS you **put.SUP** on you.OBL mitten.DEF.PL
      'Have you put mittens on?'

Figure 6.7 shows the distribution of *häva* cognates in the Cat Corpus. We see that the strongest area is Ovansiljan in Dalarna but that there are also strong points in southern Västerbotten and Ångermanland.

Eaker (1993) describes the distribution in Swedish vernaculars of the adjective *grann* and some other adjectives related to it. In this connection, the most interesting case is *laggrann* 'careful', which is in modern vernaculars found in all of Norrland and Dalarna but may have also been used earlier in Västmanland and Uppland.

6.4 Auxiliaries

Holm (1941) discusses the use of the verb *fara*, the original meaning of which is 'travel' or 'go', as an ingressive or future auxiliary. As an auxiliary with the meaning 'begin', *fara*, often in reduced forms such as *fa* or *fe*, is found in particular in the Northern Westrobothnian and the Ovansiljan areas, e.g.

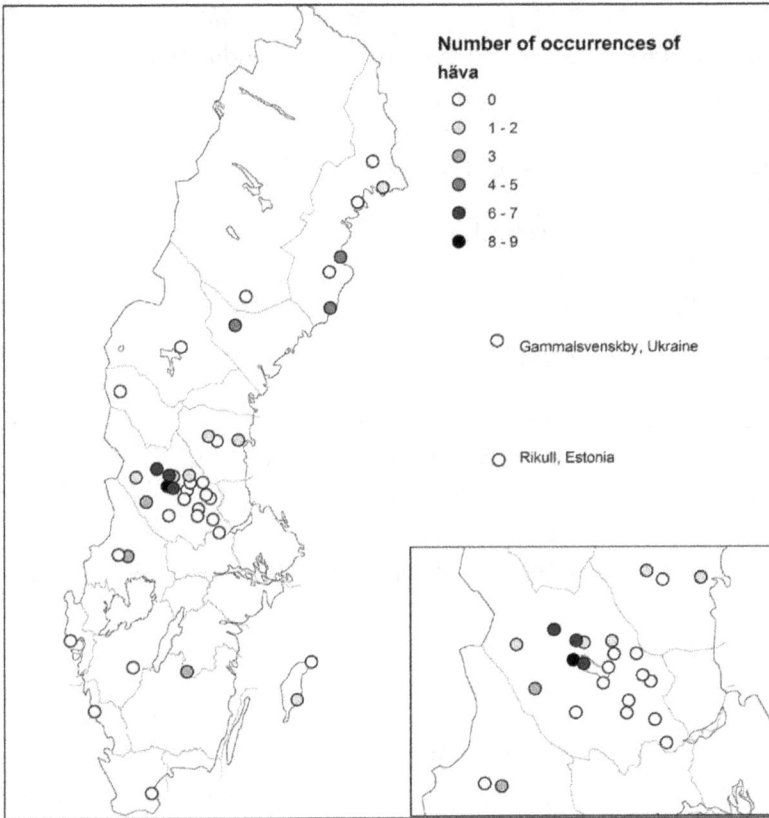

Figure 6.7: Distribution of *häva* 'raise, put' in the Cat Corpus

(5) Lövånger (Northern Westrobothnian)
   Je for   no   väL   tröyt.
   I   **start.PST PRAG** become.INF tired
   'I started to become tired.' (Holm 1942: 19)

(6) Elfdalian (Ovansiljan)
   E fa   raingen.
   it **begin.PRS** rain.INF
   'It's beginning to rain.' (Levander 1909: 115)

In Northern Västerbotten, there are also two other kinds of uses: the first one Holm characterizes as having a "futural meaning" (Holm 1941: 20):

(7) Lövånger (Northern Westrobothnian)
He kan **fara** *hall op inan sönndan.*
it may.PRS begin.INF keep.INF up before Sunday.DEF
'It may stop raining before Sunday.'

The second he labels "pleonastic" (Holm 1941: 21):

(8) Jörn (Northern Westrobothnian)
Do skul pappen **fara** *ten op do.*
then shall.PST father.DEF begin.INF light up then
'Then father was going to make a fire.'

I am not certain if the last two groups of uses are really distinct from the first. The "futural" uses are not wholly convincing as such—they often involve some other modal marker such as *kan* 'may' in (7). It is not clear if similar examples can be found in Dalecarlian.

Holm also quotes examples of *fara* as an auxiliary from Nyland, taken from Lundström (1939), such as

(9) Pojo (Nylandic)
Ja va fjȭjjo år, när ja fȭa čän bȭäno
I be.PST fourteen year.PL when I go.PST serve.INF farmer.DEF
'I was fourteen, when I started working for the farmer.' (Lundström 1939: 133)

The use in Nyland seems more restricted and may in Holm's opinion represent a transitional stage, where the auxiliary keeps part of its original meaning.

A similar use of *fara* is also found in Icelandic (both Old and Modern) and in certain Norwegian dialects. In these, however, an infinitive marker, or the preposition *til* 'to' followed by an infinitive marker, is used.

Holm notes that there seem to be no examples of auxiliary uses of *fara* in older forms of Swedish which, he says, would be expected from the general distribution of these uses in time and space. Further research is needed, he says, and it would be premature to conclude that the auxiliary uses of *fara* have been distributed as a "contiguous whole" over the whole of Scandinavia.

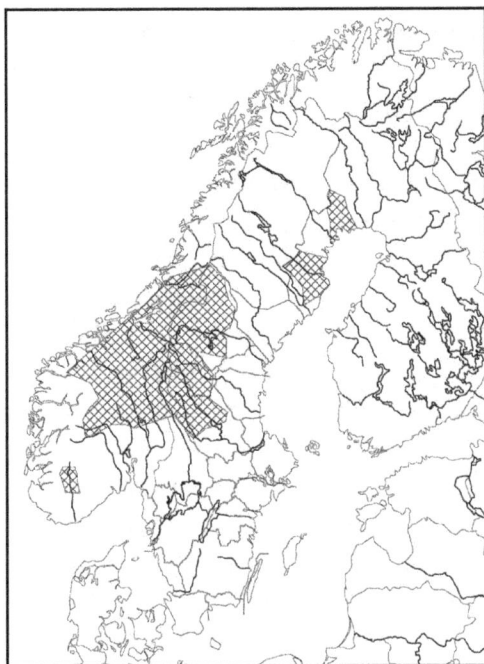

Figure 6.8: Core areas of preserved dative use according to Reinhammar (1973).

6.5 Conservative features of the Peripheral Swedish area

6.5.1 Introduction

Many of the conservative features of the Peripheral Swedish area are well-known and have been studied in detail. Most obviously, perhaps, is the retention of considerable parts of the morphology that were discarded in Central Scandinavian fairly early on.Thus, the old case system is at least partly preserved in several areas; this is particularly true for the dative case which is still alive in vernaculars in Dalarna, Härjedalen, Jämtland, Västerbotten and Norrbotten, with some remnants in Ångermanland and Medelpad (see Figure 6.8).

A three-way distinction between nominative, accusative, and dative is probably only found in the Ovansiljan area – the accusative case that has been claimed to exist in parts of Uppland is – or was – probably a general oblique case (Dahl & Koptjevskaja-Tamm 2006).

The vernaculars in Finland and Estonia do not feature dative and accusative; one might perhaps think that the vicinity to Finnish and Estonian would favour the retainment of a complex case system.

A three-gender system (rather than the two-gender system found in standard Danish and Swedish) has been generally preserved in the Peripheral Swedish vernaculars, but this is less significant, since it is true of most Peninsular Scandinavian vernaculars.

In the pronoun system, one may note various forms of the 1st person singular pronoun that contain the vowel *I*, such as *ik, ig, I*. It is somewhat unclear if this should be seen as a conservative feature or not – that is, whether the forms are derived directly from original "unbroken" forms such as Old Nordic *ek* or if they should be seen as reduced variants of "broken" forms like Standard Swedish *jag*. In any case, the *i*-forms are found, characteristically, in Norrbotten (although apparently restricted to Överkalix (Kalixmål) in the north), most of Westrobothnian, all of Ovansiljan, and Malung (Västerdalarna).

In verbal morphology, subject agreement is retained in Dalecarlian, in particular the Ovansiljan area, Northern Westrobothnian, and Norrbothnian. The distinction between singular and plural subjects is most widely marked but in Dalarna there is also special marking of the 1st and 2nd persons in the plural. It should be mentioned that verbs are also inflected for person and number in an area in Götaland (parts of Västergötland, Halland, and Småland) and in Gotland, Finland and parts of Estonia.

In phonology, the old *w*, corresponding to Central Scandinavian *v*, is retained, either only after consonants (including *h*, which later disappeared before *w/v*) or more generally in word-initial position (mainly Ovansiljan). Again, the same situation also obtains in parts of Götaland – much the same area as the one mentioned in the preceding paragraph but also including parts of Bohuslän. In another phonological development, Old Nordic *ē* became *ä* in large parts of southern Scandinavia, but is retained in Norway, northern Bohuslän, northern Dalsland, Dalecarlian, Norrlandic and in the Trans-Baltic area (Wessén 1966: 57).

There are also a number of conservative syntactic features, some of which have not been properly described in the literature. I shall discuss two of them in the following sections.

6.5.2 Infinitive constructions

Swedish employs an "infinitive marker" *att*, commonly pronounced [ɔ], which corresponds fairly well to English *to* with respect to its distribution. It is homographic to the complementizer *att* 'that' but in spoken language it is usually distinct from the latter, which is never reduced phonetically. Instead, the infinitive marker is homophonous with the reduced form of the conjunction *och* [ɔ], with which it is frequently confused. The two *att* also differ etymologically:

the complementizer is considered to derive from the demonstrative pronoun *þat*, whereas the infinitive marker comes from the preposition *at* 'to' (cf. §5.6) and was first used in final constructions:

(10) Early Written Medieval Swedish
    *Han är   i sokn farin, siukum   **at**   **hialpä.***
    he be.PRS in parish go.PP sick.DAT.PL INFm help.INF
    'He has gone to the parish to help the sick.' (Older Västgöta Law, Wessén 1956: 136)

In older forms of Swedish, the infinitive marker had a more restricted use than in Modern Swedish. In particular, we find bare infinitives as complements of adjectives as in:

(11) Early Written Medieval Swedish
    Bätra är   dyrt köpa än   swälta.
    better be.PRS dearly buy.INF than starve.INF
    'It is better to buy dearly than to starve.' (Wessén 1956: 138)

Wessén notes that in "Older Modern Swedish" the preposition *till* 'to' was frequently used as an infinitive marker. In fact, judging from the Cat Corpus material, cognates of this preposition are used very widely in vernaculars over most of Sweden (the old Danish provinces being an exception), and are in many cases the primary choice for an infinitive marker. The impression one gets is that *att*, when it does occur, is due to influence from the standard language.

In addition, a few conservative vernaculars seem to retain the older pattern where the infinitive marker is used more sparingly. Compare the following adjective complement uses of infinitives from the Cat Corpus:

(12) Elfdalian (Ovansiljan)
    *E war do fanta   me it so litt **bigrip**   **sig** o*
    it be.PST then devil_take me NEG so easy understand.INF REFL on
    kellinger, itsä!
    woman.PL NEG
    'It wasn't easy, damn it, to understand women!' (Cat Corpus)

(13) Nås (Västerdalarna)
    *Hä va   då innt lätt **begri´p**   sä   på kvinnfôłłk innt!*
    it be.PST then NEG easy understand.INF REFL on woman.PL NEG
    'It really wasn't easy to understand women!' (Cat Corpus)

(14) Skelletmål (Northern Westrobothnian)
*Hä jer   väl   bäst **pass**   sä.*
it be.PRS PRAG best **look_out.INF** REFL
'One had better look out.' (Cat Corpus)

(15) Sävar (Southern Westrobothnian)
*Hä tö   fäll   va   bäst **akt**   sä.*
it ought_to PRAG be.INF best **be_careful_about.INF** REFL
'One had probably better look out.' (Cat Corpus)

These examples come from Dalecarlian and Northern Westrobothnian, the two most conservative regions in the Peripheral Swedish area. But Källskog et al. (1993: 99) also quote examples from Roslagen along the coast of Uppland, in slightly different syntactic contexts:

(16) Väddö (Uppland)
*de håller   **spara***
it keep.PRS **save.INF**
'it will keep if you save it [lit. it keeps to save]'

(17) Hållnäs (Uppland)
*å   då   va   de **fåljâs**   åot*
and then be.PST it **follow_each_other.INF** at
'and then they had to go together'

In other words, infinitive constructions are interesting in two ways: (i) the choice of infinitive marker is one feature where modern Standard Swedish differs from most vernaculars spoken in historical Sweden but is similar to Standard Danish and the vernaculars of the previous Danish provinces; (ii) the more restricted use of infinitive markers in general is still another conservative feature common to Dalarna and Västerbotten, extending also to Uppland.

6.5.3 Temporal subjunctions

Vallmark (1937) studied the distribution of temporal subjunctions in the Swedish dialect area. In modern spoken Standard Swedish the dominant translation of English *when* is *när*, which is also used as an interrogative adverb. A more formal or bookish alternative is *då*, whose major sense is 'then', and which is attested from Runic Swedish, where it appears to have been the primary choice. *När* started to be used as a subjunction in Written Medieval Swedish but was still relatively rare there. Its subsequent spread has not been complete: many conservative vernaculars lack it, or still use *då* as a natural alternative. Elfdalian goes its own way: *mes* (etymologically identical to Swedish *medan(s)* 'while') is used for singular events or periods in the past, *da(r)* (etymologically 'there') is used in other cases (Åkerberg 2012: 152). The Cat Corpus material on the whole confirms the picture given by Vallmark. Areas that retain *då* thus include the Dalecarlian area except Älvdalen; Norrland except southern Hälsingland, Gästrikland, most of Jämtland, Pitemål and Nederkalixmål; Ostrobothnia, Åboland and Nyland; Estonia; and northern Gotland (see Figure 6.9). In Danish and Norwegian, *da* (etymologically the same as Swedish *då*) and *når* have a division of labour which resembles that between *als* and *wenn* in German.

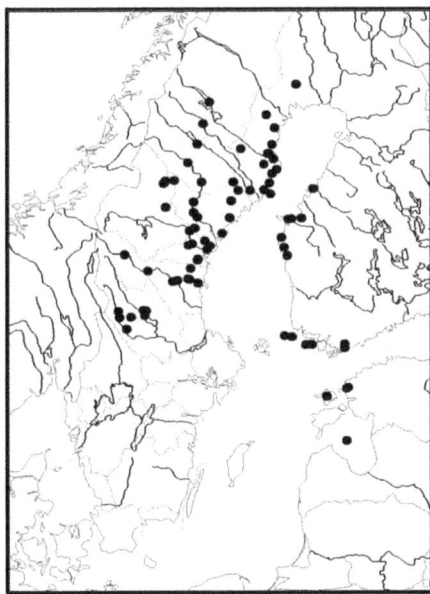

Figure 6.9: Vernaculars with predominant *då* as temporal subjunction according to Vallmark (1937).

A similar story can be told about the verbs for 'become' (Markey 1969). In the late Middle Ages, the verb *bliva* (in Modern Swedish usually *bli*), with the original meaning 'remain' and emanating from Low German *blîwen*, started to take over the domain of the verb *varda* 'become' in Scandinavian. Again, the victory was only partial. While *bli* appears to reign supreme in most of Götaland (including Gotland), southern Finland and Estonia, even colloquial Standard Swedish as spoken in the Mälar provinces retains the alternative past tense form *vart* 'became' of *varda*, although all the other forms have disappeared. Most vernaculars of Svealand and Norrland also retain the supine form *vurti* (or similar). In some areas, however, the whole paradigm still exists (see Figure 6.10, including large parts of Ovansiljan, Västerdalarna, Jämtland, Ångermanland, Västerbotten, Norrbotten, and Ostrobothnia.

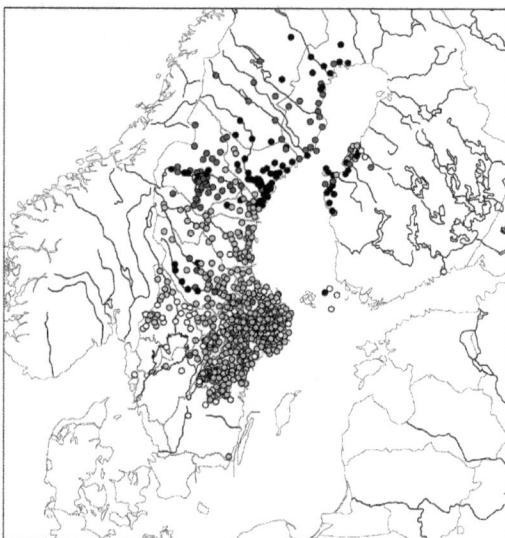

Figure 6.10: Degree of retainment of *varda* paradigm in the Swedish dialect area (Markey 1969). Black circles – full paradigm retained; grey circles – at least two forms retained; white circles – past tense only.

6.5.4 Lexical items

The vernaculars of the Peripheral Swedish area preserve many lexical items that have been discarded in Standard Swedish. As an example of an item with a wide distribution, descendants of Old Swedish *fæghin* 'happy' (cognate of English *fain*) may be mentioned as the standard counterpart of Swedish *glad*, e.g. Älvdalen *faingin*, Skellefteå *fajjen*, Färila *fäjjen*. (See Figure 6.11.) What is less conspicuous are cases where some Swedish lexical item is missing from a vernacular and replaced by a synonymous word that also exists in Swedish. Consider the words for 'find' in Swedish. While *finna* is still quite viable in written Swedish, the natural alternative in most spoken varieties is *hitta*. Both these words were found with the same meaning in Written Medieval Swedish, although *finna* may reasonably be assumed to be the older word, with cognates in all branches of Germanic. Most pertinent to our context, we find *hitta* in the preface to the Upplandic Law:

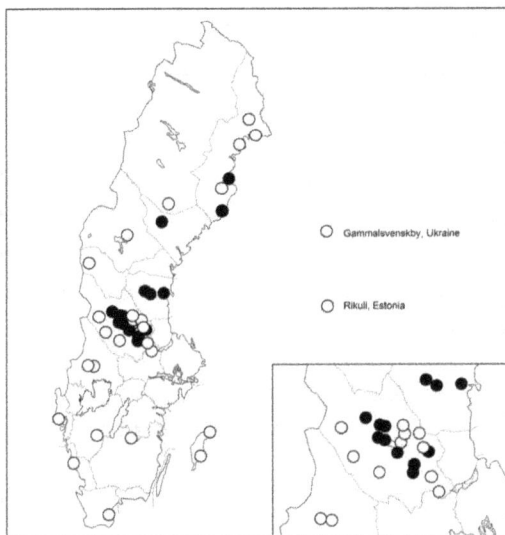

Figure 6.11: Cognates of *fæghin* in the Cat Corpus (filled circles).

(18)   Early Written Medieval Swedish
      Hwat ær wi **hittum**   *i hans laghsaghu ær allum*
      what ever we **find**.PRS.1PL in his   law.DAT   that all.DAT.PL
      mannum   *þarfflikt ær*   *þæt sætium*   *wir i bok þæssæ.*
      man.DAT.PL useful   be.PRS that put.PRS.1PL we in book this.F.ACC
      'Whatever we find in his law that is useful for everyone we include in this book.'

Turning now to the Cat Corpus, the Swedish version of the text contains three occurrences of the word *hitta* but none of *finna*, which is natural given the colloquial nature of the story. When checking how these are rendered in the other versions, we can see a widespread reluctance in the vernaculars to use the word *hitta*. At least nine versions use *finna* consistently, and about ten more do so in one or two cases of the three relevant ones. Except for Sotenäs (Bohuslän), all these versions emanate from the northern side of *limes norrlandicus*, and among the more consistent cases we find, not unexpectedly, Elfdalian (Ovansiljan) and the texts from the Northern Westrobothnian and Norrbothnian areas. In many of these texts, however, *hitta* shows up combined with the counterpart of the preposition *på* 'on' in the meaning 'to think of, make up':

(19)   Elfdalian (Ovansiljan)
       Wen al   ig itt   o i dag, truä?
       what shall.PRS I   find.INF on today think.INF
       'What shall I think of today, I wonder.'

It thus seems that *hitta* in its major use has never made its way into a significant number of Peripheral Swedish varieties. The natural conclusion would be that *hitta* was not part of the variety of Scandinavian which is the common ancestor of those varieties. In at least this respect, then, that language would differ from that of the Upplandic law.

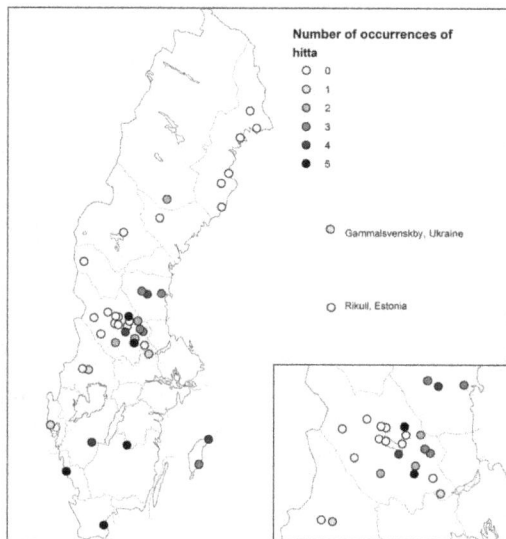

Figure 6.12: Distribution of *hitta* in the Cat Corpus.

6.6 The conservativity and innovativity indices

We have looked at a number of "archaisms" and a number of innovations in the Peripheral Swedish area. Their distributions are not identical, but certain tendencies are visible and can be made even clearer by assigning two indices to each parish: one index of "conservativity" and one of "innovativity", depending on how well the two types of features are represented in the vernacular in question. The definition of a conservative trait is one that is shared by the vernacular and the assumed common ancestor of all varieties in the Swedish dialect area, but which is not found in modern Standard Swedish. The definition of an innovative trait is one that is found neither in the assumed proto-language nor in modern Standard Swedish – and therefore must be assumed to have arisen through an innovation.

The following features enter into the conservativity index:

- Preservation of original *a* in positions where it has become *å* in Swedish

- Preservation of dative and/or accusative case in nouns

- Preservation of original diphthongs

- Preserved long stem vowels in cognates of Swedish *natt* 'night' and *döma* 'judge'

- Absence of temporal subjunction *när*

- No palatalization of *k* and *g* before front vowels in initial position

- Absence of preposed definite article

- Retainment of *varda* paradigm

- Preservation of *w*

The following features go into the innovativity index:

- Presence of demonstratives of the type *han där* and *he där*

- Absence of neutral pronouns *(h)ä(d)*

- Presence of diphthongs *ie* and *yö*

- Apocope

- *Pp* instead of *mp* in words such as *sopp* 'mushroom'

- Generic use of pronoun *han*

- Adjectival incorporation

- Deletion of *h*

- *(H)jär* 'here'

The result is shown in Figures 6.13–6.14.

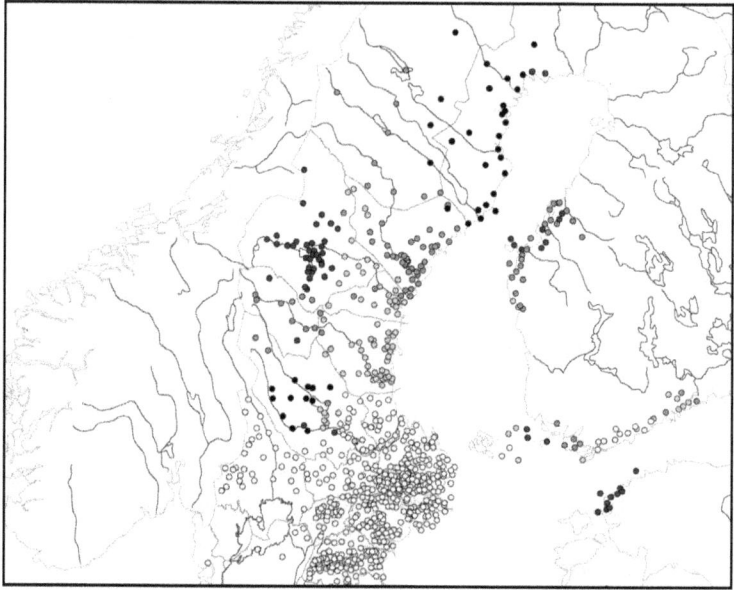

Figure 6.13: Distribution of conservative features in central and northern parts of the Swedish dialect area (darker circles – higher conservativity index).

As can be seen, the maps are similar enough for it not to be immediately obvious which map corresponds with the distribution of conservative vs. innovative features. From a visual inspection, conservativity and innovativity seem to be highly correlated. The correlation index turns out to be 0.62, which is perhaps not so impressive, but rises to 0.86 if we compare averages in dialect areas rather than values for individual parishes. The darkest areas of the maps are in Ovansiljan, northern Västerbotten and, to a lesser extent, Norrbotten. The most pronounced differences between the maps are found in Jämtland, which is more conservative than innovative, and Ostrobothnia, which is the other way around.

What conclusion should be drawn from the similarity between the maps? In my opinion, the most parsimonious way of explaining the parallels between the conservative and the innovative features is that they originally had a shared larger distribution but were later pushed back by essentially the same kinds of

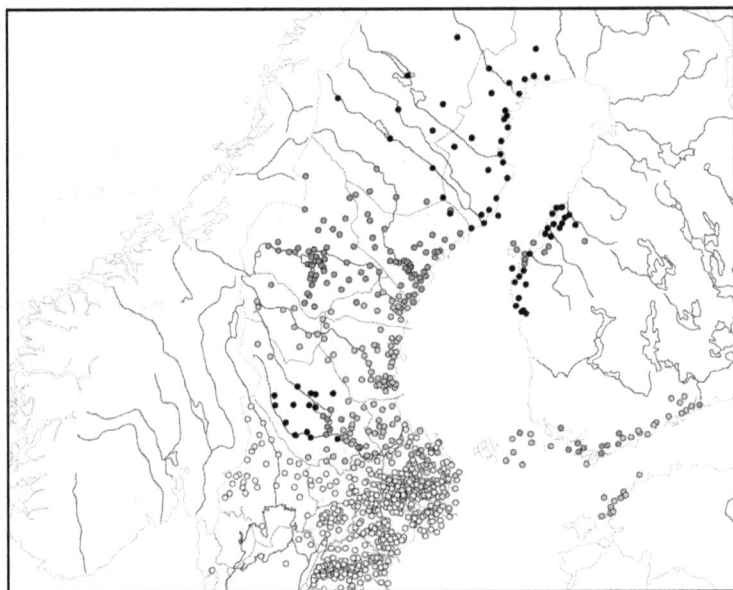

Figure 6.14: Distribution of innovative features in central and northern parts of the Swedish dialect area (darker circles – higher innovativity index).

processes. This means that the innovations must be old enough to have already been in place when these processes occurred. Given the general geographical picture, it appears that both the original spread of the innovative features and the later processes that obliterated them started in the same region, viz. in the Mälar provinces.

Now, an objection may be raised that the choice of features is somewhat arbitrary. As for the conservative traits, I have mainly tried to choose ones where there is enough reliable information to make mapping possible, but I do not think it is possible to choose a set of features that would give a radically different picture. For the innovative features, the situation is a bit different. Here, I have to a certain degree deliberately chosen ones that fit the point of view I am arguing for. This is, I think, in fact legitimate insofar as I want to show that there is a coherent set of phenomena that show a definite pattern, suggesting a common history. Other innovations may not fit into that pattern, which can be seen as an indication of a different scenario. In particular, it does seem that certain phenomena spread, not from central Sweden, but rather from Norway. These include the use of preproprial articles and of *h*-genitives, two phenomena that most likely are connected with each other.

6.7 Notes on the historical background

6.7.1 Medieval Sweden

According to the traditional view of Swedish history, during the Viking Age, if not earlier, the Svea ethnic group formed a kingdom with its centre in Uppland; this kingdom was fairly soon extended to also include the Göta ethnic group in central Götaland. developments in archaeology and history have modified this picture considerably. It is now thought that a stable central power was established in Sweden very gradually and probably not until the 13th century. The existence of "kings" in Uppland from relatively early times seems well documented, but it is unclear how far their sphere of influence extended. During the 9th and 10th centuries, the town of Birka in Lake Mälaren (which was at this time part of the Baltic Sea) was the commercial centre of the Mälar region and was apparently part of a larger network including Hedeby in southern Denmark (present-day Schleswig-Holstein) and Kaupang in Norway. Around the turn of the millennium, Birka was replaced by Sigtuna farther to the east. The 11th century is the time when most of the runic stones in Uppland were created. It appears that this was largely due to a "fashion" connected with the introduction of Christianity. There is evidence of Danish influence in Sigtuna during this period. According to the traditional account of the history of the Scandinavian languages, this was the time-point of the split between "East Nordic", comprised of Danish and Swedish, and "West Nordic", comprised of Norwegian and Icelandic. As I noted in Dahl (2001), the fact that Swedish and Danish seemed to go the same way – that is, that the same innovations were introduced in both Denmark and Sweden at the same time – is difficult to explain without assuming very intensive contact between the countries. It may be speculated that, in the Mälar provinces with Sigtuna as the centre, the introduction of Christianity was accompanied by the spread of a prestige dialect heavily influenced by Danish.

The 12th and 13th centuries are somewhat paradoxical in the sense that the "Svea" kings were mainly based in Götaland, with power alternating between the leading families of Västergötland and Östergötland. It appears that since the royal title carried considerable prestige, it was a useful resource when consolidating the developing central power in Götaland even if it was associated historically with the Mälar provinces. At the same time, these provinces were less centralized, and the ruling group of magnates (stormän) there was apparently quite happy as long as the person who was nominally their King stayed in Götaland and did not interfere in their affairs. The process of Christianization went considerably faster and apparently more smoothly in Götaland than in Svealand.

The fact that Svealand and Götaland had different monetary systems until the end of the 13th century is another sign of the incomplete integration of the two regions. In fact, most of the visible events in Swedish history during this period took place in Götaland – one gets the impression that the Mälar provinces were some kind of backwater. At any rate, there is very little written documentation from this period.

On the other hand, it does seem fairly clear that the Mälar provinces had a central part in one major economic and demographic development during this period, viz. the expansion of agriculture. Figure 6.15 shows the growth of permanently settled areas in Sweden from the Late Iron Age to the Late Middle Ages. As can be seen, it was during this period that large parts of the Peripheral Swedish area were settled. The same goes for the Swedish-speaking areas on the other side of the Baltic, which are not shown on the map. At least for the newly settled areas in Northern Sweden, it is probable that they received most of their new population from the Mälar provinces. Even areas that were already settled in the Iron Age, such as the peripheral parts of Uppland and the Middle Norrlandic provinces, greatly increased their population during this time (Broberg 1990), and it is reasonable to assume that there was considerable immigration from the central provinces.

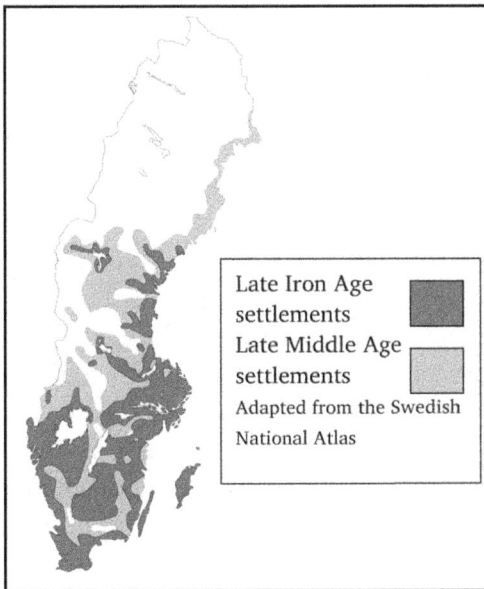

Figure 6.15: Growth of permanently settled areas between approx. 800CE and 1350CE.

At least for the northernmost parts, the expansion seems to have continued during the first half of the 14th century, when officially sanctioned colonization of the Lule and Pite river valleys took place, maybe in order to prevent Russian expansion plans in the area, and partly pushing back earlier Finnish settlements. In general, the expansion can be assumed to have been halted by the general agricultural crisis at the end of the Middle Ages, traditionally connected with the Black Death and a deterioration of the climate, and was not resumed until the 16th century (Myrdal 2003: 248). Before this, however, other important things had happened.

Whereas the political leaders of Götaland had shown a certain lack of interest in Svealand in the 12th and the beginning of the 13th century, this changed under Birger Jarl, who was never King but effectively ruled Sweden as "jarl" during the years 1248-1266. He belonged to a leading family of Östergötland but is probably most well-known as the alleged founder of Stockholm, although his role in this may have been slightly exaggerated. (The continuous rise of the land had given Stockholm a very strategic position, since this was now the only entrance to Mälaren from the Baltic.)

What is clear is that Birger Jarl used quite brutal means to take control over the Mälar provinces, and that he realized the economic potential of this region concluding among other things a treaty with the Hansa city Lübeck in order to promote the development of trade relations. The Mälar region was rapidly urbanized (see Figure 6.16). There were also considerable numbers of German merchants in the towns, and Low German was extensively used. German immigrants were also attracted to the Central Swedish mining district ("Bergslagen") which was gradually growing in importance. A major factor in this development was the copper mine in Falun in southern Dalarna. At the same time, the previously quite important production of iron from bog and lake ore in northern Dalarna lost its significance. This may have contributed to the isolation of this area which in its turn may have cemented the linguistic differences between the Dalecarlian vernaculars and the rest of the Swedish dialect area.

In the 14th century, Denmark's political influence grew, and in 1389, Denmark, Norway and Sweden were united in the Kalmar Union, which officially lasted until 1521, although in practice, Sweden was out of control for long periods.

Turning now to linguistic developments during the Middle Ages, there is a virtual break in the record between the runic stones of the 11th century and the first longer texts in Latin script in the 13th century, although there is evidence for a continuous tradition of writing with runes (mainly on wood). From the 13th century there are mainly provincial laws, the first longer text in Latin script em-

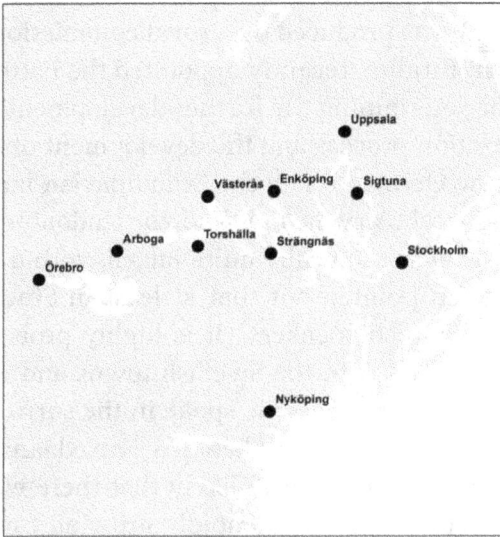

Figure 6.16: Cities and towns in the Mälar region in the late 13th century.

anating from the Mälar provinces is the Upplandic Law, which was promulgated by the King in 1296. ("Dalalagen" may be the oldest text from Svealand but its status is unclear.)

The centre of the development of Written Medieval Swedish seems to have been Östergötland, more specifically the south-west part around the town of Vadstena, which was also the origin of the ruling families of the province. Wessén (1966: 53) says that the Written Medieval Swedish was coloured by the Östergötland dialect[6], but one may surmise that it was the language of the élite that played the major role rather than that of the rank-and-file population. There has been little discussion of possible social variation in the language during this period, but given that society was highly stratified and that the ruling groups had intimate connections outside the area, it is to be expected that there were quite significant differences between the social classes. But Written Medieval Swedish, in particular the language of the legal texts, may also reflect older writing traditions.

There is relatively little dialectal variation in the provincial laws. This could be taken as an indication of the absence of such variation also in the spoken language, but in my opinion it rather suggests that there was in fact a relatively standardized way of writing such documents. We should therefore not expect,

---

[6] "fornsvenskt skriftspråk är östgötskt färgat; det är väsentligen Vadstenaspråk"

for example, the Upplandic Law to reflect spoken 13th century Upplandic to any great extent. After all, it was produced by a royal commission (headed by Birger Persson, father of Saint Birgitta, recently appointed the Patron Saint of Europe).

The strongest factor determining the further development of Swedish was undoubtedly the urbanization process and the development of trade relations. The strong influence of Low German on all the Scandinavian languages during this period, especially the vocabulary, is well known. Undoubtedly, the population of many Swedish towns was ethnically quite mixed, with a large proportion of Germans. It is also often pointed out that at least in Stockholm there was a fairly large number of Finnish speakers. It is highly probable that special urban varieties would have arisen in the Swedish towns and would have differed quite considerably from the ways people spoke in the surrounding countryside. Scholars such as Wessén (1954) have spoken of a "mixed language" as a result of German-Swedish contacts. But it is also likely that there were other non-local influences, since the population of the rapidly growing towns in the 13th and 14th century Mälar provinces would have also been recruited from other parts of Sweden. Birger Jarl's taking control of the Mälar provinces must also have meant a movement of people from Östergötland to Stockholm and other towns in the area, and this may have especially had consequences for the prestige variety.

In addition, the role of Danish has probably been underestimated. The 19th century scholar Esaias Tegnér, Jr. voiced the opinion that "even if, as is natural, Swedish received many loans directly from German during the Low German period..., it is the Danish influence during the period of the Kalmar union which to a quite essential extent has contributed to the establishment of such Low German words and to the form in which they appear".[7] Tegnér points to the high degree of correspondence between the Low German grammatical and lexical elements in Danish and Swedish and to the fact that the same deviations from the original Low German forms tend to show up in both languages. Such differences that are found, he says, are usually attributable to later High German influences. I checked Tegnér's claims by looking at the words listed as Low German loans in Hellquist (1922); as it turns out, a very high proportion (perhaps something like 90 per cent) do exist or have existed also in Danish. Scholars after Tegnér, however, have not paid too much attention to his hypothesis. Wessén (1954) is sceptical: according to him, the high degree of correspondence, which he does

---

[7] "En granskning af de tyska lånorden i vårt språk har bibragt mig det intrycket, att om ock svenskan naturligtvis under den lågtyska perioden (intill reformationstiden) mottagit många lån omedelbart från tyskan, så är det likväl i ganska väsentlig grad danskarnas inflytande i Sverige under Kalmarunionens tid, som bidragit därtill att dylika lågtyska ord blivit bofasta hos oss och att de uppträda i den form, som vi finna dem hava." (Tegnér 1889: 159)

not deny, can be explained by the common "cultural and linguistic preconditions" for borrowings in Danish and Swedish. I would personally tend to side with Tegnér on this issue. It is, furthermore, possible to establish quite a long list of points where Standard Swedish and urban Central Swedish join Standard Danish against most of the vernaculars in Peninsular Scandinavia, at least those north of the Southern Swedish/East Danish dialect area, such as the restructured gender system, the feminine definite suffix -en, the use of att (rather than till as an infinitive marker and man as a generic pronoun, consistent preposed placement of possessive pronouns etc.

It is commonly said that Standard Swedish arose from the dialects of the Mälar region, but it is often not made clear exactly which these dialects were. Källskog et al. (1993: 67), in their discussion of the similarity between Standard Swedish and Upplandic, claim that the base for the former is to be found in medieval "high-status dialects, primarily Upplandic and östgötska [the speech of Östergötland]".[8] Thus, they say, it is not the case that Upplandic has been influenced by the standard language in Stockholm and Uppsala, it is rather the other way around. The Swedish expression they use for 'high-status dialects', "folkmål med hög status", sounds almost like an oxymoron, given that "folkmål" is usually understood as denoting rural, non-standard varieties. In fact, their claim does not make a lot of sense if the flow of influence is not supposed to go from rural to urban varieties. In the next section, we shall look more closely at the dialect situation in Uppland.

6.7.2 Uppland

To understand the dialectological situation in Uppland, it is of some importance to relate it to the administrative and demographic structure of the province.

The present-day province of Uppland has, strictly speaking, never functioned as an administrative unit. The judicial province (lagsaga) of Uppland that was created in 1296 also included the province of Gästrikland, and was formed by merging three so-called "folklands", Fjädrundaland (Fjärdhundraland), Tiundaland, and Attundaland. These names mean "the land of four (ten, eight) hundreds" and refer to the number of hundare,[9] smaller administrative units, suggesting that the names were created as a bureaucratic measure from above rather than developing naturally. The coastal region nowadays called Roslagen had a

---

[8] "Stommen i detta språk utgjordes av folkmål med hög status, främst uppländska och östgötska..."

[9] The word hundare corresponds etymologically to English hundred, used in medieval England as a term for a division of a shire The hundare were later on identified with the judicial districts called härad.

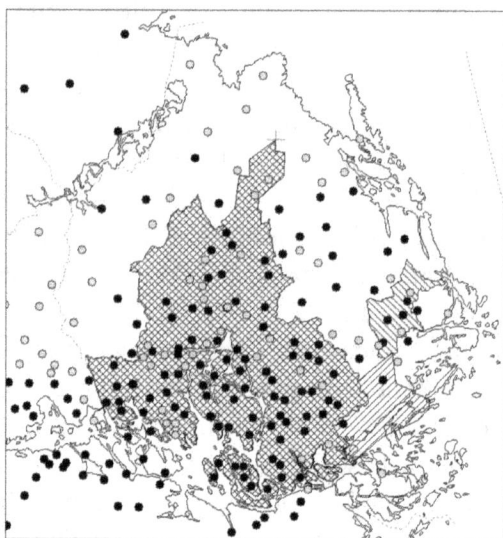

Figure 6.17: Uppland with "high-activity" areas and medieval churches (black cir‐
cles represent churches built 1000–1250, grey circles churches built
1250-1500; left hatching – hundreds with >20 runic stones, right
hatching – >50 per cent land with tax-relief in the mid 16th century).

somewhat uncertain status: it was divided into two halves, referred to as "Norra
Roden" and "Södra Roden", and loosely attached to Tiundaland and Attundaland
respectively.

The population of Uppland has always been unevenly distributed. Figure 6.18
shows the present-day situation, with a heavy concentration in the urban areas
around Stockholm and Uppsala. The medieval distribution was not that different,
in fact. The hatched areas in Figure 6.17 (after Broberg 1990) show the following
indicators of social stratification (and thus, presumably the areas with the great‐
est economic activity and densest population) in earlier times: (i) the hundreds
with more than 20 runic stones, (ii) the hundreds which had more than 50 per
cent land with tax-relief (that is, land owned by the state, the church or the nobil‐
ity) in the mid 16th century. It is somewhat remarkable that these two indicators
coincide almost completely, and are not too different from what we find today.

Figure 6.17 also shows the medieval churches in the area, according to the
database of the Swedish National Heritage Board (www.raa.se). These data are
of some interest because they show a possible model for the way linguistic in‐
novations may have spread in this period. We can see that there is a concentra‐

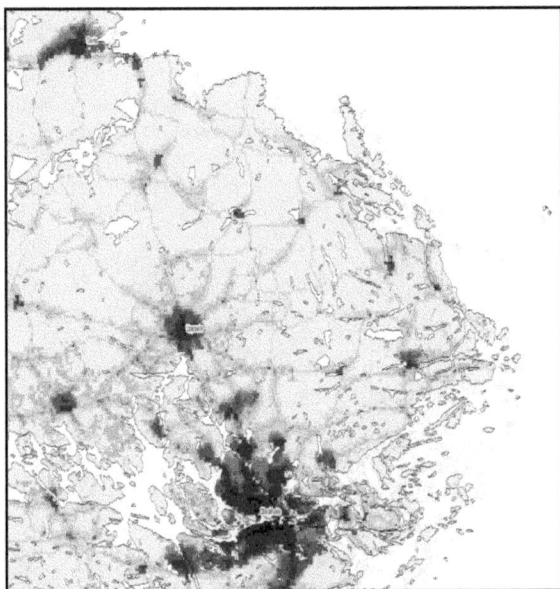

Figure 6.18: Distribution of population in present-day Uppland.

tion of early churches in the southern part of the hatched area, whereas church construction in the Late Middle Ages took place to a much larger extent in the peripheral areas.

The conclusion that can be drawn is that medieval Uppland, like Uppland of today, can be understood as having consisted of a centre in the middle south, in the areas adjacent to Lake Mälaren, and a periphery around it. Crucially, this persistent division cross-cuts the old administrative division into folklands, as can be seen when comparing Figure 6.18–Figure 6.17 with Figure 6.19. The structure of Uppland is somewhat like (half) a pizza, with each folkland representing one slice, all of which meet in the most densely populated area in the south in the immediate vicinity of the medieval towns Uppsala and Sigtuna. Each folkland itself thus consists of a central and a peripheral part.

The first and in some ways still most complete account of the Upplandic dialects is that of Kruuse (1908).[10] Kruuse is somewhat hesitant to divide Uppland into dialect areas, being well aware that "the area of one linguistic feature very seldom coincides with the area of another, and strictly speaking we cannot speak of a certain number of dialects with definite borders". After having stated this

---

[10] Kruuse says that he bases his account on word lists collected in a survey led by A. Erdmann, in addition to various written works. (The later fate of these word lists is unclear.)

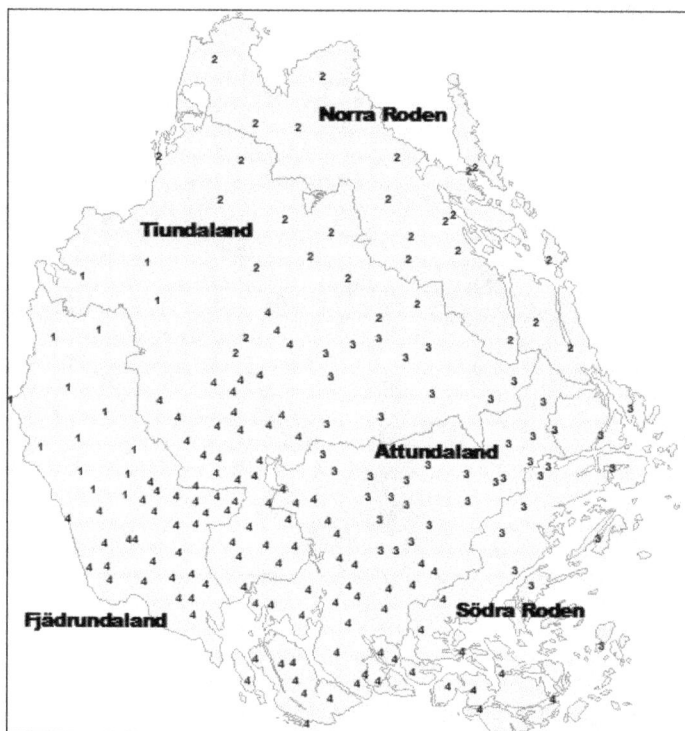

Figure 6.19: Kruuse's dialect areas and the Upplandic folklands

reservation, he presents a division of the province into four areas, based on a number of important isoglosses. There is a map provided with Kruuse's article, but it shows the isoglosses rather than the areas – neither Kruuse nor anybody else seems to have drawn a map of the areas themselves, so Figure 6.19 is my own reconstruction from the description in Kruuse's text.

A different division is given by Hesselman (1920: 1194) in his article on Upplandic dialects in the encyclopedia *Nordisk familjebok*. He proposes to divide the Upplandic vernaculars "in three larger groups, whose borders by and large follow those of the ancient folklands".[11] This statement is echoed in later treatments. Thus, in Källskog et al. (1993: 75), it is said that Uppland can be divided "into three dialect areas, which to some extent coincide" with the folklands.[12] The change

---

[11] "En god indelning är den, som sammanför upplandsmålen i tre större grupper, hvilkas gränser i stort sedt följa de gamla uppländska folklandens."

[12] "Landskapet Uppland kan grovt delas in i tre dialektområden som i någon mån sammanfaller

rom "by and large" to "to some extent" may reflect a certain uneasiness on part of the authors. In their ensuing presentation, however, the names of the folklands are used as labels of the three areas, with which they are in practice identified. In my opinion, such a practice is rather misleading. As can be seen from Figure 6.19, the placement of the borders of the folklands, does not coincide very well with the areas proposed by Kruuse, and indeed, if one looks at the borders of individual phenomena, they tend not to honour the actual folkland borders. What is particularly important here is that three of Kruuse's areas that "to some extent" coincide with the folklands (Areas 1-3) are actually mainly located on their periphery, while Kruuse's Area 4 equals the demographic and economic centre of the province, which as we have seen, also includes the pivot points of all three folklands. Note that Kruuse's Area 4 is wholly included in the central area indicated in Figure 6.17 and in fact follows its borders relatively closely, except in the east. This does not warrant the conclusion that Kruuse's areas directly reflect the demographic and economic situation in the Middle Ages. The explanation is rather that the centre-periphery division of Uppland has been relatively constant over the last millennium and that it is this division that underlies the modern dialectological make-up of Uppland, being a result of the expansion of innovations from a centre towards a periphery as much as an ancient division into subprovinces. In particular, some of the borderlines drawn by Kruuse may be snapshots of a moving boundary.

Wessén (1966: 77), having first pointed to the possibility of an influence of "German sound formation and German linguistic habits" on medieval Stockholm speech, says that medieval documents suggest that the spoken language in Stockholm was "to a striking extent" coloured by Central Swedish and Götamål (see §2.3.2). (He explains this by immigration from the "inner Mälar provinces", but does not say where the Göta influence would come from.)

Among the traits characterizing parts of Uppland, there is a subset which shows some interesting and partly baffling characteristics. To start with, most treatments, beginning with Kruuse (or even earlier, in Rydqvist 1868), tell us that there have been changes in the pitch accent systems in parts of Uppland: the acute accent has been generalized in the northeast (the eastern part of Kruuse's Area 2), while the grave accent is generalized in large parts of southern Uppland and also in the eastern part of Södermanland (most of Kruuse's Area 4 and parts of his Area 1, see Figure 6.20). The generalized grave accent is discussed in some detail in Nyström (1997).[13] (For an account of the present-day

---

med de tre s.k. folklanden från vikingatid och medeltid..."

[13] It is not always clear if the generalization means that all words are pronounced with a grave

situation, see Ericsson 2006). Nyström mentions two logical possibilities: either the grave accent was productive at the time when the definite article became an affix (see §3.1.4) and monosyllabic words became bisyllabic through the insertion of a "svarabhakti" vowel, or the generalization is a later innovation, taking place some time between the changes just mentioned and the mid 19th century, when the phenomenon was first documented. In the latter case, which he seems to lean towards, it is plausible to assume, he says, that the generalized grave accent was also found in the urban varieties spoken in Stockholm (as was also suggested by Otterbjörk 1982) and that maybe Stockholm was in fact the origin of the development. If the contiguous area shown in Figure 6.20 could not include its geographical centre, Stockholm, this would be hard to explain "from the point of view of dialect geography". A possible scenario would then be as follows: the "massive Low German influence" in the city during the late Middle Ages would have triggered the coalescence of the two pitch accents, and this would then have spread to neighbouring areas. Later on, the pitch accent distinction would have been re-introduced in Stockholm during the expansion of the city from the 18th century onwards, as a combined result of the influx of people from other parts of the country and the rise of a national spoken standard. In the context of our discussion, this hypothesized development is highly interesting in that it illustrates how innovations from a centre could be canceled by later spreads from the same centre. In fact, there are a few more features that have a rather peculiar distribution in the Mälar area and which could be ascribed to similar processes.

One such feature is the preservation of *k* before initial front vowels, reported by Kruuse (1908) (he gives examples such as *kepp* 'stick' and *körä* 'drive' from the Vätö vernacular). This feature was found in areas almost enclosing Stockholm (see Figure 6.20) but has probably more or less disappeared by now. It certainly looks as a conservative feature, but the donut shape of the area would rather suggest an expansion from Stockholm outwards. In the speech of the capital, it might be due to foreign, possibly Danish, influence.

The other feature to be noted here is the definite endings of feminine nouns. In Written Medieval Swedish, the definite form of a word such as *bok* 'book' was *bokin*. In the modern vernaculars of most parts of Sweden and Norway, feminine words would take a definite suffix -*a* or -*i*, but there is an area to the north and south of Lake Mälaren where the ending is -*en*. In Figure 6.20, the borderlines

---

accent or that just more of them are than in the standard language. Thus, Nyström enumerates some standard minimal pairs such as *ánden* 'the duck': *ànden* 'the spirit' and says that they are all pronounced with a grave accent, and then adds that "also polysyllabic words such as *betàla* 'pay', *indiàner* 'indians'..." are pronounced "more often" with a grave accent.

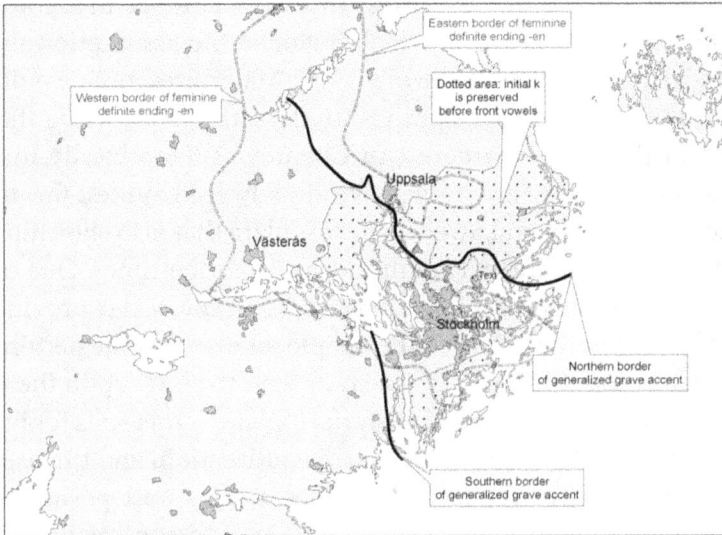

Figure 6.20: Some mysterious dialect phenomena in the Mälar area.

of this area are shown in accordance with Modéer (1946). This is often seen as a conservative feature, but the fact that it is also found in Denmark and the South Swedish dialect area, as well as in Standard Swedish, suggests that it could also be the result of an import from the south into the Stockholm area, from which it then expanded. In this connection, it is not irrelevant that the *-en* ending tends to be connected with a breakdown of the old three-gender system and the rise of the new two-gender one – a development which is common to Stockholm speech and varieties in Denmark and Southern Sweden.

It may be seen as a difficulty for this hypothesis that the *-en* area extends as far as Gästrikland in the north. On the other hand, the distribution of the *-en* ending is not too different from that of the generalized grave accent, as described by Kruuse, which goes at least as far north as the border between Uppland and Gästrikland.

It is not excluded, however, as assumed by Lindström & Lindström (2006: 239), that even if there is influence from the south in the high-prestige varieties, the *-en* ending in the more peripheral parts of the area is a conservative trait.

As was noted above, the settlement of the Peripheral Swedish area took place mainly during the period between 1200 and 1350. If the assumption that the Mälar provinces were the major contributors to this expansion, we might expect the Peripheral Swedish vernaculars to reflect the varieties that were spoken in those provinces in the 13th-14th centuries. This would also be in accordance with the view expounded above in §6.1, which included the assumption that at least the more standard varieties of the present-day Mälar provinces would preserve the traits of those varieties to a significantly lesser extent. While the phenomena that were at the focus of interest in Chapters 3-5 are hardly found in the Mälar provinces at all, there are, as we have already seen, quite a few other traits characteristic of the Peripheral Swedish vernaculars that also show up in at least parts of Uppland and even further south, at least in earlier times. One might hope that the geographical distribution of those traits in the Mälar provinces would tell us something about the origin of the people who settled the periphery. What we see, however, is that the traits in question tend to show up in the peripheral parts, that is, primarily northern and eastern Uppland – this goes for innovations such as the distribution of *h*-pronouns, medial affrication, and the use of *han* as a generic pronoun, and for conservative traits such as post-position of possessive pronouns, omission of infinitive markers, retained consonant clusters such as *mb* (as in *lamb* 'lamb') and various others. It is less likely that these somewhat sparsely populated parts of Uppland were the major source for the emigration to the Peripheral Swedish area – rather, they were themselves at least partly settled during the same period (Broberg 1990). The settlers will have come primarily from the more populous regions in the southern and western parts of Uppland, and the reason that there are not more similarities between the vernaculars of those areas and the ones in the Peripheral Swedish has to be that those similarities were obliterated under external influence.

In their treatment of the critical historical period in the Mälar provinces, Lindström & Lindström (2006) argue for a somewhat different picture. According to them, the resistance against Birger Jarl's strivings to control the Mälar provinces was concentrated in the southwestern part of Uppland – Fjädrundaland (Fjärdhundraland) (which also may have included parts of Västmanland at the time). They argue that this area is characterized by a linguistic conservatism, assumed to reflect the unwillingness of the medieval population to accept foreign innovations. Moreover, they say that there is evidence that the emigration to the peripheral areas was concentrated in this area: "From a purely linguistic point of view there are several common traits to these newly settled regions and precisely the peculiar dialect of the Fjärdhundra area."

These claims are a bit unexpected in the light of what I have just said about the distribution of linguistic traits in Uppland. The empirical evidence they provide also turns out to be a bit thin. The trait that they discuss in some detail[14] is the

---

[14] The other trait they mention is the "pure å-sound for old short >o<" ("det rena å-ljudet för

definite feminine noun ending -*en* discussed above, which is in their opinion a conservative trait in Fjädrundaland. Even if we assume that they are right on this point, the -*en* ending can hardly be used as evidence for the connection between Fjädrundaland and the peripheral areas, since the feminine definite suffix generally ends in a vowel rather than in -*n* in the Peripheral Swedish vernaculars except the vernaculars spoken in Finland. In most of the area, the general ending is -*a*, the exception being the Ovansiljan area, where it is -*i*/-*e* or (nasalized) -*i̯*/-*e̯*. In this respect, there is a connection between Ovansiljan, coastal vernaculars in Roslagen (Uppland) and Södertörn (Södermanland) as well as Gotland, where the ending -*i* is also found. Given that -*i* is also found as a feminine definite ending in some vernaculars in the inner parts of Norway, the total picture of the distribution of feminine definite suffixes is rather confusing.

In fact, the Ovansiljan area shares other traits with the coastal areas of Uppland and Södermanland that are not found further north in Sweden, including the diphthongs *ie* and *yö*, corresponding to Swedish long *e* and *ö*, and the disappearance of the *h* phoneme, although the last-mentioned feature is admittedly probably a late innovation in the Dalecarlian area. In any case, the linguistic evidence for an early strong connection between south-western Uppland and Dalarna, as suggested by Lindström & Lindström (2006: 237), and as might prima facie seem natural from the geographical point of view, is rather scanty.[15]

---

gammalt kort >o<" (Lindström & Lindström 2006: 315). I am not sure what this refers to, possibly to the pronunciation of the feminine plural ending -*or*.

[15] Lindström & Lindström (2006: 237) also indirectly admit this by saying that if the contact between Uppland and Dalarna had not been "cut off" by the immigration to the high-mobility mining district, the connection would have been "much more apparent" ("mycket mer uppenbart").

7 Concluding discussion

What we have seen in this book is a variety of developments within the grammar of noun phrases in the vernaculars of the Peripheral Swedish area. Some of these developments are astonishingly uniform across this vast area, suggesting an early origin. But at the same time we find diversity in details, and in some domains, perhaps most strikingly in the marking of possessive constructions, a bewildering number of alternative ways of expressing the same content.

What can we find here that is of interest beyond the purely dialectological description of phenomena?

Let us begin with a look at the grammaticalization of definite articles. This is a topic that has been studied in some detail, but the particular patterns we find in the Peripheral Swedish area are relatively unusual typologically and have not been studied from a cross-linguistic or diachronic point of view. It was shown in Greenberg's classical work (Greenberg 1978) that definite articles can develop beyond what we would normally think of as their final stage of development, the "full-blown" definite article as we find it for instance in English. In the cases discussed by Greenberg, the articles eventually develop into general affixes on nouns, carrying gender and number information. Another possible further stage is found in the "specific" articles in Austronesian languages (see §3.1.3. In Peripheral Swedish vernaculars, we now see another development: definite articles – or definite suffixes on nouns – are extended to a number of uses commonly associated with articleless indefinites – non-delimited ("partitive") uses, uses with quantifiers and low-referentiality uses of singular count nouns. I hypothesized in Chapter 3 that these developments, for which the clearest parallels are found in Moroccan Arabic, are mediated by generic uses of definite noun phrases, which are more pervasive in the Peripheral Swedish vernaculars than in Central Scandinavian. Evidence from Romance, in particular Italian and Italian vernaculars, was given in support of this.

As I argued in Dahl (2003), there have been several different grammaticalizations of definite articles in the North Germanic area, and in a large part of the area, this led to competition between preposed and suffixed articles, with different solutions in different varieties. The notion of a "buffer zone" which was used in Stilo (2004) to refer to the more general phenomenon of a typologically "inconsistent" zone between two areas with consistent typological patterns. may be applied here.

In the Peripheral Swedish area, the suffixed articles are in general the strongest, the preposed being rather marginal, but we also find "non-standard" developments of demonstratives into preposed definites, a somewhat neglected topic in the literature.

Adjective incorporation, which is another pervasive phenomenon in the Peripheral Swedish area, represents a type of incorporation which differs from other more well-known cases such as noun incorporation. Most notably, it is in many varieties obligatory in the sense that it is the only way of combining an adjective with a definite noun. Regrettably, the origin of the incorporation construction remains rather obscure, and due to the lack of data from earlier periods we may never be able to find out exactly how it came about. It does seem, however, that the incorporating construction arose through a process in which combinations of weak attributed adjectives with apocopated endings and definite head nouns were reinterpreted as compounds. In the vernaculars where incorporated adjectives compete with syntactic constructions, the division of labour between the alternatives is reminiscent of that between, for example, preposed and postposed attributive adjectives in Romance, in that incorporated and preposed adjectives tend to be chosen primarily from the set of "prototypical" adjectives identified by Dixon (1977). Further research is needed to elucidate the principles by which choices between alternative attributive constructions are made in the languages of the world.

A common feature to the phenomena studied in this book is that these are innovations, relative to older forms of North Germanic, and are usually more or less restricted to the Peripheral Swedish area or parts of it. This also means that as the standard language – Swedish – advances or at least increases its influence on local varieties, the features in question tend to retreat and eventually disappear. This is a kind of situation which has not received due attention in the literature on grammatical change (see Dahl (2004) for a discussion). What is peculiar about it is that it represents a seeming reversal of the original grammaticalization process, and could thus be said to be a kind of degrammaticalization – a notion which has usually been taken to necessarily involve a development from grammatical to lexical morphemes. More concretely: in some language variety, a grammatical construction is extended to a new use, but after some time this use disappears under the pressure of some neighbouring language variety in which the original change never took place. An interesting problem then is what exactly happens if the reversal takes place gradually rather than all at once – is this process in any way comparable to the original grammaticalization?

There is in fact some evidence to suggest that this is the case. More specifically, if we look at the extended uses of definite forms in the Peripheral Swedish area, there is at least one fairly clear case where the contexts which survive longest when the uses are disappearing are those that most probably were the first to appear when the extension took place. It was suggested in Chapter 3 that the non-delimited uses of definite forms developed out of generic uses of such forms. It was also noted that there are intermediate cases where it is possible to choose between a generic noun phrase and an indefinite one, and that such cases are presumably the bridgehead for the further expansion of definites into the non-delimited territory. For example, both in Standard Italian and Italian vernaculars, definite noun phrases corresponding to English bare NPs are more likely to show up in habitual contexts. Thus, (1)(a) is more natural than (b).

(1) Italian

    a. *Papà beve*   *la birra* ogni mattina.
        father drink.PRS.3SG DEF **beer** every morning

        'Father drinks beer every morning.'

    b. father PROG.3.SG drink.GER DEF **beer** exact hour

        'Father is drinking beer right now.' (Pier Marco Bertinetto,
        pers.comm.)

But in a similar way, in the vernacular of Sollerön (Ovansiljan), (2), repeated here, the choice of the definite form induces a habitual interpretation:

(2) Sollerön (Ovansiljan)
    An drikk   *mjotji.*
    he drink.PRS milk.DEF

    'He drinks milk.' (questionnaire)

The difference between the two cases is that for the vernacular of Sollerön, we have reason to assume that (2) represents a receding use, that is, it is likely that the definite forms were used more generally in non-delimited contexts, whereas there is no such evidence for Italian – rather, we have to see Italian as a language which has undergone only the initial stages of the extension of definite marking that we see in the Peripheral Swedish area.

    It is not unreasonable that the contexts first hit by an expanding construction should also be the last ones to remain when the use of that construction contracts. More empirical evidence is needed, however, to establish whether this is a general phenomenon. I want to mention here a somewhat similar case from the literature on language change. In their discussion of Cappadocian Greek, Thomason & Kaufman (1988), quoting Dawkins (1916), note that the use of the definite article has "declined drastically". That this has taken place under the influence of Turkish rather than independently is seen from the fact that the Greek article is retained "only in the single morphosyntactic context where Turkish marks definiteness – on direct objects (i.e., in the accusative case)". This is not a perfect parallel, and it is also not clear that the accusative in Turkish is a marker on definiteness on direct objects rather than a direct object marker on definite NPs However, what it shows is the following. Differential marking of definite and indefinite objects commonly arises as an extended use of some case marker or adposition, e.g. a marker of indirect objects. But as we see here, there is another possibility where, under the influence of patterns in a neighbouring language such marking is the result of shrinking the domain of use of a grammatical morpheme.

A somewhat related problem arises with the incorporated adjectives. As we have seen, in some areas, adjectival incorporation is restricted to a few "prototypical" adjectives such as 'big' and 'new'. At least in the Ovansiljan area, this appears to be a fossilized state of a more general construction which was used more indiscriminately with definite attributive adjectives, and which has been pushed back by a competing construction (with a demonstrative pronoun in the function of preposed article). The question is if this is the only way in which such lexically restricted incorporation can arise. In some Romance languages, some "prototypical" adjectives, when preposed to a noun, behave in a way that looks very much like the incorporated adjectives of Peripheral Swedish in that the final ending may be elided, as in Spanish *un gran hombre* 'a great man' (as compared to *un hombre grande* 'a big man', with the adjective in a non-reduced form). In the absence of evidence that this has been a more general process, it seems most natural to assume that it is a process that has hit these particular adjectives exclusively. Likewise, it is questionable whether adjectival incorporation has ever been a more general process for instance in the varieties of Norwegian where it occurs with a few adjectives such as *ny* 'new'. It would thus seem that there is more than one path to the synchronic state in which prototypical adjectives enter into a tighter relationship with a head noun. What I have said here does not preclude that there may be other aspects of the developments that make the patterns in Scandinavian and Romance differ (such as a differentiation in meaning between the preposed and postposed variants).

The other field for which this investigation may be relevant is the history of the Scandinavian languages. Traditional accounts of this history tend to see it as a linear development in which the various vernaculars grow out of relatively unified older stages; for the ones spoken within the original Swedish provinces, it is usually assumed that they derive from what is referred to as *fornsvenska* or "Old Swedish", which was gradually differentiated into Svea and Göta vernaculars. However, the traits that were involved in this differentiation, such as the lengthening of short syllables, are relatively late and can be attributed to the period after Birger Jarl's taking control of the Svea provinces – which among other things is reflected in the fact that these developments were only partly implemented in the Peripheral Swedish area. On the other hand, a large number of innovations, including the ones which this book focuses on, are widespread in the same area and also sometimes other more central parts of the old Svea provinces. Historically, some of these developments, such as the innovations of the pronoun system, can be shown to go back to medieval times, and must thus be the result of an early spread in the Svea area of influence. Since these developments show a very different geographical pattern from the innovations that differentiated Svea vernaculars from the Göta ones, it is unlikely that they took place at the same time or spread along the same routes. Rather, I would argue, we should assume that they are older, having spread during a period when the influence from the south had not yet become very strong in the Mälar provinces, from which they were later pushed back. The development of the language of the Mälar region has thus not been linear in the sense that the modern varieties of that region are to be seen as direct descendants of the varieties spoken there in the early Middle Age. If this is the case, one may wonder why it has not been obvious to earlier researchers. It may be noted that the assumption of a linear development fits well with the traditional view of Sweden as having always had a natural political and economic center in Svealand. The more recent view, that the main center of power has at times been located in Götaland, can be more easily combined with a non-linear view of linguistic developments. It may also be the case that the focus on sound change in traditional historical linguistics has detracted attention from phenomena of a more grammatical (particularly syntactic) character, phenomena which the Peripheral Swedish developments tend to demonstrate.

I thus hope to have demonstrated that the study of grammatical phenomena in traditional non-standardized varieties can uncover typologically interesting patterns as well as suggest paths of development and spread of linguistic phenomena.

Appendix A: Quotations from older texts

7.1 Some cases of extended uses of definite articles in Written Medieval Swedish

Mistha klöffwana

> Misther falken klöffwana, Tha tak paper oc *tänth elden thär j* oc bren the thaana som klöffwen wil aff falla, oc smör sidhan äffther mädh honagh oc bint bombas thär wm j nyo dagha etc:-

[S7], #142

Göra en sten som tänder eld aff spwteno

> Tak osläktan kalk tw lod, tuciam som ey är tilredh ij lod, salpeter ij lod, brennesten ij lod, camfora ij lod, calamitam ij lod, Stötis alth ganskans granth oc sammanblandis sictandis gönom en haardwk. Sidan läth thet alth j en posa aff nyth oc täth lärofft trykkiandis harth samman oc täth före knytandis, sidan läg then posan j ena leer krwko, oc eth lok lwtera tättelika oc starkelika affwan wpp swa ath jngen ande kan wthkomma, oc säth swa pottona äller leerkrwekona j oghnen *görandis eldhen* wmkringh, oc när alt är bränth wthtakes oc ypnas krwkan oc tw findher alth wara giorth j en steen som tändher eld aff sig när som spwttas pa honom...
>
> Sidhan tak then kalken vth oc mal smaan som grannaste myöl, Sidhan läth thz myölith j glasith mz hwilko plägha distilleras hängiandis thz j en kätil affwan wathnith tw twär fingher, Swa ath thz ey taker wathnith, oc *gör elden* wndy kätillen, swa smälter qwekselffwens kalker j the warmo bastwffwonne, oc flyther j glaseno,

[S7], #154

> ...tha gik then goda Blandamær
> och løstæ allæ the fanger ther

wæræ, riddare och swenæ,
badæ fatigæ och rikæ,
och *stikkade* swa *elden* j borgenæ och brende henne nidh j røter.

[S27]

7.2 The presumed oldest attestation of an extended use of a definite article in Dalecarlian

... Ötwerd tarwer ok / sosse tita / full /
misusmör ok skiwåråsod /
Lunssfiskren / Qwotta / Miokblötu wridäl / ...
ålt såmå gäwe gwot mod.

Swedish translation (Björklund 1994: 166): "Aftonvard tarvar också, såsom tina full, messmör och (skivor å såd?), surfisk(en), grisar, mjölkblöta, knotskål, allt-samman give gott mod."

7.3 A medieval Norwegian text demonstrating the use of preproprial articles (Diplomatarium Norvegicum XVI:94)

Thet se ollum godom monnum kunnokt sem þetta bref sia
æder høra at ek Aslak Aslaksson wæt þet firi gudi sant wara
at Andris Ormsson gud hans sæil haui war at allo skilgætæn ok
swa hans synir Orm ok **han Olaf** jtem hørdæ ok ek ofta ok
morgom sinnom at þe brødernæ Ormer ok **han Olaf Andrissa**
syni wora rætta aruinga æftir **hænne Groa Aslaks dotter** badhe
aff **hænnæ Groa** fyrda ok sua af **hanom Guduluæ Clæmætssyni**
bonde **henna Groa** fyrda þa hørde ek þøm þet oftæ lyusa til san-
nanda hær om sæter ek mit insigle firi þetta bref.

(Year: c. 1430. Location: unknown.)

Appendix B: Text sources

[S1] "Öfversättning af Den förlorade sonen" Jämten 1964, 119-20. [Translation of The Prodigal Son].

[S2] Äldre Västgötalagen (c. 1220) (FTB) [Older Västgöta Law]

[S3] Arngart, Olof. 1968. The Middle English Genesis and Exodus. Lund studies in English, 36. Lund: Gleerup. [Quoted after Allen (1997).]

[S4] Arvidsjaurs kommuns hemsida [Website of Arvidsjaur municipality] (http://www.arvidsjaur.se/sve/kommun/forvaltningar/ kultur_fritid/barn kultur/bondska/bondska_naturen.asp)

[S5] Bergvall, Frans, Nyman, Åsa and Dahlstedt, Karl-Hampus. 1991. Sagor från Edsele. Skrifter utgivna genom Dialekt- och folkminnesarkivet i Uppsala. Ser. B, Folkminnen och folkliv, 20. Uppsala: Dialekt- och folkminnesarkivet. [Folktales from Edsele (Angermannian)]

[S6] Bonaventuras betraktelser över Kristi leverne (FTB) [translation of Bonaventure's Meditationes Vitæ Christi, about 1400].

[S7] Bondakonst. A translation (about 1515) by Peder Månsson of Lucius Junius Moderatus Columella's De re rustica. (FTB)

[S8] Codex Bureanus [medieval Swedish manuscript, second half of 14th century, containing a collection of legends, "Fornsvenska legendariet"]

[S9] Ekman, Kerstin. 2000. Rattsjin. [The dog.] Älvdalen: Juts böcker. [Translation by Bengt Åkerberg of Kerstin Ekman's novel Hunden]. (Älvdalen Ovansiljan)

[S10] En bröllopsdikt från 1736, Nederluleå socken. Publicerad av Bengt Hesselman. Norrbotten 1929, 33-43. [A wedding poem from Nederluleå (Lulemål) 1736.]

[S11] En byskomakares historia. Upptecknad av Herman Geijer. Svenska landsmål. Svenska landsmål och svenskt folkliv 1920, 6-20. (Kall Jamtska) [A village shoemaker's story transcribed by Herman Geijer]

[S12] En jakt. Dalarna, Älvdalens socken. Sagesperson: Hård Alfred Eriksson, f. 1906. Inspelningsår: 1984. In Thelin, Eva and Språk- och folkminnesinstitutet. 2003. Lyssna på svenska dialekter! : cd med utskrifter och översättningar. Uppsala: Språk- och folkminnesinstitutet (SOFI), pp. 20-21. (Älvdalen Ovansiljan) [A hunting story from Älvdalen by Hård Alfred Eriksson, b. 1906]

[S13] Erikskrönikan [medieval Swedish chronicle, first half of 14th century]

[S14] Et mässer ien juolnot, a Christmas poem by Anna Dahlborg, b. 1879. ULMA 37541 (Älvdalen Ovansiljan)

[S15] Från Stöde i Medelpad. Trollkunniga finnar i Lomarken. Av A.G. Wide, 1877 (ULMA 88:53). Svenska Landsmål och Svenskt Folkliv III.2:186-189. (Stöde Md) [Finnish magicians in Lomarken, text by A.G. Wide]

[S16] Fäbodlivet i gamla tider. Berättad av Vikar Margit Andersdotter i Klitten, född 26 april 1852. (ULMA 10149). (Älvdalen Ovansiljan) [Shieling life in old times, told by Vikar Margit Andersdotter from Klitten, b. 1852]

[S17] Han Jåck-gubben. Af kyrkoh. A.H. Sandström (Från Öfver-Kalix i Västerbotten). Svenska landsmål och svenskt folkliv III.2:32-34. (Överkalix (*Kalixmål*) [Text from Överkalix written by the Rev. A.H. Sandström]

[S18] Hjelmström, Anna. 1896. Från Delsbo: Seder och bruk, folktro och sägner, person- och tidsbilder upptecknade. Bidrag till kännedom om de svenska landsmålen ock svenskt folkliv. 11:4. 1896. Stockholm. [Texts from Delsbo (Helsingian)]

[S19] Holmberg, Karl Axel. 1990. Siibooan berettar: bygdemål från Sideby, Skaftung och Ömossa i Österbotten. Stockholm & Vasa: Almqvist & Wiksell International, Scriptum. [Texts from (Sideby Southern Ostrobothnian)]

[S20] Jonsson, Linda. 2002. Mormålsbibeln. [The Bible in Mormål.] Mora: Mora hembygdslag. [Bible texts translated into various village varieties from Mora parish (Ovansiljan)]

[S21] Larsson, Hjalmar. 1985. Kunundsin kumb: lesubuok o dalska. Älvdalen. (Älvdalen Os) [The King is Coming: An Elfdalian Reader]

[S22] Letter from Peder Throndssön, "Lagrettemand" in Österdalen, Norway. Diplomatarium Norvegicum 9:795. http://www.dokpro.uio.no/

[S23] Lidman, Sara. 1953. Tjärdalen ['The tar pit', a novel]. Stockholm: Bonnier.

[S24] Lite om min båndom å ongdom, by Anders Ahlström. In En bok om Estlands svenska, del 3B: Estlandssvenskar berättar. Dialekttexter med översättning och kommentar. Stockholm: Kulturföreningen Svenska Odlingens Vänner 1990. 79-85. [Text from Ormsö (Estonian Swedish vernaculars)]

[S25] Lyckönskningsdikt av Jacob Danielsson till Gustavus A. Barchæus disputation 'De Fortitudine Mulierum' försvarad i Upsala den 19 juni 1716 under presidium av professor Joh. Upmarck.) H101-102. [Congratulatory poem from a doctoral defense in Uppsala 1716]

[S26] Lyckönskningsdikt till Olof Siljeström Larssons (dalecarlus) dissertation 'De Lacu Siljan', försvarad i Uppsala den 13 juni 1730 under presidium av Andreas Grönwall. H197. [Congratulatory poem from a doctoral defense in Uppsala 1730]

[S27] Nampnlos och Falantin. (Kritische Ausgabe mit nebenstehender mittelniederdeutscher Vorlage, herausgegeben von Werner Wolf. SFSS Bd 51. Uppsala 1934.) [Medieval novel, translated from Low German.]

[S28] Nordlinder, E. O. Bärgsjömål. Anteckningar från Bärgsjö socken i Hälsingland på socknens mål (1870-talet). 1909. Svenska landsmål och svenskt folkliv 1909.39-77. [Texts from Bergsjö (Helsingian)]

[S29] Norsk Tekstarkiv [Norwegian Text Archive] http://www.hit.uib.no/nta/

[S30] Nya Testamentet 1526 [Translation of the New Testament into Swedish 1526].

[S31] Om seende. Från Luleå i Västerbotten. Svenska landsmål och svenskt folkliv III.2, 43-44. [Text from Luleå (Lulemål)]

[S32] Pentateuchparafrasen [Pentateuch paraphrasis] (about 1335). (FTB)

[S33] Recording from Edefors (Lulemål) on the website of DAUM
http://www2.sofi.se/daum/dialekter/socknar/edefors.htm

[S34] Recording made by L. Levander of Erkols Anna Olsdotter in Åsen 1917
(Älvdalen Ovansiljan)

[S35] Runic stone (Sö 164) from Spånga, Råby (Södermanland).

[S36] Siälinna Tröst. [A translation (about 1460) of the Low German text Seelen
trost.] (FTB)

[S37] Steensland, Lars. 1989. Juanneswaundsjila: Johannesevangeliet på älvdalska. [The Gospel of John in Elfdalian] Knivsta: L. Steensland. (Älvdalen
Ovansiljan)

[S38] Stensjö-Kråka. Av Alfred Vestlund (1891-1954) efter N O Höglund i Järkvissle f. 1859 (ULMA 1631). In Hellbom (1980: 17-19). [Text from Liden (Medelpadian)]

[S39] Strånde å sjoen, by Edvin Lagman. In En bok om Estlands svenska, del 3B
Estlandssvenskar berättar. Dialekttexter med översättning och kommentar
Stockholm: Kulturföreningen Svenska Odlingens Vänner 1990. 61-66 [Text
from Nuckö (Estonian Swedish vernaculars)]

[S40] Text written down in 1874 by the clergyman O.K. Hellzén, a native of
Njurunda (ULMA 88:53). It has been published at least twice: in Svenska
Landsmål och Svenskt folkliv III.2 .175-185 and in Hellbom (1980: 92-107). I
am here using Hellbom's spelling. (Njurunda Medelpadian)

[S41] Thelin, Eva. 2003. Lyssna på svenska dialekter cd med utskrifter och översättningar [Listen to Swedish dialects – a CD with transcriptions and trans-
lations]. Uppsala: Språk- och folkminnesinstitutet (SOFI).

[S42] Transcribed text by Alfred Vestlund (1891-1954) originating from N.O. Höglund in Järkvissle (Medelpadian), born in 1859 (ULMA 1631).

[S43] Transcribed text from Ersmark (Northern Westrobothnian) (ULMA 26833)

[S44] Transcribed text from Hössjö (Southern Westrobothnian) (speaker Oskar
Norberg) (DAUM4245).

[S45] Transcribed text from Svartlå, Överluleå (*Lulemål*) (speaker: Pettersson,
Thorsten) (DAUM 4164)

[S46] Två rättegångsmål. Av G.F.A. Palm, på Bonäsmål 1876 (ULMA 90:42:1). Svenska landsmål III.2.118-119 (1881-1946). [Texts from Mora (Ovansiljan)]

[S47] Vidhemsprästens krönika. [The chronicle of the Vidhem priest.] A chronicle from about 1280 found together with the Younger Västgöta Law. (FTB)

[S48] Wennerholm, John, ed. 1996. Många av Spegel Annas historier jämte hennes levnadshistoria författad av Per Johannes [Various stories by Spegel Anna and her life-story told by Per Johannes]. Tällnäs: J. Wennerholm. (Leksand Nedansiljan).

Abbreviations used in the list of sources

FTB Fornsvenska textbanken [Old Swedish Text Bank]: http://www.nordlund. lu.se/Fornsvenska/FsvFolder/index.html

ᴬAUM Dialekt-, ortnamns- och folkminnesarkivet i Umeå [Dialect Archive in Umeå]

ᵁLMA refers to the Dialect Archive in Uppsala.

H Hesselman, Bengt and Lundell, Johan August. 1937. Bröllopsdikter på dialekt och några andra dialektdikter från 1600- och 1700-talen. Nordiska texter och undersökningar, 10. Stockholm: Geber.

ᴸTEXT an Old Swedish corpus comprising about 2 million words, available at http: //spraakbanken.gu.se/ (partly coinciding with FTB)

Bibliography

Allen, Cynthia L. 1997. The origins of the 'group genitive' in English. *Transactions of the Philological Society* 95. 111–131.

Allen, Cynthia L. 2008. *Genitives in early English typology and evidence.* Oxford: Oxford University Press.

Andersson, Margit & Suzanne Danielsson. 1999. *Färdär frå Soldn. Spår från Sollerön: en ordbok på soldmål.* Sollerön: M. Andersson & S. Danielsson.

Axelsson, Monica. 1994. *Noun phrase development in Swedish as a second language: a study of adult learners acquiring definiteness and the semantics and morphology of adjectives.* Stockholm: Univ.

Behaghel, Otto. 1923. *Deutsche Syntax: eine geschichtliche Darstellung* (Germanische Bibliothek. Abteilung 1, Sammlung germanischer Elementar- und Handbücher. Reihe 1, Grammatiken, 10.). Heidelberg.

Behrens, Leila. 2005. Genericity from a cross-linguistic perspective. *Linguistics* 43. 275–344.

Bergholm, Erika, Maria Linder & Cecilia Yttergren. 1999. *Nordsvenska nominalfraser – analyser av en enkätundersökning.* Umeå: Inst för filosofi och lingvistik, Umeå universitet C-uppsats 10 p.

Berglund, Erik & Gun Lidström. 1991. *Pitemålet: ållt mila àagg å ööx.* Piteå: ABF Piteåbygden.

Bergman, Gustaf. 1893. Alundamålets formlära. *Svenska landsmål och svenskt folkliv* XII(6).

Bertinetto, Pier Marco & Mario Squartini. 2000. The simple and compound past in the Romance languages. In Östen Dahl (ed.), *Tense and aspect in the languages of Europe*, 403–440. Berlin: Mouton de Gruyter.

Björklund, Stig. 1994. *Dalmålsstudier: festskrift till Stig Björklund på 75-årsdagen den 19 februari 1994* (Skrifter utgivna genom Dialekt- och folkminnesarkivet i Uppsala. Ser. A, Folkmål 24). [Studies in the Dialects of Dalarna: an anthology in honour of Stig Björklund on his 75th birthday, 19 February 1994]. Uppsala: Dialekt- och folkminnesarkivet.

Boas, Franz & Ella Deloria. 1941. *Dakota grammar.* Vol. 23 (National Academy of Sciences. Memoirs 2). Washington.

Bibliography

Bogren, Petrus. 1921. *Torpmålets ljud- och formlära.* Stockholm: Norstedt.

Broberg, Anders. 1990. *Bönder och samhälle i statsbildningstid: en bebyggelsearke ologisk studie av agrarsamhället i Norra Roden 700–1350* (Rapporter från Bark nåreprojektet 3). Uppsala: Upplands fornminnesfören.

Broberg, Richard. 1936. *Syntaktiska företeelser i Östmarksmålet.* ULMA 9856.

Broberg, Richard. 1980. *Invandringen från Finland till mellersta Skandinavien före 1700. Finska språket i Sverige.* Fören. Norden; Finn-Kirja. Stockholm: Fören.

Brännström, Ingvar. 1993. *Grammatik på pitemålet.* Piteå: Piteå museum.

Bull, Tove. 1995. Language contact leading to language change: The case of North ern Norway. Jacek Fisiak (ed.). 15–34.

Carlson, Gregory N. 1977. A unified analysis of the English bare plural. *Linguistics and Philosophy* 1. 413–458.

Caubet, Dominique. 1983. Quantification, négation, interrogation: les emplois de la particule "ši" en arabe marocain. *Arabica* 30. 227–245.

Clark, H. H. & S. E Haviland. 1974. Psychological processes as linguistic explana tion. In D. Cohen (ed.), *Explaining linguistic phenomena,* 91–124. Washington Hemisphere Publishing Corp.

Croft, William & Efrosini Deligianni. 2001. *Asymmetries in NP word order.* http //www.unm.edu/{\Tilde}wcroft/Papers/NPorder.pdf.

Dahl, Östen. 1973. On generics. In Edward Keenan (ed.), *Formal semantics of nat ural language,* 99–111. Cambridge: Cambridge University Press.

Dahl, Östen. 2001. The origin of the Scandinavian languages. In Östen Dahl & Maria Koptjevskaja-Tamm (eds.), *The Circum-Baltic languages: past and present* 215–235. Amsterdam & Philadelphia: John Benjamins.

Dahl, Östen. 2003. Competing definite articles in Scandinavian. In Bernd Kort mann (ed.), *Dialectology meets typology,* 147–180. Berlin: Mouton de Gruyter.

Dahl, Östen. 2004. *The growth and maintenance of linguistic complexity* (Studies in language companion series 71). Amsterdam: John Benjamins.

Dahl, Östen. 2005. Att sätta älvdalskan på kartan. In Gunnar Nyström (ed.), *Rap port från Fuost konferensn um övdalsku (första konferensen om älvdalska).* Upp sala: Institutionen för nordiska språk, Uppsala universitet. http://www.nordisk uu.se/arkiv/konferenser/alvdalska/konferensbidrag/Dahl.pdf.

Dahl, Östen. 2008. The degenerate dative in southern Norrbothnian. In Greville G. Corbett & Michael Noonan (eds.), *Case and grammatical relations. Studies in honor of Bernard Comrie,* 105–126. Amsterdam: John Benjamins.

Dahl, Östen & Maria Koptjevskaja-Tamm. 2001. Kinship in grammar. In Irène Baron, Michael Herslund & Finn Sørensen (eds.), *Dimensions of possession.* Am sterdam: John Benjamins.

Dahl, Östen & Maria Koptjevskaja-Tamm. 2006. The resilient dative and other re-markable cases in Scandinavian vernaculars. *Sprachtypologie und Universalienforschung* 59. 56–75.

Dahlstedt, Karl-Hampus. 1956. Inledning till Pitemålet. *Norrbottens läns hembygsförenings årsbok.* 9–46.

Dahlstedt, Karl-Hampus. 1962. *Det svenska Vilhelminamålet: språkgeografiska studier över ett norrländskt nybyggarmål och dess granndialekter* (Kvantitet. Apokope, A, Text 2). Uppsala: Lundequistska.

Dahlstedt, Karl-Hampus. 1971. *Norrländska och nusvenska: tre studier i nutida svenska.* Lund: Studentlitteratur.

Dawkins, R. M. 1916. *Modern Greek in Asia Minor: A study of the dialects of Silli, Cappadocia and Phárasa, with grammar, texts, translations and glossary.* Cambridge: Cambridge Univ. Press.

Delsing, Lars-Olof. 1993. *The internal structure of noun phrases in the Scandinavian languages: a comparative study.* Lund University PhD thesis.

Delsing, Lars-Olof. 2002. The morphology of Old Nordic II: Old Swedish and Old Danish. In Oskar Bandle & Kurt Braunmüller (eds.), *The Nordic languages: an international handbook of the history of the North Germanic languages,* 924–939. Berlin: de Gruyter.

Delsing, Lars-Olof. 2003a. Perifrastisk genitiv i nordiska dialekter. In Øystein Alexander Vangsnes, Anders Holmberg & Lars-Olof Delsing (eds.), *Dialektsyntaktiska studier av den nordiska nominalfrasen,* 65–84. Oslo: Novus.

Delsing, Lars-Olof. 2003b. Syntaktisk variation i nordiska nominalfraser. In Øystein Alexander Vangsnes, Anders Holmberg & Lars-Olof Delsing (eds.), *Dialektsyntaktiska studier av den nordiska nominalfrasen,* 11–64. Oslo: Novus.

Dixon, Robert M. W. 1977. Where have all the adjectives gone? *Studies in Language* 1. 19–80.

Dryer, Matthew. 2005. Definite articles. In Martin Haspelmath, Matthew S. Dryer, David Gil & Bernard Comrie (eds.), *World atlas of language structures,* 154–156. Oxford: Oxford University Press.

Eaker, Birgit. 1993. *Adjektivet grann i svenska dialekter: en semantisk och dialektgeografisk undersökning* (Skrifter utgivna genom Dialekt- och folkminnesarkivet i Uppsala. Ser. A, Folkmål 21). Uppsala: Dialekt- och folkminnesarkivet.

Ebert, Karen H. 1971. *Referenz, Sprechsituation und die bestimmten Artikel in einem nordfriesischen Dialekt.* Braist/Bredstedt: Nordfriisk Instituut.

Ericsson, Anna M. 2006. *Generaliserad grav accent i Sorundadialekten: en studie av tre generationer.* B.A. thesis. Stockholm.

Eriksson, Gunnar & Anne-Charlotte Rendahl. 1999. *Nominalfraser norr om Dalälven Österbotten. Rapport från fältkurs vt-ht 1998.* Tech. rep. Department of Linguistics, Stockholm University.

Faarlund, Jan Terje, Svein Lie & Kjell Ivar Vannebo. 1997. *Norsk referansegrammatikk.* Oslo: Universitetsforlaget.

Franck, Håkan. 1995. *Forsamålet: ordlista och grammatik.* Hudiksvall: Monfors.

Fraurud, Kari. 1992. *Processing noun phrases in natural discourse.* Stockholm: Univ.

Freudenthal, Axel Olof. 1878. *Über den Närpesdialekt.* Helsingfors.

Geijer, H. & E Holmkvist. 1930. Några drag ur Västmanlands språkgeografi. *Svenska landsmål och svenskt folkliv* 18. 1–28.

Greenberg, Joseph H. 1978. How does a language acquire gender markers? In Joseph H. Greenberg (ed.), *Universals of human language*, 48–81. Stanford: Stanford University Press.

Hagfors, Karl Johan. 1891. *Gamlakarlebymålet: ljud- och formlära samt språkprov.* Stockholm: Norstedt.

Harling-Kranck, Gunilla & Johanna Mara. 1998. *Från Pyttis till Nedervetil: tjugonio prov på dialekter i Nyland, Åboland, Åland och Österbotten.* Helsingfors: Svenska litteratursällskapet i Finland.

Haugen, Einar. 1970. The language history of Scandinavia: A profile of problems. In Hreinn Benediktsson (ed.), *The Nordic languages and modern linguistics: Proceedings of the international conference of Nordic and general linguistics, University of Iceland, Reykjavik July 6-11, 1969*, 41–86. Reykjavík: Visindafélag íslendinga.

Hawkins, John A. 2004. *Efficiency and complexity in grammars.* Oxford: Oxford University Press.

Hedblom, Folke. 1978. *En hälsingedialekt i Amerika: hanebomål från Bishop Hill, Illinois: text och kommentar* (Skrifter utgivna genom Dialekt- och folkminnesarkivet i Uppsala. Ser. A, Folkmål 15). Uppsala: Lundequistska bokh.

Hellbom, Algot. 1961. Dativböjning i Medelpads bygdemål. *Svenska landsmål och svenskt folkliv* 1961. 101–130.

Hellbom, Algot. 1980. *Sant och diktat på dialekt* (Medelpad berättar 1). Sundsvall: Sundsvalls museum.

Hellevik, Alf. 1979. *Språkrøkt og språkstyring: eit utval av artiklar: festskrift til Alf Hellevik på 70-årsdagen, 28. juni 1979.* Oslo: Det norske samlaget.

Hellquist, Elof. 1922. *Svensk etymologisk ordbok.* Lund: Gleerup.

Hesselman, Bengt. 1905. *Sveamålen och de svenska dialekternas indelning.* Uppsala.

Hesselman, Bengt. 1908. Uppländskan som skriftspråk. In Karl Hildebrand & Axel Erdmann (eds.), *Uppland*, 499–536. Stockholm: Wahlström & Widstrand.

Hesselman, Bengt. 1920. Upplands folkmål. In Bernhard Meijer (ed.), *Nordisk familjebok, konversationslexikon och realencyklopedi*, 1192–1195. Stockholm: Nordisk familjeboks förlags aktiebolag.

Hesselman, Bengt. 1936. Några nynordiska dialektformer och vikingatidens historia: En undersökning i svensk och dansk språkutveckling. In Bengt Hesselman (ed.), *Ordgeografi och språkhistoria*, 127–162. Stockholm & Copenhagen: Gebers & Levin & Munksgaard.

Himmelmann, Nikolaus P. 1997. *Deiktikon, Artikel, Nominalphrase: zur Emergenz syntaktischer Struktur* (Linguistische Arbeiten 362). Tübingen: Niemeyer.

Himmelmann, Nikolaus P. 1998. Regularity in irregularity: Article use in adpositional phrases. *Linguistic Typology* 2. 315–353.

Hjelmström, Anna. 1896. *Från Delsbo: Seder och bruk, folktro och sägner, person- och tidsbilder upptecknade* (Svenska landsmål ock svenskt folkliv. Vol. 11 4). Stockholm.

Holm, Gösta. 1941. Västerbottniska syntaxstudier. *Svenska landsmål och svenskt folkliv* 235.

Holm, Gösta. 1942. Lövångersmålet. In Carl Holm (ed.), *Lövånger: En sockenbeskrivning under medverkan av flere fackmän*. Umeå: Aktiebolaget Nyheternas Tryckeri.

Holmberg, Anders & Görel Sandström. 2003. Vad är det för särskilt med nordsvenska nominalfraser? In Øystein Alexander Vangsnes, Anders Holmberg & Lars-Olof Delsing (eds.), *Dialektsyntaktiska studier av den nordiska nominalfrasen*, 85–98. Oslo: Novus.

Hummelstedt, Eskil. 1934. Om användningen av substantivets bestämda form i Österbottniskt folkspråk. *Folkmålsstudier* 2. 134–136.

Ivars, Ann-Marie. 2005. Sydösterbottnisk nominalfrassyntax. *Svenska landsmål och svenskt folkliv* 2005. 73–93.

Iversen, Ragnvald. 1918. *Syntaksen i Tromsø bymaal: en kort oversigt*. Kristiania: Bymaals-laget.

Janda, Richard D. 1980. On the decline of declensional systems: the overall loss of OE nominal case inflections and the ME reanalysis of *-es* as *his*. In Elizabeth Closs Traugott, Rebecca Labrum & Susan Shepherd (eds.), *Papers from the 4th International Conference on Historical Linguistics*, 243–252. Amsterdam: John Benjamins.

Janzén, Assar. 1936. *Studier över substantivet i bohuslänskan* (Göteborgs Kungl Vetenskaps- och Vitterhets-Samhälles handlingar. Ser. A, Humanistiska skrifter Följd 5 5:3). Göteborg: Wettergren & Kerber.

Juvonen, Päivi. 2000. *Grammaticalizing the definite article: a study of definite ad nominal determiners in a genre of spoken Finnish*. Stockholm: Dept. of Linguistics, Stockholm University PhD thesis.

Kammerzell, Frank. 2000. Egyptian possessive constructions. *Sprachtypologie und Universalienforschung* 53. 97–108.

Knudsen, Trygve. 1941. *Kasuslære*. Oslo: Universitetets studentkontor.

Koptjevskaja-Tamm, Maria. 2001. "A piece of the cake" and "a cup of tea": Partitive and pseudo-partitive nominal constructions in the Circum-Baltic languages. In Östen Dahl & Maria Koptjevskaja-Tamm (eds.), *The Circum-Baltic languages: typology and contact*, 523–568. Amsterdam: John Benjamins.

Koptjevskaja-Tamm, Maria. 2003. Possessive noun phrases in the languages of Europe. In Frans Plank (ed.), *Noun phrase structure in the languages of Europe* 621–722. Berlin: Mouton de Gruyter.

Krifka, Manfred, Francis Jeffry Pelletier, Greg N. Carlson, Alice ter Meulen, Gennaro Chierchia & Godehard Link. 1995. Genericity: An introduction. In Greg N Carlson & Francis Jeffry Pelletier (eds.), *The generic book*. Chicago: University of Chicago Press.

Kruuse, E. 1908. De lefvande folkmålen. In Karl Hildebrand & Axel Erdmann (eds.), *Uppland*, 537–552. Stockholm: Wahlström & Widstrand.

Källskog, Margareta. 1992. *Attityd, interferens, genitivsyntax: studier i nutida Överkalixmål Ny utg* (Skrifter utgivna genom Dialekt- och folkminnesarkivet i Uppsala. Ser. A, Folkmål 18). Uppsala: Dialekt- och folkminnesarkivet.

Källskog, Margareta, Gerd Eklund, Bo Danielsson, Kristina Hagren, Anna Westerberg, Rune Västerlund & Maj Reinhammar. 1993. *Uppländska: språkprov med kommentar* (Skrifter utgivna genom Dialekt- och folkminnesarkivet i Uppsala Ser. A. Folkmål 22). Uppsala: Dialekt- och folkminnesarkivet.

Lagman, Edvin. 1979. *En bok om Estlands svenskar* (Estlandssvenskarnas språkförhållanden 3A). Stockholm: Kulturföreningen Svenska odlingens vänner.

Landtmanson, Samuel. 1952. *Västgötamålet* (Västergötland. A, 8). Stockholm: Almqvist & Wiksell.

Larm, Karl. 1936. *Den bestämda artikeln i äldre fornsvenska: en historisk-semologisk studie* (Stockholm studies in Scandinavian philology 2). Stockholm: Bonnier.

Larsen, Amund B. 1895. Antegnelser om substantivböiningen i middelnorsk. *Arkiv för nordisk filologi* 13. 244–253.

Larsson, Seth. 1929. *Substantivböjningen i Västerbottens folkmål: jämte en exkurs till ljudläran.* Uppsala: s.n.

Laury, Ritva. 1997. *Demonstratives in interaction: the emergence of a definite article in Finnish* (Studies in discourse and grammar 7). Amsterdam & Philadelphia: John Benjamins.

Levander, Lars. 1909. *Älvdalsmålet i Dalarna: ordböjning ock syntax* (Nyare bidrag till kännedom om de svenska landsmålen ock svenskt folkliv). Stockholm.

Levander, Lars. 1925. *Dalmålet: beskrivning och historia.* Vol. I. Uppsala: Appelbergs boktryckeri.

Levander, Lars. 1928. *Dalmålet: beskrivning och historia.* Vol. II. Uppsala: Appelbergs boktryckeri.

Levander, Lars, Gunnar Nyström & Stig Björklund. 1961. *Ordbok över folkmålen i övre Dalarna* (Skrifter utgivna genom Dialekt- och folkminnesarkivet i Uppsala. Ser. D, Dialektordböcker från Dalarna, Gotland och andra landskap 1). Uppsala: Dialekt- och folkminnesarkivet.

Lindkvist, Einar. 1942. Om Gästriklands folkmål. *Från Gästrikland. Gästriklands Kulturhistoriska Förenings meddelanden* 1942. 5–102.

Lindström, Henrik & Fredrik Lindström. 2006. *Svitjods undergång och Sveriges födelse.* Stockholm: Bonnier.

Lundell, Johan. 1936. *Skandinaviska folkmål i språkprov.* Stockholm: Norstedt.

Lundström, Gudrun. 1939. *Studier i nyländsk syntax* (Svenska landsmål och svenskt folkliv. B 38). Stockholm: Norstedt.

Lyons, Christopher. 1999. *Definiteness* (Cambridge textbooks in linguistics). Cambridge: Cambridge Univ. Press.

Löfström, Jonas. 1988. *Repliker utan gränser: till studiet av syntaktisk struktur i samtal.* Göteborg.

Markey, Thomas L. 1969. *The verbs varda and bliva in Scandinavian* (Studia philologiae Scandinavicae Upsaliensia 7). Uppsala, Stockholm: Almqvist & Wiksell.

Marklund, Thorsten. 1976. *Skelleftemålet: grammatik och ordlista: för lekmän - av lekman.* Boliden.

Modéer, Ivar. 1946. *Studier över slutartikeln i starka femininer* (Uppsala universitets årsskrift 2). Uppsala: Lundequistska bokh.

Mosel, Ulrike & Even Hovdhaugen. 1992. *Samoan reference grammar* (Instituttet for sammenlignende kulturforskning. Serie B, Skrifter 85). Oslo: Scandinavian Univ. Press.

Muravyova, Irina A. 1998. Chukchee (Paleo-Siberian). In Andrew Spencer & Arnold Zwicky (eds.), *Handbook of morphology*, 521–538. Oxford: Blackwell.

Myrdal, Janken. 2003. *Digerdöden, pestvågor och ödeläggelse: ett perspektiv på senmedeltidens Sverige.* Runica et mediaevalia (Scripta minora 9). Stockholm: Sällsk. http://www.ekon.slu.se/forsknin/agrar/forskning/Artiklar/Digerdoden. pdf.

Neckel, Gustav. 1924. Die Entwicklung von schwachtonigem altnordischem u (o) vor m aus helleren Vokalen und der altnordische Substantivartikel. In *Festschrift für E. Mogk*, 387–418. Halle.

Nikula, Kristina. 1997. Species i finlandssvensk dialekt. In Maj Reinhammar (ed.), *Nordiska dialektstudier: föredrag vid femte nordiska dialektologkonferensen, Sigtuna 17–21 augusti 1994*, 203–213. Uppsala: Språk- och folkminnesinstitutet.

Norde, Muriel. 1997. *The history of the genitive in Swedish: a case study in degrammaticalization.* Amsterdam: Vakgroep Skandinavisch Taal- en Letterkunde, University of Amsterdam PhD thesis.

Nordling, Anna. 2001. *Pa swänsko: studier i lexikalisk förnyelse hos Peder Månsson.* Göteborg: Institutionen för svenska språket, Göteborgs Universitet PhD thesis.

Nordström, August. 1925. *Luleåkultur.* Luleå.

Nyström, Jan-Olov. 1993. *Ordbok över Lulemålet: på grundval av dialekten i Antnäs by, Nederluleå socken* (Skrifter utgivna av Dialekt-, ortnamns- och folkminnesarkivet i Umeå. Serie A, Dialekter 10). Umeå: Dialekt- ortnamns- och folkminnesarkivet.

Nyström, Staffan. 1997. *Grav accent i östra Svealands folkmål.* Maj Reinhammar (ed.). Uppsala: Språk- och folkminnesinstitutet.

Näsman, Reinhold E. 1733. *Historiola linguæ Dalekarlicæ Upsala.* Literæ Wernerianæ.

Olofsson, Jon Olof. 1999. *Tännäsmålet: grammatik och ordlista.* Tännäs: J.O. Olofsson.

Oscarsson, Bo. 2007. *Jamska: Jamtarnas språk – Språke at jamtom.* http://www. mdh.se/ima/personal/lln01/jamtamot/dokument/jubileumsskrift1985/js1985_ nr07_jamska.html.

Otterbjörk, Roland. 1982. *Boki om sondemåhle eller Sorundamålet i teori och praktik.* Sorunda: Sorunda hembygdsfören.

Perridon, Harry. 1989. *Reference, definiteness and the noun phrase in Swedish.* Amsterdam: Univ. of Amsterdam.

Perridon, Harry. 2002. Dialects and written language in Old Nordic II: Old Danish and Old Swedish. In *The Nordic languages: An international handbook of the history of the North Germanic languages*, 924–939. Berlin: de Gruyter.

Plank, Frans. 2003. Double articulation. In Frans Plank (ed.), *Noun phrase structure in the languages of Europe*, 337–396. Berlin & New York: Mouton de Gruyter.

Reinhammar, Maj. 1973. *Om dativ i svenska och norska dialekter. Studier till en svensk dialektgeografisk atlas.* Uppsala: Almqvist & Wiksell.

Reinhammar, Maj. 2002. *En 1700-talsordlista från Piteå* (Acta Academiae Regiae Gustavi Adolphi 80). Uppsala: Gustav Adolfsakademien.

Reinhammar, Vidar. 1975. *Pronomenstudier* (Studier till en svensk dialektgeografisk atlas 7). Uppsala: Almqvist & Wiksell.

Reinhammar, Vidar. 1988. Om uppkomsten av svenskt *den här. Svenska landsmål och svenskt folkliv* 1988. 72–101.

Reinhammar, Vidar. 2005. *Hammerdalsmålet. Folklivsskildringar och bygdestudier.* Uppsala: Kungl. Gustav Adolfs akademien för svensk folkkultur.

Rendahl, Anne-Charlotte. 2001. Swedish dialects around the Baltic Sea. In Östen Dahl & Maria Koptjevskaja-Tamm (eds.), *The Circum-Baltic languages: typology and contact,* 137–178. Amsterdam: John Benjamins.

Rießler, Michael. 2002. Der partitive Artikel in nordskandinavischen Dialekten. *Tijdschrift voor Skandinavistiek* 23. http://rjh.ub.rug.nl/tvs/article/view/10603, 43–62.

Rutberg, Hulda. 1924. Folkmålet i Nederkalix och Töre socknar. *Svenska landsmål och svenskt folkliv.* Vol. H:3.

Rydqvist, Johan Erik. 1868. *Svenska språkets lagar: kritisk afhandling.* Stockholm: Norstedt.

Saltveit, Laurits & Didrik Arup Seip. 1971. *Norwegische Sprachgeschichte. Grundriss der germanischen Philologie.* Berlin: de Gruyter.

Sandström, Görel & Anders Holmberg. 2003. Ett polysyntetiskt drag i svenska dialekter. In Øystein Alexander Vangsnes, Anders Holmberg & Lars-Olof Delsing (eds.), *Dialektsyntaktiska studier av den nordiska nominalfrasen,* 99–112. Oslo: Novus.

Schagerström, August. 1882. *Upplysningar om vätömålet i Roslagen* (Nyare bidrag till kännedom om de svenska landsmålen ock svenskt folkliv 2:4). Stockholm.

Sick, Bastian. 2004. *Der Dativ ist dem Genitiv sein Tod: ein Wegweiser durch den Irrgarten der deutschen Sprache.* Köln: Kiepenheuer & Witsch.

Skautrup, Peter. 1944. *Det danske sprogs historie.* København: Det Danske Sprog- og Litteraturselskab, Gyldendalske boghandel.

Skubic, Mitja. 1973–1974. Le due forme del preterito nell'area siciliana. *Atti della Accademia di Scienze, Lettere e Arti di Palermo.* 225–293.

Steensland, Lars. 1994. *Älvdalska växtnamn: förr och nu* (Skrifter utgivna genom Dialekt- och folkminnesarkivet i Uppsala. Ser. A, Folkmål). Uppsala: Dialekt- och folkminnesarkivet.

Stenberg, Margit. 1971. *Äldre och yngre Kalixmål. Tvåbetygsuppsats i nordiska språk.*

Stenbom, Eric. 1916. Njurundamålets formlära. *Svenska landsmål och svenskt folk liv* 1916. 49–71.

Stilo, Donald. 2004. Iranian as buffer zone between the universal typologies of Turkic and Semitic. In Éva Ágnes Csató, Bo Isaksson & Carina Jahani (eds.) *Linguistic convergence and areal diffusion: Case studies from Iranian, Semitic and Turkic,* 35–63. London: Routledge Courzon.

Syrett, Martin. 2002. Morphological developments from Ancient Nordic to Old Nordic. In Oskar Bandle & Kurt Braunmüller (eds.), *The Nordic languages: an international handbook of the history of the North Germanic languages,* 719–729 Berlin: de Gruyter.

Söderwall, Knut Fredrik. 1884. *Ordbok öfver svenska medeltids-språket* (Samlingar utgivna av Svenska fornskriftssällskapet. Serie 1, Svenska skrifter). Lund. http //spraakbanken.gu.se/fsvldb/index2.html.

Tarkiainen, Kari. 1990. *Finnarnas historia i Sverige. 1, inflyttarna från Finland un der det gemensamma rikets tid* (Nordiska museets handlingar 109). Stockholm Helsingfors: Nordiska museet; Finska historiska samf.

Tegnér, Esaias d.y. 1889. Tyska inflytelser på svenskan. *Arkiv för nordisk filologi* 5. 155–167.

Teleman, Ulf, Staffan Hellberg & Erik Andersson. 1999. *Svenska akademiens grammatik.* Stockholm: Svenska akademien, Norstedts ordbok.

Thomason, Sarah Grey & Terrence Kaufman. 1988. *Language contact, creolization and genetic linguistics.* Berkeley: University of California Press.

Thompson, Sandra A. 1988. A discourse approach to the cross-linguistic category "adjective". In John Hawkins (ed.), *Explaining language universals,* 167–185. Oxford: Blackwell.

Tiberg, Nils. 1962. *Estlandssvenska språkdrag* (Acta Academiae Regiae Gustavi Adolphi 38). Uppsala & Köpenhamn: Kungl. Gustav Adolfs akademien för folklivsforskning.

Tiselius, Gustav Adolf. 1902. Ljud- ock formlära för Fasternamålet i Roslagen. *Svenska landsmålen och svenskt folkliv* 18(5).

Törnqvist, Elin. 2002. *Prepropriell artikel i norrländska dialekter.* Stockholm: Inst för lingvistik, Stockholms universitet MA thesis.

Vallmark, Sven. 1937. Fördelningen av de temporala konjunktionerna *då* ock *när* i svenskt talspråk. *Svenska landsmål och svenskt folkliv* 1936. 119–159.

Vangsnes, Øystein Alexander. 2003. 'identifikasjon' og morfologiens rolle i den nordiske nominalfrasen. In Øystein Alexander Vangsnes, Anders Holmberg &

Lars-Olof Delsing (eds.), *Dialektsyntaktiska studier av den nordiska nominalfrasen*, 99–112. Oslo: Novus.

Vendell, Herman. 1882. *Runömålet: ljud- ock formlära samt ordbok* (Nyare bidrag till kännedom om de svenska landsmålen ock svenskt folkliv). Stockholm.

Vestlund, Alfred. 1923. *Medelpads folkmål* (Svenska landsmål och svenskt folkliv. B 48).

Västerlund, Rune. 1988. Alundamål. *Svenska landsmål och svenskt folkliv*. 25–64.

Wallerström, Thomas. 1995. *Norrbotten, Sverige och medeltiden: problem kring makt och bosättning i en europeisk periferi* (Lund studies in medieval archaeology 15). Norrbotten, Sweden and the Middle Ages: problems concerning power and settlement on a European periphery. Stockholm: Almqvist & Wiksell International.

Wessén, Elias. 1954. *Om det tyska inflytandet på svenskt språk under medeltiden* (Skrifter utgivna av Nämnden för svensk språkvård). Stockholm.

Wessén, Elias. 1956. *Svensk språkhistoria. III: Grundlinjer till en historisk syntax*. Stockholm: Almqvist & Wiksell.

Wessén, Elias. 1966. *Våra folkmål*. 7th edn. Stockholm.

Wessén, Elias. 1968. *Svensk språkhistoria. I: Ljudlära och ordböjningslära*. Stockholm: Almqvist & Wiksell.

Westerberg, Anna. 2004. *Norsjömålet under 150 år* (Acta Academiae Regiae Gustavi Adolphi 86). Uppsala: Swedish Science Press.

Westerlund, Ernst. 1978. *Folkmål i Skelleftebygden: en liten ordlista till bygdemålen i norra länsdelen jämte ett urval visor, gåtor, härm, ramsor, öknamn och åtskilligt annat*. Skellefteå: Studieförb. Vuxenskolan.

Widmark, Gun. 1994. Birkasvenskan - fanns den? *Arkiv för nordisk filologi* 109. 173–216.

Widmark, Gun. 2001. *Det språk som blev vårt: ursprung och utveckling i svenskan: urtid, runtid, riddartid* (Acta Academiae Regiae Gustavi Adolphi 76). Uppsala: Swedish Science Press.

Wikberg, Dagmar. 2004. *Rånemålet i Böle = ranmale opa Böle*. Råneå: Böle hembygdsfören.

Wälchli, Bernhard, Mikael Parkvall & Nawzad Shokri. 1998. *The use of the definite article in the Swedish dialects of Västerbotten and Ångermanland*. Stockholm: Department of Linguistics, University of Stockholm.

Zamparelli, Roberto. 2002. Definite and bare kind-denoting noun phrases. In Claire Beyssade, Reineke Bok-Bennema, Frank Drijkoningen & Paola Monachesi (eds.), *Romance languages and linguistic theory 2000; selected papers from*

'*Going Romance*' *2000.* http://semanticsarchive.net/Archive/zViY2I5N/Def-bare-kinds.pdf. Amsterdam: John Benjamins.

Ågren, Per-Uno & Karl-Hampus Dahlstedt. 1954. *Övre Norrlands bygdemål: berättelser på bygdemål med förklaringar och en dialektöversikt.* Umeå: Vetenskapliga bibl.

Åkerberg, Bengt. 2012. *Älvdalsk grammatik. Under medverkan av Gunnar Nyström.* Mora.

Name index

Language index

Subject index

www.ingramcontent.com/pod-product-compliance
Lightning Source LLC
Chambersburg PA
CBHW080543110426
42813CB00006B/1194